SYDNEY
DRAUGHT
BATSMEN OUT F OF W
14
37
29
17
DYSON 2 23
G.CHAPPELL 11 38
WESSELS 53 82
HOOKES 19 113
BORDER 83 262
31
40
46
SUNDRIES 7
have a Winfield 25
G AREA IS PROHIBITED
EDGES Company
LADIES
ESANDA
THE POWER
TOOHEYS

THE WISDEN ILLUSTRATED HISTORY OF CRICKET

THE WISDEN ILLUSTRATED HISTORY OF CRICKET

VIC MARKS

RECORDS COMPILED BY BILL FRINDALL

WHSMITH
EXCLUSIVE
· BOOKS ·

A Queen Anne Press BOOK

First published in Great Britain in this edition in 1990 by
Queen Anne Press, a division of
Macdonald & Co (Publishers) Ltd
3rd Floor
Greater London House
Hampstead Road
London
NW1 7QX

A member of Maxwell Pergamon Publishing Corporation plc

British Library Cataloguing in Publication Data

The Wisden illustrated history of cricket
1.Cricket, 1985
I.Frindall, Bill, 1939
II.Marks, Victor

796.35′8′09

ISBN 0-356-17123-x

Typeset by Tradespools Ltd., Frome, Somerset
Printed and bound in Hong Kong by Leefung-Asco Limited

CONTENTS

ACKNOWLEDGEMENTS

I would like to thank Paddy Armstrong and Peter Robinson for unlimited access to their cricket libraries, and John Claughton for thumbing through *Wisdens*

PICTURE CREDITS

Aldus Archive: 9bl *All-Sport:* 18r, 34r, 66b, 77, 105r, 172t, 173b 180bl & tr, 191, 199, 200, 201 both, 202br, 204t & bl, 205t, 207 both, 208 both, 211, 214, 215 both, 217, 219 both, 222b, 224t, 226, 228t, 229b, 232 both, 233 both *BBC Hulton:* 141, 18r, 191, 22t, 24c, 24b, 31, 32, 35 both, 39t, 42r, 42br, 45 tl & tr, 51, 56, 581, 59, 67r, 70b, 71t, 72, 73b, 73c, 74, 75t, 77t, 84t, 84–5, 87, 90b, 91 t & c, 92–3, 95b, 98t, 107, 108, 110, 111b, 112t, 113t, 114t, 116b, 121b, 129t, 132b, 135, 142t, 150t, 151, 152b, 158, 167b, 168t, 170t, 187b *George Beldam Collection:* 50 both, 53b, 57, 63, 64, 65 *Burlington Gallery:* 12 tr & b, 15b, 17, 30, 40t, 58r *Patrick Eagar:* front endpaper, 161 both, 162 both, 163, 164, 165br, 172b, 173t, 174b, 175, 176 both, 177 bl, tr, tl, 179t, 180t, 181b, 183 both, 1841, 185 both, 186 both, 187t, 188, 189, 190, 192, 193 tl & tr, 194, 197, 201t, 2031, 204b, 205b, 209 both, 210, 212, 213, 216, 218t, 220 both, 221, 222t, 224b, 227, 230 both, back endpaper *Alf Gover:* 19r, 26t, 111t *Imperial War Museum:* 82, 119t *India Office Library (British Library):* 21t, 23, 25, 33 both *Kent County Cricket Club:* 8, 80–1, 85b *Keystone:* 83b, 84b, 86, 88 both, 89 both, 91b, 97t, 98b, 99, 101, 102, 106r, 112bl & br, 115, 116t, 117b, 118, 119b, 120b, 122, 123, 1241, 126, 127 both, 128, 131 all, 132t, 136b, 138, 139, 140r, 141 both, 142, 147b, 152t, 153, 156, 1651, 166t, 169 both, 170b, 184r *London Express News & Feature Services:* 134 both *Mansell Collection:* 10 both, 16, 181, 20, 21b, 22b, 25, 28, 29, 36, 47, 52, 61, 78, 79t, 1061 *MCC:* 8, 9 t & br, 12, 13t, 14r, 26b, 39b, 421, 44bl, 62, 75b, 83t, 88t, 92 both, 94, 97b *Robert Opie:* 60b, 121t *Popperfoto:* 11, 125–6, 128–9, 136t, 145, 195 *Punch:* 27 both, 45b, 53t, 71b, 80bl *Sport and General:* 104–5, 147t, 148 both, 149 both, 150b, 154, 155, 167, 173b, 174t, 177br *Sporting Pictures:* 181t *The Times:* 156b, 168b *Telegraph and Argus:* 179b *Bob Thomas:* 202b, 218b, 225 *Tom Webster/Daily Mail:* 90t, 95t, 100, 157

The publishers would like to thank David Frith for his kind cooperation with picture research in this book.

1 THE EARLY YEARS

In 1864 *Wisden Cricketers' Almanack* was published for the first time. Apart from its name, it bears little resemblance to the monster whose publication now heralds the arrival of another cricket season. The 1864 *Wisden* was 112 pages long and contained information that would certainly not be deemed essential to the modern cricket enthusiast. For instance the winners of the Derby, Oaks and St Leger races since 1779 are listed, along with the fact that China was first visited by a European in 1517. The book recorded the results of the University Boat Race and the dates of the principal battles of the Wars of the Roses (not the annual skirmishes at Headingley and Old Trafford).

Obviously John Wisden had difficulty in filling his book up. In 1987, however, *Wisden*'s editor was confronted with the opposite dilemma – what to leave out – despite having 1,296 pages at his disposal. As I embark upon this brief history, I suspect that my problems will have more in common with more recent editors of *Wisden*, than with its enterprising founder.

It would be particularly convenient to record that an idle Englishman sat down in the spring of 1863 and devised the game of cricket – like the originators of Monopoly or Trivial Pursuit. Of course, the game is far too complicated for that to have happened. It took centuries to evolve, possibly six of them if the reference to 'Creag' in the reign of Edward I, involving a club and a ball, was a primitive form of our modern game. A more trustworthy reference, this time to 'crickett', appears at the end of the reign of Henry VIII in 1598. A certain John Derrick, when giving evidence about a disputed piece of land at Guildford, wrote that he and some of his friends 'did play there at crickett and other plaies'.

We can surmise that Oliver Cromwell was not particularly enthused by the game, as in 1654 the churchwardens and overseers of Eltham in Kent fined seven of their parishioners two shillings each for playing cricket on the Lord's Day. In Ireland, it is alleged, Cromwell's major generals went one step further and banned the game completely, ordering all 'sticks' and balls to be burnt. It took the Irish a long time to recover from such severity. Some would say they never have – but for their triumph at Londonderry on 2 July, 1969, when they bowled West Indies out for 25.

In the first half of the eighteenth century the game was most popular in the south east of England. It even moved some to poetry. In 1706 an old Etonian composed an account in Latin of a game of cricket (which I shan't quote now), and 30 years later the story of a game between Kent and All England began with a flourish:

> Hail Cricket! Manly British game!
> First of all sports! Be first alike with fame!

For the writer, James Love, the charms of cricket clearly won precedence over any other game. The nation was yet to be subjected to televised snooker.

The patrons of the game were often wealthy landowners who were anxious to ensure that their estates were well manned with gardeners and gamekeepers who could bat and bowl. They were desperate to win as considerable bets were frequently placed on the outcome of the match. It is, however, not just an eighteenth-century phenomenon that institutions take due – or undue – consideration of an employee's cricketing prowess. Recently I saw an advertisement from a church diocese in need of reinforcement, 'Curate required, slow left-arm spinner preferred'. Naturally I assume that on this occasion it was not money that was at stake.

In the middle of the eighteenth century the centre of the cricketing universe was the tiny Hampshire village of Hambledon and its ground, the charmingly rustic 'Broadha'penny Down'. Richard Nyren was both captain and secretary of the local team, as well as being landlord of the Bat and Ball Inn, and he somehow contrived to attract the main patrons of the game and its best players to this little village, which even today is off the beaten track.

John Nyren, Richard's son, wrote *The Young Cricketer's Tutor* recording the Hambledon days. He tells of John Small, a bat maker and one of the first exponents of playing with a straight bat (showing the maker's name, no doubt); of 'Lumpy' Stevens, renowned for the accuracy of his bowling, who caused the introduction of the third stump, having bowled the ball through Small's wicket three times in one innings; and of the greatest bowler of the age, David Harris. The Rev John Mitford describes Harris in action:

> His attitude when preparing to deliver the ball was masculine, erect and appalling. First he stood like a soldier at drill, upright. Then with a graceful and elegant curve, he raised the fatal ball to his forehead and, drawing back his right foot, started off.

Mitford was a devoted enthusiast, but not a great player – which may explain why the prospect of facing Harris sounds such an awesome task. Indeed, perhaps Harris was the forerunner of Lillee and Marshall, but the batsman did have the consolation of knowing the ball was going to be delivered 'under-arm'. It wasn't until 1835 that round-arm bowling was legalised, when the law was amended to allow the ball to be delivered below the level of the shoulder, and only in 1864 was the bowler given complete freedom regarding the height of his arm.

Inevitably the village of Hambledon could not hold centre stage for long – no more than three decades in fact. In 1787 Thomas Lord, an enterprising Yorkshireman, leased a piece of land in London, where Dorset Square now stands, and on 31 May 1787 the first ball was bowled at Lord's. In the same year the Marylebone Cricket Club was formed, and within 12 months the MCC had revised the laws of the game. Thereafter the club was accepted as the unchallenged guardian of the laws of cricket.

A cricket match about 1760 at Kenfield Hall, Petham, near Canterbury

Above *Some of the early giants*

Top *The Artillery Ground, Finsbury, by Francis Hayman*

Right *John Nyren*

Twenty years later Lord was obliged to move premises and after three years at Lisson Grove he moved the ground, turf and all, to the present headquarters of cricket in St John's Wood. Soon Lord's became the prime venue of the great amateur fixtures of the day: in 1805 came Eton v Harrow, Gentlemen v Players in 1806 and Oxford v Cambridge in 1827, and it became the ambition of every upstanding young cricketer to play at Lord's – just as it is today.

Gradually the game began to flourish – not least because it gave those with nothing better to do an excuse to indulge in one of their favourite pastimes: betting. Spare a thought for William Lambert, acknowledged as the best all-rounder of his day and a mighty adversary in the popular single-wicket contests. In 1817, after a game between England and Nottingham, he was said to have 'sold the match', and his career came to an abrupt, inglorious end. Thereafter the bookmakers were banned from Lord's: it took them 160 years to return.

By the middle of the nineteenth century several county sides had been formed, the best of which was undoubtedly Kent, who possessed two of the giants of the game in Alfred Mynn and Fuller Pilch. Aside from county cricket there was one other equally important development within the game, which was later to inspire 'W.G.' himself – the advent of the 'professional circus'.

I wonder whether in 1977 Kerry Packer was aware that his idea of employing professionals to play in his own games was not a new one. William Clarke, a bricklayer from Nottingham, had a similar notion which caused far fewer ructions back in 1846. Clarke, a handy underarm bowler, whose effectiveness doesn't appear to have been reduced by the loss of an eye, was probably even more shrewd as a businessman. He employed a team of professionals, known as the All England XI, to tour the countryside, playing against local XVIIIs and XXIIs. No doubt modern public relations officers would stress the missionary nature of such an enterprise, and indeed the arrival of the All England XI would have created tremendous interest around the shires, but the prime motivation for Clarke's scheme was undoubtedly profit.

Below left and right *The title and final pages of the 1774 document that laid down the laws of the game*

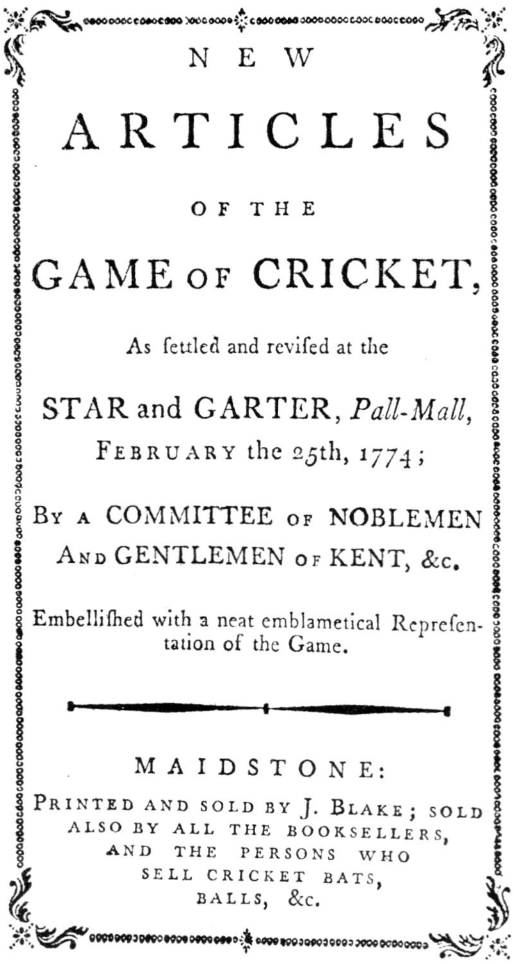

NEW

ARTICLES

OF THE

GAME OF CRICKET,

As ſettled and reviſed at the

STAR and GARTER, *Pall-Mall*,

FEBRUARY the 25th, 1774;

BY A COMMITTEE OF NOBLEMEN AND GENTLEMEN OF KENT, &c.

Embelliſhed with a neat emblametical Repreſentation of the Game.

MAIDSTONE:

PRINTED AND SOLD BY J. BLAKE; SOLD ALSO BY ALL THE BOOKSELLERS, AND THE PERSONS WHO SELL CRICKET BATS, BALLS, &c.

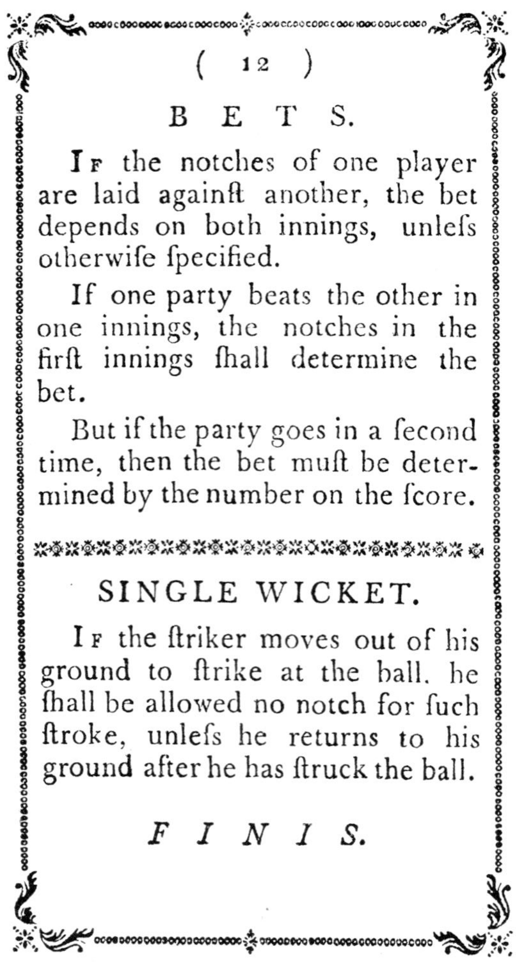

(12)

BETS.

IF the notches of one player are laid againſt another, the bet depends on both innings, unleſs otherwiſe ſpecified.

If one party beats the other in one innings, the notches in the firſt innings ſhall determine the bet.

But if the party goes in a ſecond time, then the bet muſt be determined by the number on the ſcore.

SINGLE WICKET.

IF the ſtriker moves out of his ground to ſtrike at the ball, he ſhall be allowed no notch for ſuch ſtroke, unleſs he returns to his ground after he has ſtruck the ball.

FINIS.

A handbill advertising an early 19th-century game at Lord's. Team celebrities included Lord Frederick Beauclerk and Squire Osbaldeston

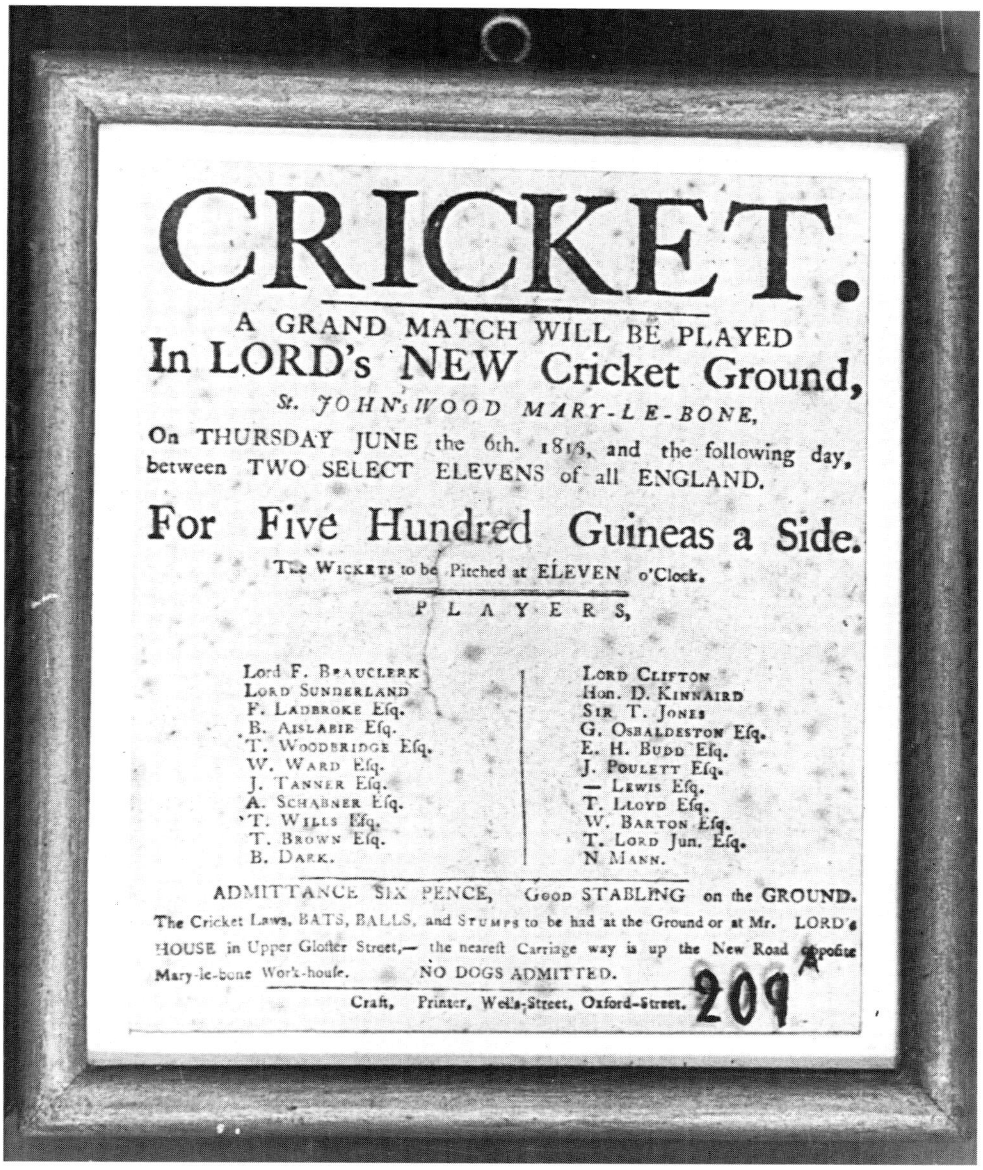

CRICKET.

A GRAND MATCH WILL BE PLAYED
In LORD's NEW Cricket Ground,
St. JOHN's WOOD MARY-LE-BONE,
On THURSDAY JUNE the 6th. 1816, and the following day,
between TWO SELECT ELEVENS of all ENGLAND.

For Five Hundred Guineas a Side.

The WICKETS to be Pitched at ELEVEN o'Clock.

PLAYERS,

Lord F. BEAUCLERK	LORD CLIFTON
LORD SUNDERLAND	Hon. D. KINNAIRD
F. LADBROKE Eſq.	SIR T. JONES
B. AISLABIE Eſq.	G. OSBALDESTON Eſq.
T. WOODBRIDGE Eſq.	E. H. BUDD Eſq.
W. WARD Eſq.	J. POULETT Eſq.
J. TANNER Eſq.	— LEWIS Eſq.
A. SCHABNER Eſq.	T. LLOYD Eſq.
T. WILLS Eſq.	W. BARTON Eſq.
T. BROWN Eſq.	T. LORD Jun. Eſq.
B. DARK.	N MANN.

ADMITTANCE SIX PENCE, Good STABLING on the GROUND.
The Cricket Laws, BATS, BALLS, and STUMPS to be had at the Ground or at Mr. LORD's HOUSE in Upper Gloſter Street,— the neareſt Carriage way is up the New Road oppoſite Mary-le-bone Work-houſe. NO DOGS ADMITTED.

Craft, Printer, Wells-Street, Oxford-Street. 209

Some more recent England players might well have been grateful for Punch's *19th-century protective clothing*

NEW CRICKETING DRESSES, TO PROTECT ALL ENGLAND AGAINST THE PRESENT SWIFT BOWLING

Leech 1854

Above *Thomas Lord*

Above *Alfred Mynn, the 'Lion of Kent'*

Below *An early women's cricket match*

Right *A commemorative handkerchief, marking the MCC's 50th Anniversary Match in July 1837. The South beat the North*

Below *Cricket on the Goodwin Sands, about 1840*

Amongst his band were Mynn and Pilch, George Parr, who was to succeed him in 1856, 'Tear 'em' Tarrant, who could be relied upon to terrify the locals, a lively all-rounder who really was called Julius Caesar and John Wisden, five feet four and fast. Theirs was definitely a strenuous occupation, travelling around the countryside, often on an embryonic railway system, which could not by any stretch of the imagination be considered to be 'getting there'. I doubt whether they lost many games – though how the likes of Fuller Pilch and George Parr managed to penetrate a field of 22 baffles me.

In 1852 internal quarrels caused a split. Some of the players, particularly the southern professionals, felt that they were being underpaid and that Clarke was taking too large a share of the profits. Everything came to a head at a meeting at Sheffield, but Clarke was not the compromising sort, and as a result Wisden and 'Ploughboy' Dean founded a rival team, the United England XI. For a while both sides co-existed happily, since there were plenty of teams eager to entertain them. Indeed, one of the highlights of the season was the game between the two rival XIs. We can imagine that it was certainly keenly contested.

John Wisden, founder of the Almanack

CRICKET.

A GRAND MATCH
WILL BE PLAYED IN
LORD'S GROUND,
MARYLEBONE,
On Monday, June 28th, 1847, & following Day.
Kent against England.

PLAYERS.

Kent.	England.
E. L. BAYLEY, Esq.	Sir F. BATHURST
E. BANKS, Esq.	A. M. HOARE, Esq.
N. FELIX, Esq.	R. T. KING, Esq.
A. MYNN, Esq.	O. C. PELL, Esq.
ADAMS	BOX
DORRINTON	CLARK
HILLYER	DEAN
MARTIN	GUY
MARTINGEL	LILLYWHITE
PILCH	PARR
W. PILCH	SEWELL

MATCHES TO COME.

Thursday, July 1st, at Eton, the Marylebone Club against the Gentlemen of Eton.
Monday, July 5th, at Lord's, the Marylebone Club and Ground against the Bury and Suffolk Club.
Thursday, July 8th, at Lord's, the Marylebone Club and Ground against the Undergraduates of Oxford. Return Match.
Monday, July 12th, at Lord's, the Marylebone Club and Ground against the Cambridge Town and County Club
Thursday, July 15th, at Kennington Oval, the Marylebone Club and Ground against the County of Surrey. Return Match.
Saturday, July 17th, at Harrow, the Marylebone Club against the Gentlemen of Harrow
Monday, July 19th, at Lord's, the Gentlemen against the Players
Monday, July 26th, at Lord's, a Grand Match in honor of A. Mynn, Esq.
Wednesday, July 28th, Thursday, July 29th Friday, July 30th, & Saturday, July 31st, the Annual Matches between the Gentlemen of Harrow, Eton, and Winchester.

DARK's newly-invented Leg Guards.

Also his TUBULAR and other INDIA-RUBBER GLOVES, SPIKED SOLES FOR CRICKET SHOES, CRICKET BALLS, and DENISON's CRICKETER'S COMPANION, to be had of R. Dark, at the Tennis Court.

R. Dark being the Manufacturer of all the various articles which are here enumerated, and therefore assured of the excellence of the quality of the different materials with which they are constructed, can with the utmost confidence recommend them to the cricketing world.

Cricket Bats and Stumps to be had of M. Dark, at the Manufactory on the Ground.

Admittance 6d.......Stabling on the Ground......Ordinary at 3 o'clock.

Morgan Printer, 38, Church-st, adjoining the Theatre

A match at Lord's, including many 19th-century notables

Above *A match between the Army and the Navy, near Portsmouth, about 1840*

Below *A commemorative handkerchief illustrating the All England XI of 1847*

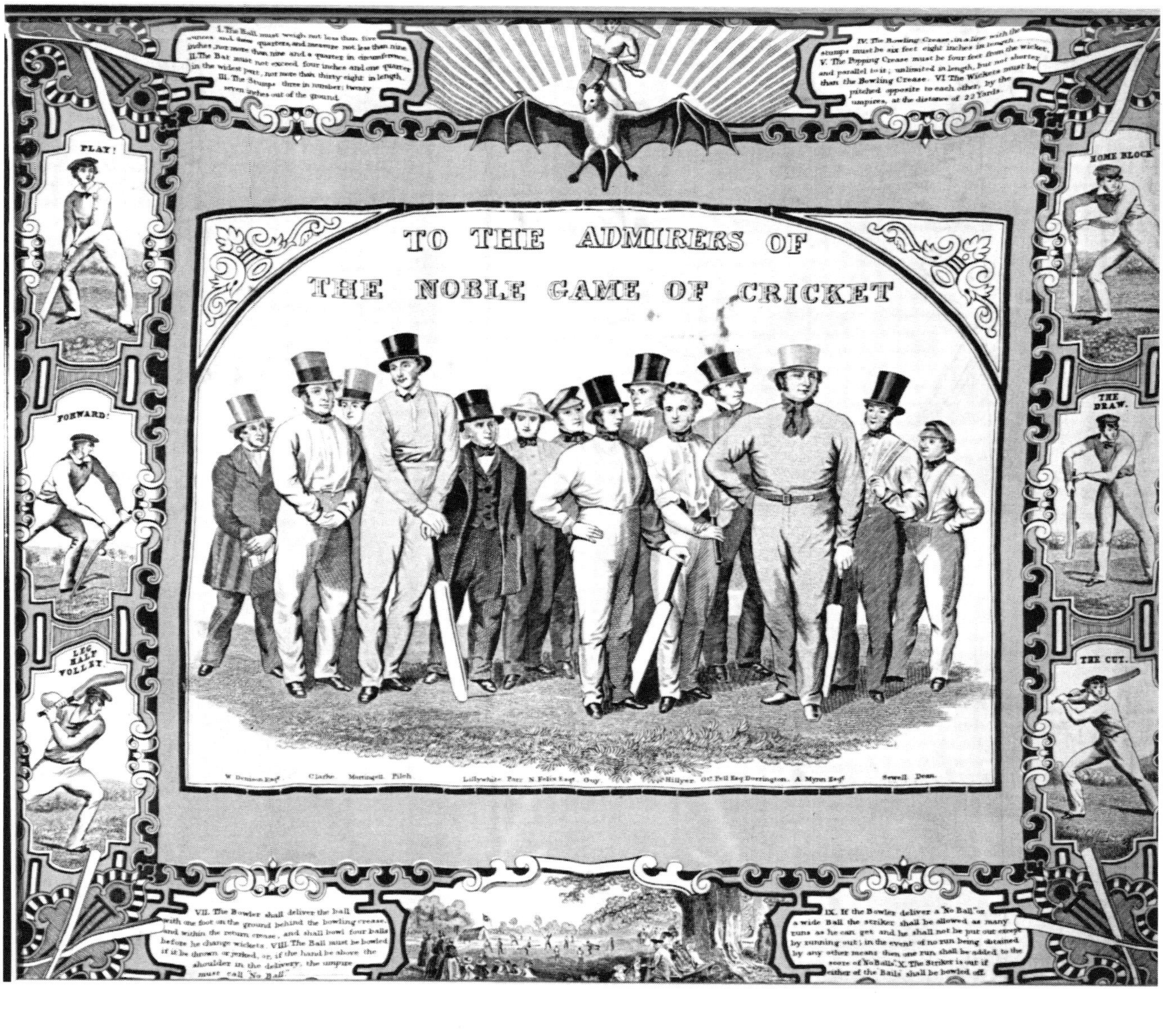

FULLER PILCH,
BORN MARCH 17TH 1803, AT HORNINGTOFT, NORFOLK.
WM LILLYWHITE,
BORN JUNE 13TH 1792, AT GOODWOOD, SUSSEX.
THOS BOX,
BORN FEBY 7TH 1809, AT ARDINGLY, SUSSEX.
JAS COBBETT,
BORN JANY 12TH 1804, AT FRIMLEY, SURREY.
To Benjamin Aislabie, Esqre the Zealous Supporter of the Noble Game of Cricket, these Sketches of Celebrated Player
are by permission most respectfully Dedicated by his obliged & obedient Servant, W. H. Masch

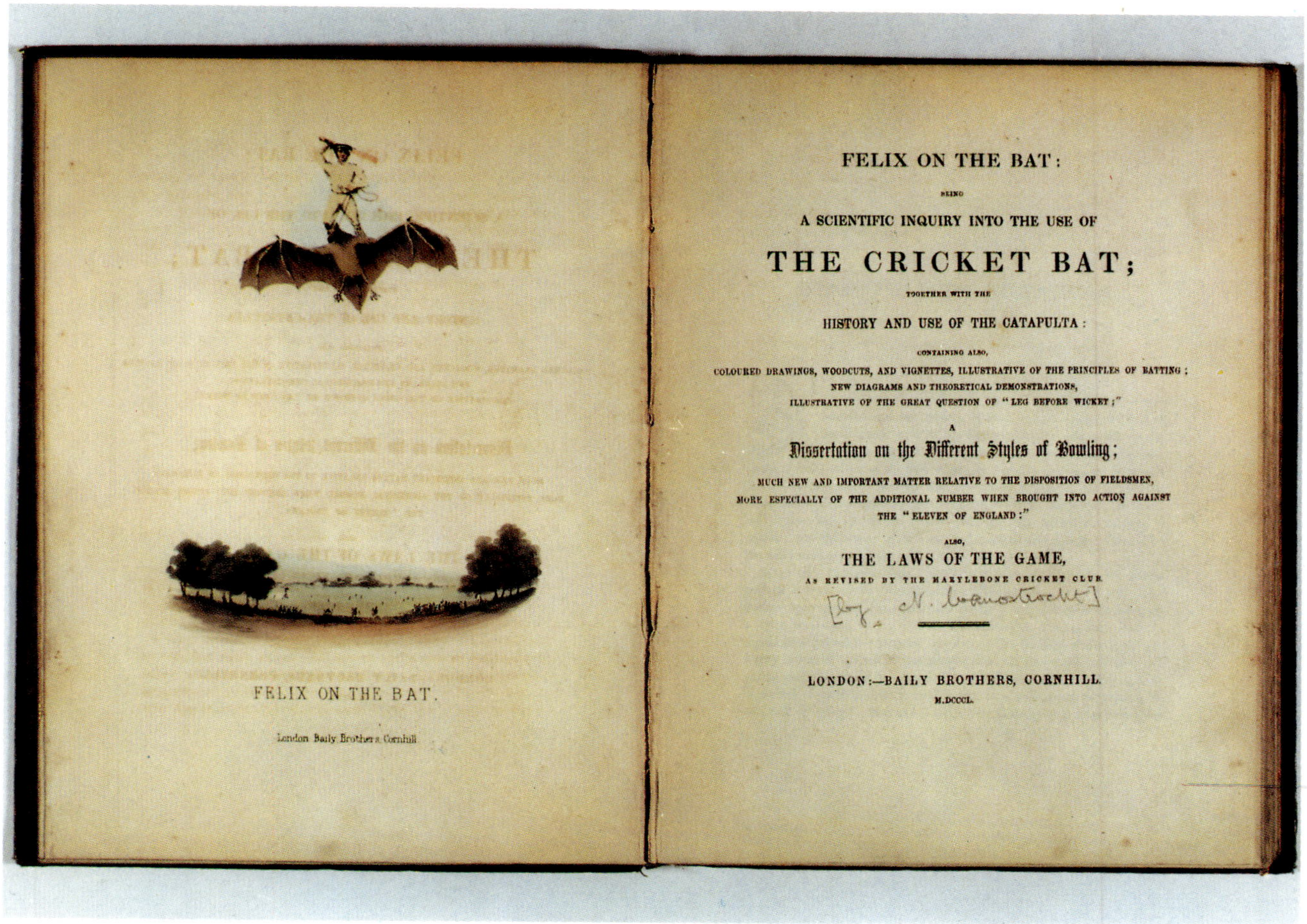

On 22 June 1854 the All England XI came to Bristol to play XXII of West Gloucestershire. I don't suppose they were too excited by the prospect: apart from these 'circus' games they still represented their counties and there the cricket would have been more challenging. None the less they performed 'professionally', defeating their opponents by 149 runs and impressing the locals in the process. The game, though, was to have rather more far-reaching consequences than could have been predicted at the time, for amongst the crowd was a six-year-old boy who watched every ball. No one present, except perhaps his mother, Martha, could have known that this child was to become the greatest cricketer in the history of the game. His name, of course, was William Gilbert Grace.

This little boy – and it is hard to imagine W.G. Grace without a beard and a paunch – was to dwarf all others in the period from 1865 to 1900. If this chapter dwells upon him to the exclusion of almost everyone else, it will at least reflect the standing of W.G. in relation to his contemporaries. He became as celebrated as Queen Victoria herself, and we can be sure that signs were indeed erected outside the cricket grounds of England stating, 'Admission threepence. If W.G. Grace plays sixpence'. Unwittingly Grace carried the game of cricket into the modern era almost single-handed. So it is worth exploring how the doctor's son from Downend began his cricketing career.

Dr Henry Grace and his wife Martha were cricket fanatics. Dr Henry formed and captained the West Gloucestershire side, and when the All England XI returned in 1855 he included his two eldest sons, Alfred (aged 15) and Edward Mills (13), as well as his brother-in-law, Alfred Pocock. 'E.M.' so impressed William Clarke by his fielding that he was presented with a bat, whilst Mrs Grace was given a book with practical hints on cricket. These gifts must have provided an extra stimulus for the family practices in the orchard – not that one was needed. The practices were conducted with true Victorian discipline – 15 minutes batting for the adults, five for the children. Mrs Grace looked on, no doubt occasionally consulting her handbook, and the three dogs retrieved the ball from the undergrowth. E.M. probably kept them the busiest, as he frequently

Top *Felix's early coaching manual*

Opposite *Four pioneers of the early 19th century*

played a vicious pull shot – even to straight balls – which was to become the hallmark of his game. Despite – or because of – this unorthodoxy, E.M. swiftly gained a reputation as a devastating hitter. In 1862, when he played as a last-minute replacement for the MCC against the Gentlemen of Kent, he proceeded to score 192 not out and take all 10 wickets in the second innings. This performance prompted Martha to write to George Parr, who was now the manager of the All England XI, to suggest a trial. She added the prophetic words that her younger son would be even better because he had a sounder defence. This 'sound' defence owed much to the patient tuition of Uncle Alfred, who, whilst he admired the deeds of E.M., was pained by his heretical style.

In 1863 George Parr brought his All England side back to the west country to play against XXII of Bristol and District. Four Graces played – father Henry, Alfred, E.M. and W.G. The locals defeated the All England XI by an innings and 20 runs. E.M. scored 37 and took most of the wickets. W.G., at 15 years old, scored 32. Already it was clear that Martha's boys were going to make an impact on the game beyond the boundaries of Gloucestershire: indeed E.M. joined George Parr's professionals on their tour of Australia in 1863–64.

Over the next three seasons W.G. established himself as one of the best cricketers in England – and therefore the world. By the end of the 1866 season, when he was 18 years old, he was acknowledged as the best. At this time he had to travel long distances to play top-class cricket, because Gloucestershire CCC had yet to form; the most prestigious matches were the Gentlemen v Players fixtures. In 1865 W.G. played in them both for the first time,

Right *Martha Grace*

Below *Three celebrated bats: (left) one used by Alfred Mynn, about 1850; (centre) the left-handed Merser's 18th-century bat and (right) that belonging to C. Bagot in 1793*

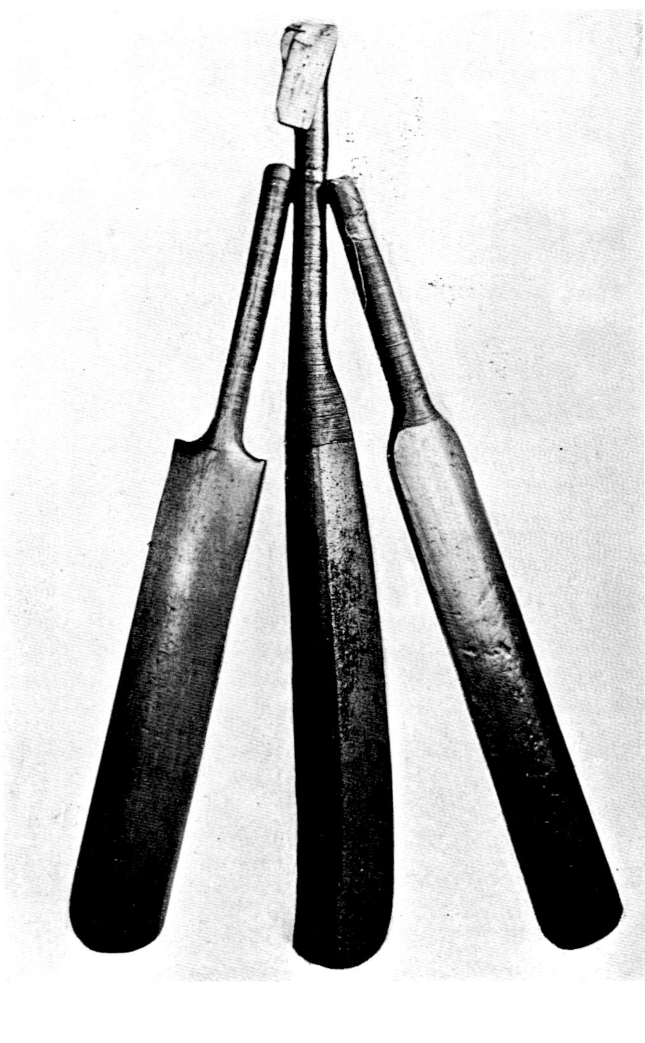

excelling more with the ball than the bat. In 1866 Surrey played an England XI and W.G., batting at number five, amassed 224 not out as England won by an innings and 300 runs. On the last afternoon his captain gave him permission to pop off to Crystal Palace to run in a 440-yard hurdle race – he won. Three weeks later he scored 173 not out for the Gentlemen of the South against the Players of the South at The Oval, having already taken seven wickets whilst bowling unchanged throughout the Players' innings. W.G. was creating new standards that no one else could reach. To appreciate the enormity of these batting performances here is W.G.'s own assessment of the wickets:

> Many of the principal grounds were so rough as to be positively dangerous to play upon and batsmen were commonly damaged by the fast bowling. When the wickets were in this condition the batsmen had to look out for shooters and leave the bumping balls to look after themselves. In the sixties it was no unusual thing to have three shooters in an over.

Hereafter it is possible to pinpoint only a few pinnacles in a staggering career. In 1871 he amassed 2,739 runs at an average of 78.25 per innings. Two years later he became the first man to perform the double. As early as 1876, there were murmurs that he had passed his best, until the month of August when he scored 1,279 runs with consecutive scores of 344, 177 and 318 not out. And as late as 1895, when he was 46 years old, he scored a thousand runs in May, finishing the season with an aggregate of 2,346 runs, more than anyone else. Bear in mind that even Geoffrey Boycott had later withdrawn from the fray by this age. These were truly remarkable deeds.

Right *Tom Humphrey (left) and Harry Jupp: Humphrey was the first man to score 1,000 runs in a first-class season*

Below *A young W. G. Grace, in the 1860s*

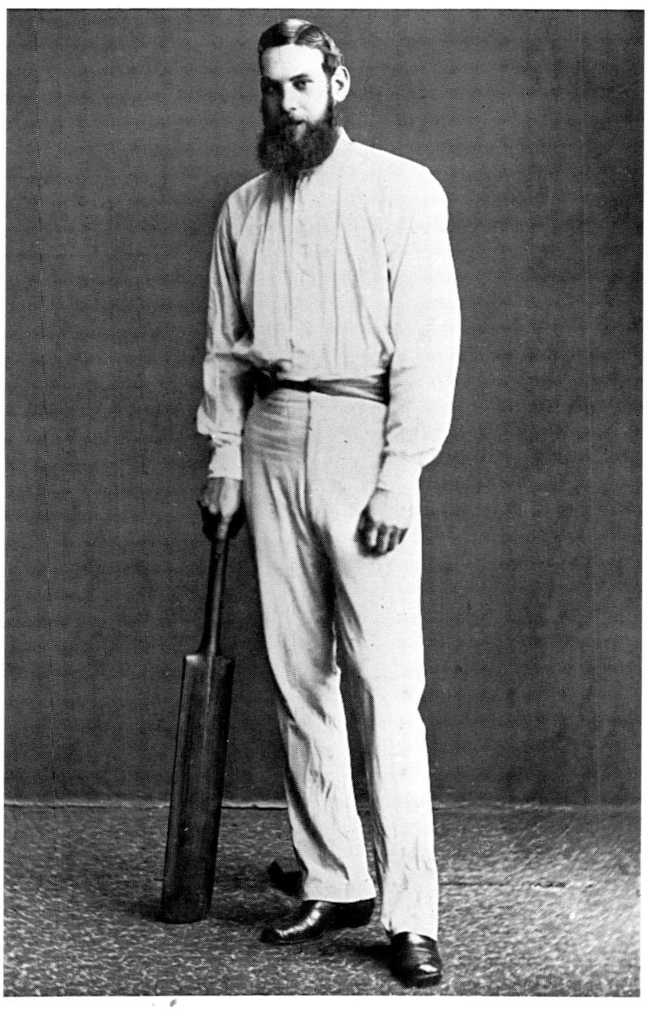

'Spy's' vision of the 'Champion', originally captioned merely 'Cricket' – the embodiment of the game

Above *Calcutta Cricket Club in 1861. Cricket was by now flourishing in the colonies*

Below *Melbourne Cricket Ground in 1864*

Above *The Household Brigade XI at Lord's in 1863*
Below *Richard Daft, a fine player in the 1860s and 1870s and George Parr's successor as Notts captain*

What, then, made Grace so much better than his contemporaries? Ranji, in *The Jubilee Book of Cricket*, gives us part of the answer:

> He revolutionized batting. He turned it from an accomplishment into a science .... Before W.G. batsmen were of two kinds; a batsman played a forward game or he played a back game .... It was bad cricket to hit a straight ball; as for pulling a long hop, it was regarded as immoral. What W.G. did was to unite in his mighty self all the good points of all the good players and to make utility the criterion of style. He founded the modern theory of batting by making forward and back play of equal importance, relying neither on one nor on the other, but both .... I hold him to be, not only the finest player born or unborn, but the maker of modern batting. He turned the old one stringed instrument into a many chorded lyre.

Allied to this new technical awareness was an insatiable appetite for runs. In a tribute in the 1915 *Wisden* Lord Harris recalls that he was just as anxious and watchful when his score was 200 as when he was on 0 – and just as reluctant to leave the wicket on dismissal. In 1895 he scored his 100th hundred against Somerset at Bristol. A magnum of champagne was brought out on to the square to celebrate the record, which everyone assumed would never be surpassed. Maybe the Somerset bowlers had more than their fair share. At any rate W.G. was obviously more interested in batting than in any immediate celebration, for he went on to amass 288 out of a total of 474, a measure of his hunger for runs as well as his stamina.

One other aspect of W.G.'s batting that would endear him to modern cricketers and critics is the fact that he was at his best against fast bowling. Nowadays, whenever a potential prodigy arrives with a flourish, the wiseacres invariably ask, 'But can he play fast bowling?'. There's no doubt that W.G. relished the challenge, and a contemporary, A.G. Steel, noted that 'his power of playing fast bowling was the greatest feature of his game'. His duels with Fred Spofforth, the 'Demon' from Australia, must have excited even the most luke-warm enthusiast.

As well as the 54,896 runs that Grace compiled in his career we must also account for 2,876 wickets. He was not a revolutionary bowler. He started off as a medium-paced slinger, but in the seventies soon saw the virtues of bowling more slowly. He kept an immaculate length and cut the ball from leg to off. Clearly he must have enjoyed bowling, as there are numerous occasions when we read that W.G. bowled right through the innings. In addition to his obvious stamina and eagerness to be constantly involved, there are two other factors that explain why he should occupy one end for an entire innings. The first is that an over in those days consisted of just four balls and was therefore a less demanding undertaking. The second is that during the latter part of his career W.G. was invariably captain of the side he was playing in. Occasionally he might startle his colleagues by announcing that he would agree to change the bowling, but invariably this meant that he had decided to have a go from the other end.

As well as being the canniest of bowlers he was also 'the pluckiest field to his own bowling'. In addition, I have no doubt that he won his fair share of lbw decisions. Writing in 1895 Lord Harris, captain of Kent and England, could not avoid making the following observation:

> I always thought the old man depended rather too much on the umpire for leg before, particularly when I was on the opposite side. He crossed the wicket so far to the off himself that he could not in many instances judge with any accuracy whether the ball pitched straight or not and I don't think a bowler ought to ask for leg before unless he is pretty sure as to the pitch.

Cricket in Kohat (now Pakistan) in 1862

Above *Professionals – and scholars! Four great Yorkshire cricketers of the 1880s don some fancy dress for the camera (left to right): Ephraim Lockwood, Ted Peate, George Ulyett, Bobby Peel*

Right *Cricket at Port Elizabeth, the Cape of Good Hope, in 1871*

Right *Nets on a corner of The Close at Clifton College in the 1880s. This was the scene of Sir Henry Newbolt's 'A bumping pitch and a blinding light' in his* Vitae Lampada. *The ground also witnessed A.E.J. Collins' 628 not out in a house match in 1899, the highest-ever score in an organised game*

Not a philosophy that W.G. would have pursued. Indeed he was known on occasions to add insult to injury by murmuring to a batsman who had just been sent back to the pavilion 'lbw Grace'. 'You weren't out, you know'. I don't suppose this would have endeared him to his opponents, yet when we try to discover from the writings of his contemporaries what he was like, it is hard to find anyone who is not full of affection for the 'Old Man'.

We all know what he looked like, a figure instantly recognised by the nation even in those far-off pre-television days. He spoke with an incongruous high-pitched voice that must have surprised first-time acquaintances. He didn't care much for appearances; his dress was intended to be comfortable rather than fashionable, even though the whole world would want to observe him – he invariably dressed in a broad hat, a long and ample lounge coat, more than ample trousers and a massive pair of boots to support him.

He was neither a villain nor an angel. His contemporaries record that there were several occasions when he was unable to hide his displeasure at unfavourable umpiring decisions – but as we are now well aware that is quite a common trait amongst the truly great players. There is a moment of disbelief that cannot be disguised. Though an amateur, he was not an aristocrat and he was anxious to reap financial rewards from his prowess. His testimonials gathered something in the region of £14,000, an unprecedented sum in the nineteenth century. He manipulated expenses and demanded considerable remuneration from those who wanted him to participate on tours or in special matches. Modern cricketers would regard this as simply good business, but it probably provoked some envy and bitterness amongst his fellows. Yet he was known to travel miles to support some lowly beneficiary. He could be stubborn and autocratic, as his stormy relationship with the Gloucestershire committee in the 1890s demonstrates, but he would not be the last cricketer to be frustrated by the administrators. Nor would he have claimed to be a great intellect, though he did finally qualify as a doctor at the age of 31.

Cricket was popular at girls' schools in the Victorian era. This is a team at Wycombe Abbey

W.G. Grace and the ex-Australian captain, Billy Murdoch. They were stalwarts of W.G.'s London County team in the early 1900s

Right *W.G. with his sons W.G. Grace, junior (left), and C.B. Grace (right)*

Colonel Philip Trevor wrote that 'W.G. was a great big baby. Is that a libel? If it is a good many of us would like to be libelled all day long and every day of the week'. Trevor clearly intended this as a compliment. It is a theme that Bernard Darwin takes up in his excellent biography of W.G., though he prefers to compare his subject to an overgrown schoolboy:

> He had all the schoolboy's love for elementary and boisterous jokes; his distaste for learning; his desperate and undisguised keenness; his guilelessness and his guile; his occasional pettishness and pettiness; his endless power of recovering his good spirits. To them may be added two qualities not as a rule to be found in schoolboys; a wonderful modesty and lack of vanity; an invariable kindness to those younger than himself, 'except' as one of his most devoted friends has observed, 'that he tried to chisel them out lbw'.

I know that comparisons can be futile, but Darwin's assessment of W.G. could easily apply to Ian Botham. They have both shared an unquenchable and uncomplicated thirst for life, which often exhausted their colleagues. Even as he approached the age of 60 W.G. would wear out friends 30 years his junior. After three long days of early-morning shooting and cricket, he was 'honestly perplexed' when his companions refused to join him in the billiard room at midnight. I have seen Botham similarly stunned and dismayed by his colleagues' lack of stamina. However, not even Botham can be considered to have transformed the game of cricket and the public's awareness of it in the same way as W.G. Grace.

NINETY IN THE SHADE—NOT OUT!

UMPIRE PUNCH (*to* W. G. SOL). "BY JOVE, OLD MAN, YOU'VE 'BEATEN THE RECORD' *THIS* TIME, AND NO MISTAKE!"

["The Record-breaker was greatly gratified with the greeting, but did not fail to remember that his long innings might be declared 'closed' at any moment by that most capricious of Captains, the Clerk of the Weather."—*Punch's Epitome of History*.]

LORD'S IN DANGER. THE M. C. C. GO OUT TO MEET THE ENEMY.

["Sir EDWARD WATKIN proposes to construct a Railway passing through Lord's Cricket Ground."]

Above right *W.G., seen by* Punch *as the incarnation of the sun, during the long hot summer of 1898*

Right Punch *sees W. G. take on a new enemy*

Lord Harris, by 'Spy'. One of cricket's great administrators and 'missionaries', Harris remained involved in the game all his life

The young C.B. Fry, in 1894, originally seen by 'Spy' as 'Oxford Athletics'

The cricket season in W.G.'s heyday was less structured and more varied than today's, which is formulated by a soulless computer hidden away at Lord's. In 1873, which is regarded as the inaugural year of the County Championship, Gloucestershire and Nottinghamshire shared the title, having both played six games. Surrey, who were bottom of the table, played 14 matches, so it was obviously a haphazard affair. However, county cricket was just one element of a season, rather than being its focal point. In amateur circles the Eton v Harrow match at Lord's and the Varsity matches were undoubted highlights. A dip into the *Wisden* of 1876 confirms this:

That Eton v Harrow maintains its popular position in fashionable society as 'the match of the season', was abundantly proved by the facts that all the seats in The Grand Stand at Lord's were secured so early that the MCC Committee resolved to have erected another Stand . . . and that a clear week prior to the match the following notice was issued *via* the public press:-

'The whole available space having been filled up, no further applications for carriage or enclosure tickets can be entertained.'

Similarly, we learn that during that year's Varsity match 'on the tops of all walls commanding a sight

Cricket and Football Times

VOL. I.—EXTRA NUMBER.] SEPTEMBER 1878. [PRICE 3d., POST FREE 3½d

THE AUSTRALIAN ELEVEN.

:o:

REVIEW OF THEIR PERFORMANCES.

No day during the past few months has caused greater interest amongst the cricketers of this seagirt land than the second Monday in May last; it was on the evening of that day that the "City of Berlin," one of the Inman line, arrived in the Mersey, having amongst the passengers on board a gallant little band from far away Australia, a brave aspiring party who had travelled this great distance with a view to testing their capabilities in the cricket field, and throwing down the gauntlet against the cream of Old England's elevens. As all know, this was their first visit to this country, although in previous years several of our teams had travelled to the Antipodes, and then results proved

that the Colonials were opponents by no means to be despised, their calibre at cricket being but little inferior to our own, and in one memorable instance, against Lillywhite's team in '76, they were, even-handed, able to hold their own, and administer a defeat to the English eleven.

On arriving in England our guests at once made their way to Nottingham, the place chosen for their *début*, where their reception was most cordial and enthusiastic; many supporters of cricket in the lace town welcoming them at the railway station. The remainder of the week was devoted to practice at Trent Bridge, where, criticised by many old frequenters of that ground, they were at once pronounced well able to hold their own in the generality of matches, and likely to prove most formidable opponents to any county team. The opinions then expressed have been borne out to the letter, their play throughout the season having been consistently sound, though perhaps latterly their constant exertions have had the effect of makin them somewhat stale and worn out.

Trent Bridge was crowded on Monday morning, May 20th, and genuine English cheer welcomed the brothers Bannerman as they walke to the wickets as the first Australian representatives. The weath was cold and showery, consequently the wickets were very dead an slow, exactly suiting Alfred Shaw, who was in fine form with th leather. His analysis shows 36 overs, 3 balls, 25 maidens, 20 run 5 wickets, and Morley was not far behind him in his return; conse quently it is not to be wondered at that the Australians made but a indifferent stand, Midwinter and Garrett alone making double figure the innings only totalling 63. Assisted by some vigorous play by Selb who put together 66 in fine style, the "Lambs" totalled 153 on the dismissal, so that the visitors had a lot of leeway to make up, b

Shaw would not allow them to get on even terms, his analysis—58 ov 40 maidens, 35 runs, and 6 wickets—being extraordinary. Australians could only reach 76, thus leaving Nottinghamshire victors by an innings and 14 runs. The match being over somew early, a single wicket game, four on each side, was played, in which Australians were victorious; the way in which Spofforth ripped up stumps auguring ill for some of our batsmen in the future. Many cuses have been made for so disastrous a defeat, and to a great ext they are allowable, as the visitors had certainly not recovered from effects of their long voyage, and were out of practice, whilst treacherous nature of our climate militated against their chance.

Lord's was the next battlefield in the following week, and here th performance fairly took the cricketing world by storm, as an eleven Marylebone, containing such names as Messrs. W. G. Grace, Horn Ridley, Webbe, with Shaw and Morley, was easily defeated by ni

The Cricket and Football Times *of September 1878, describing the performances of the summer's Australian visitors* men clustered as closely as they could'. Today these traditional fixtures still take place at Lord's, but only the die-hards watch them.

Any two sides might be formed to provide an entertaining cricket match. For instance in 1884 the Smokers were defeated by the Non Smokers at Lord's, a result that would have given modern medics great satisfaction, though the decisive factor was probably that W.G., whilst he liked a drink, abstained from smoking all his life. In 1870 the Right Handed of England beat the Left Handed and the Married played the Single. *Wisden* even records a bizarre match at Islington in 1867 between One Arm and One Leg.

However, undoubtedly the most important fixture of the season, particularly before the advent of touring sides, was the match between the Gentlemen and the Players. During the period from 1806 to the coming of Grace in 1865 the Players dominated the fixture; indeed from 1855 to 1864 the Gentlemen avoided defeat just once. During the twenties and thirties, in order to make the contest worthy of a bet, the Gentlemen often played with teams of 15 or 18. In 1821 the Gentlemen were dismissed for 60; the Players responded with a score of 278 for six, whereupon we learn that the Gentlemen 'gave up' and the match was abandoned. I wonder whether the Players would have been allowed to take the same action if they had found themselves in such a hopeless situation. Once in 1837 the Gentlemen were permitted to defend conventional wickets, whilst the Players had to bat in front of four stumps measuring 36 inches by 12 inches; and the Gentlemen still lost by an innings.

Only during the Grace era did the Gentlemen dominate the fixture – and that is no coincidence. W.G. seemed to save his best performances for the occasion, which serves to emphasise the fact that it was the most important game in the cricket calendar. In all he scored a total of 6,008 runs for the Gentlemen v Players – more than twice the next man – and he took 276 wickets.

Gloucestershire in 1877. Back row (left to right): W.O. Moberley, W. Fairbanks, G.F. Grace, F.G. Monkland, W.R. Gilbert, W. Midwinter, C.K. Pullin (umpire). Front row: H.B. Kingscote, F. Townsend, R.F. Moles, W.G. Grace, E.M. Grace

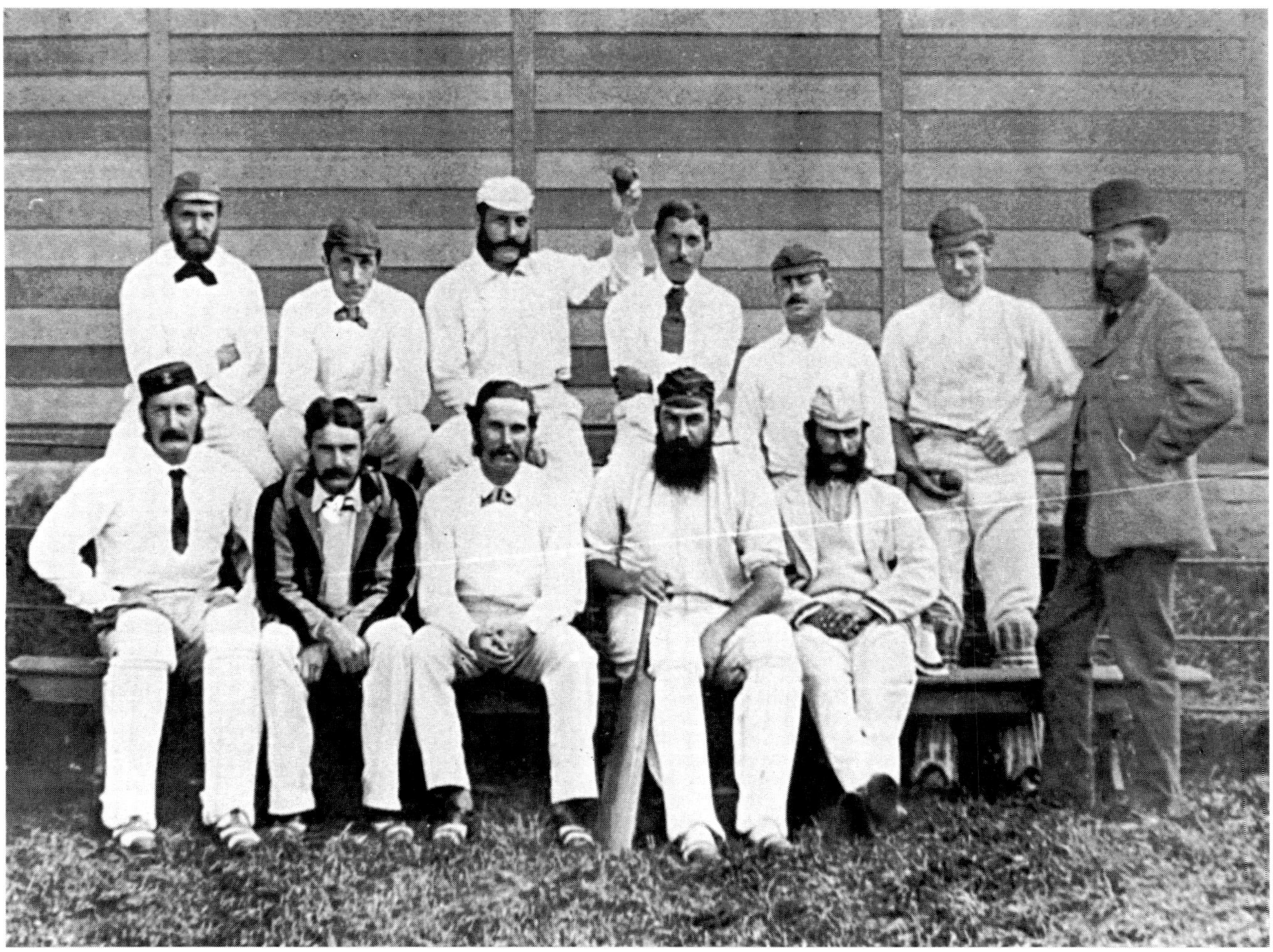

THE GENTLEMEN V THE PLAYERS

Played at Lord's, 3, 4, 5 July, 1876
Result: The Gentlemen won by an innings and 98 runs

The Gentlemen: First innings

C.J. Ottaway c Pooley b Emmett	42
W. G. Grace c Hill b Shaw	169
A.J. Webbe b Hill	26
A.N. Hornby c Shaw b Morley	13
A.W. Ridley c Emmett b Morley	103
F. Penn b Shaw	12
G.F. Grace not out	68
Lord Harris c Greenwood b Morley	0
W. H. Hadow b Morley	0
Hon A. Lyttelton b Morley	0
A. Appleby b Morley	0
Extras (b 6, lb 7, w 3)	16
Total	449

Fall of Wickets: 1/126, 2/230, 3/258, 4/262, 5/294, 6/433, 7/437, 8/437, 9/448.

Bowling: Shaw 83-38-106-2, Emmett 43-14-99-1, Morley 42·3-19-73-6, Hill 27-6-66-1, Lockwood 20-8-38-0, Oscroft 18-3-28-0, Daft 6-0-23-0.

The Players: First innings

R. Daft c W. G. Grace b Appleby	28
E. Lockwood c Lyttelton b Appleby	6
H. Jupp b Appleby	34
W. Oscroft b Appleby	58
A. Shrewsbury run out	9
A. Greenwood c Harris b Appleby	28
E. Pooley c Hornby b W. G. Grace	7
T. Emmett not out	14
A. Shaw c Harris b Appleby	4
A. Hill c Webbe b W. G. Grace	18
F. Morley c Webbe b W. G. Grace	5
Extras (b 6, lb 2)	8
Total	219

Fall of Wickets: 1/28, 2/57, 3/86, 4/105, 5/164, 6/171, 7/183, 8/193, 9/214.

Bowling: Appleby 57-28-96-6, W. G. Grace 55·2-23-81-3, G. F. Grace 19-6-26-0, Ridley 16-10-8-0.

The Players: Second innings

R. Daft not out	39
E. Lockwood b G.F. Grace	26
H. Jupp c Harris b W. G. Grace	21
W. Oscroft c Lyttelton b W. G. Grace	7
A. Shrewsbury b W. G. Grace	10
A. Greenwood c Appleby b G.F. Grace	3
E. Pooley c and b W. G. Grace	2
T. Emmett c Lyttleton b W. G. Grace	0
A. Shaw c Penn b W. G. Grace	2
A. Hill b G.F. Grace	11
F. Morley run out	8
Extras (b 1, lb 1, w 1)	3
Total	132

Bowling: Appleby 7-0-30-0, W. G. Grace 42-19-41-6, G.F. Grace 29-15-45-3, Ridley 6-2-13-0.

Let me give one example of Grace's domination by printing in full the scorecard of the 1876 match at Lord's. On this occasion W.G. was ably supported by his younger brother, Fred, an extremely gifted cricketer, who was much mourned by his elder brother when he died suddenly in 1880. The Gentlemen were led by the famous Lancashire captain, A.N. Hornby, but this didn't stop W.G. bowling 97 overs in the match. Richard Daft, arguably the best professional batsman of the sixties and seventies led the Players, for whom Arthur Shrewsbury was making his debut. Shrewsbury and W.G. became good friends and when, later in his career, the Old Man was asked which of his contemporaries he rated highest, he would reply without delay 'Give me Arthur'.

W.G.'s final appearance at Lord's for the Gentlemen was in 1899. Naturally he was captain, but one sure sign of advancing years – he was now 51 – is that he didn't bowl and he batted at number seven instead of his customary position at number one. None the less he scored 78, and was doubtless confident of a century until his partner, J.R. Mason, called for a run, which, 'in view of his weight and age, was beyond W.G.'s compass'. It doesn't take much imagination to envisage the Old Man's immediate reaction. The Gentlemen won by an innings, which was hardly surprising since the side contained many of the men who were to become legendary figures of the Edwardian era, MacLaren, Fry, Ranjitsinhji and F.S. Jackson. On the Players side was a 21-year-old Yorkshireman, Wilfred Rhodes, who was to have the rare privilege – and

Top *George Parr's English side which toured North America in 1859*

Right above *Kandy cricket ground in 1889, where (**right below**) English and Ceylonese elevens played regularly*

AUSTRALIA v ENGLAND

Played at Melbourne, 15, 16, 17, 19 March, 1877.
Result: Australia won by 45 runs.

Australia: First innings

C. Bannerman retired hurt	165
N. Thompson b Hill	1
T.P. Horan c Hill b Shaw	12
D.W. Gregory* run out	1
B.B. Cooper b Southerton	15
W.E. Midwinter c Ulyett b Southerton	5
E.J. Gregory c Greenwood b Lillywhite	0
J.M. Blackham† b Southerton	17
T.W. Garrett not out	18
T. Kendall c Southerton b Shaw	3
J.H. Hodges b Shaw	0
Extras (b 4,lb 2,w 2)	8
Total	245

Fall of Wickets: 1/2, 2/40, 3/41, 4/118, 5/142, 6/143, 7/197, 8/243, 9/245.
Bowling: Shaw 55.3-34-51-3, Hill 23-10-42-1, Ulyett 25-12-36-0, Southerton 37-17-61-3, Armitage 3-0-15-0, Lillywhite 14-5-19-1, Emmett 12-7-13-0.

England: First innings

H. Jupp lbw b Garrett	63
J. Selby† c Cooper b Hodges	7
H.R.J. Charlwood c Blackham b Midwinter	36
G. Ulyett lbw b Thompson	10
A. Greenwood c E.J. Gregory b Midwinter	1
T. Armitage c Blackham b Midwinter	9
A. Shaw b Midwinter	10
T. Emmett b Midwinter	8
A. Hill not out	35
James Lillywhite* c and b Kendall	10
J. Southerton c Cooper b Garrett	6
Extras (lb 1)	1
Total	196

Fall of Wickets: 1/23, 2/79, 3/98, 4/109, 5/121, 6/135, 7/145, 8/145, 9/168, 10/196.
Bowling: Hodges 9-0-27-1, Garrett 18.1-10-22-2, Kendall 38-16-54-1, Midwinter 54-23-78-5, Thompson 17-10-14-1.

Australia: Second innings

C. Bannerman b Ulyett	4
N. Thompson c Emmett b Shaw	7
T.P. Horan c Selby b Hill	20
D.W. Gregory* (9) b Shaw	3
B.B. Cooper b Shaw	3
W.E. Midwinter c Southerton b Ulyett	17
E.J. Gregory c Emmett b Ulyett	11
J.M. Blackham† lbw b Shaw	6
T.W. Garrett (4) c Emmett b Shaw	0
T. Kendall not out	17
J.H. Hodges b Lillywhite	8
Extras (b 5,lb 3)	8
Total	104

Fall of Wickets: 1/7, 2/27, 3/31, 4/31, 5/35, 6/58, 7/71, 8/75, 9/75, 10/104.
Bowling: Shaw 34-16-38-5, Hill 14-6-18-1, Ulyett 19-7-39-3, Lillywhite 1-0-1-1.

England: Second innings

H. Jupp (3) lbw b Midwinter	4
J. Selby† (5) c Horan b Hodges	38
H.R.J. Charlwood (4) b Kendall	13
G. Ulyett (6) b Kendall	24
A. Greenwood (2) c Midwinter b Kendall	5
T. Armitage c Blackham b Kendall	3
A. Shaw st Blackham b Kendall	2
T. Emmett (9) b Kendall	9
A. Hill (1) c Thompson b Kendall	0
James Lillywhite* b Hodges	4
J. Southerton not out	1
Extras (b 4,lb 1)	5
Total	108

Fall of Wickets: 1/0, 2/7, 3/20, 4/22, 5/62, 6/68, 7/92, 8/93, 9/100, 10/108.
Bowling: Hodges 7-5-7-2, Garrett 2-0-9-0, Kendall 33.1-12-55-7, Midwinter 19-7-23-1, D.W. Gregory 5-1-9-0.

pain – of bowling to both W.G. and his Australian counterpart of the next generation, Donald Bradman.

In time the Gentlemen v Players fixture had to yield centre stage to international matches, and it is to Australia and the beginnings of Test cricket that we now turn.

A band of enterprising professionals had crossed the Atlantic in 1859 to play a short series of games in Canada and the United States. Two years later the altogether more ambitious project of travelling with a side to Australia was undertaken, and the venture was a great success, arousing tremendous interest amongst the natives and providing a healthy profit for the promoters: Messrs Spiers and Pond. In 1863 the second team, under George Parr, set sail with a professional side plus E.M. Grace, and nine years later W.G. himself went down under along with his wife, for whom the trip was intended to be a honeymoon. Let's hope she was a cricket enthusiast.

Alfred Shaw, bowler of Test cricket's first delivery

So far all the games had been played 'against the odds'. However, on 15–19 March 1877 a Combined Australian XI played the visiting English side on level terms at Melbourne and this match is now regarded as the first Test match. Charles Bannerman scored 165, and even though none of his colleagues was able to pass 20 in either innings, his effort was sufficient to earn the Australian XI victory by 45 runs. In the nineteenth century England just managed to maintain the ascendancy, winning 26 matches to Australia's 20, but the latter still remain ahead in terms of overall victories.

Spurred on by their success, the Australians came to England for the summer of 1878. There were no internationals but an extraordinary match between the MCC and the tourists is worthy of mention. It began and ended on 27 May on a treacherous Lord's wicket. The MCC, with their illustrious openers W.G. and A.N. Hornby, were dismissed for 33 and 19 leaving the tourists, who themselves had been tormented by Alfred Shaw's accuracy, just 12 runs to win, a task they completed for the loss of one wicket. The architects of the Australian victory had been Boyle and Spofforth, noble antecedents of Lindwall and Miller and Lillee and Thomson. The result caused a sensation and prompted *Punch* to these lines:

> The Australians came down like a wolf on the fold,
> The Marylebone cracks for a trifle were bowled;
> Our Grace before dinner was very soon done,
> And Grace after dinner did not get a run.

However, order was restored in the first international on English soil in 1880. Remarkably the Australians had landed in England unannounced and without any sort of fixture list. With the domestic programme already organised, they had to play a series of matches 'against the odds' with local clubs

The great Australian bowler Hugh Trumble, in 1886

Harry Boyle, Spofforth's partner at The Oval in 1882

The 'Demon' Spofforth

An artist's impression of the England versus Australia Test at Lord's in 1886

W.G.'s image, used to sell mustard in the 1890s

ENGLAND v AUSTRALIA

Played at The Oval, 6, 7, 8 September 1880.
Result: England won by five wickets.

England: First innings

E.M. Grace c Alexander b Bannerman	36
W.G. Grace b Palmer	152
A.P. Lucas b Bannerman	55
W. Barnes b Alexander	28
Lord Harris* c Bonnor b Alexander	52
F. Penn b Bannerman	23
A.G. Steel c Boyle b Moule	42
Hon. A. Lyttelton† not out	11
G.F. Grace c Bannerman b Moule	0
A. Shaw b Moule	0
F. Morley run out	2
Extras (b 8, lb 11)	19
Total	420

Fall of Wickets: 1/91, 2/211, 3/269, 4/281, 5/322, 6/404, 7/410, 8/410, 9/413, 10/420.
Bowling: Boyle 44-17-71-0, Palmer 70-27-116-1, Alexander 32-10-69-2, Bannerman 50-12-111-3, McDonnell 2-0-11-0, Moule 12.3-4-23-3.

Australia: First innings

A.C. Bannerman b Morley	32
W.L. Murdoch* c Barnes b Steel	0
T.U. Groube b Steel	1
P.S. McDonnell c Barnes b Morley	27
J. Slight c G.F. Grace b Morley	11
J.M. Blackham† c and b Morley	0
G.J. Bonnor c G.F. Grace b Shaw	2
H.F. Boyle not out	36
G.E. Palmer b Morley	6
G. Alexander c W.G. Grace b Steel	6
W.H. Moule c Morley b W.G. Grace	6
Extras (b 9,lb 3)	12
Total	149

Fall of Wickets: 1/28, 2/39, 3/59, 4/84, 5/84, 6/89, 7/97, 8/113, 9/126, 10/149.
Bowling: Morley 32-9-56-5, Steel 29-9-58-3, Shaw 13-5-21-1, W.G. Grace 1.1-0-2-1.

Australia: Second innings

A.C. Bannerman c Lucas b Shaw	8
W.L. Murdoch* (3) not out	153
T.U. Groube (4) c Shaw b Morley	0
P.S. McDonnell (5) lbw b W.G. Grace	43
J. Slight (6) c Harris b W.G. Grace	0
J.M. Blackham† (7) c E.M. Grace b Morley	19
G.J. Bonnor (8) b Steel	16
H.F. Boyle (2) run out	3
G.E. Palmer c and b Steel	4
G. Alexander c Shaw b Morley	33
W.H. Moule b Barnes	34
Extras (b 7,lb 7)	14
Total	327

Fall of Wickets: 1/8, 2/13, 3/14, 4/97, 5/101, 6/143, 7/181, 8/187, 9/239, 10/327.
Bowling: Morley 61-30-90-3, Steel 31-6-73-2, Shaw 33-18-42-1, W.G. Grace 28-10-66-2, Barnes 8.3-3-17-1, Lucas 12-7-23-0, Penn 3-1-2-0.

England: Second innings

E.M. Grace (6) b Boyle	0
W.G. Grace (7) not out	9
A.P. Lucas c Blackham b Palmer	2
W. Barnes (5) c Moule b Boyle	5
F. Penn (4) not out	27
Hon. A. Lyttelton† (1) b Palmer	13
G.F. Grace (2) b Palmer	0
Extras (nb 1)	1
Total. (5 wickets)	57

Lord Harris*, A. G. Steel, A. Shaw and F. Morley did not bat.

Fall of Wickets: 1/2, 2/10, 3/22, 4/31, 5/31.
Bowling: Boyle 17-7-21-2, Palmer 16.3-5-35-3.

in the north and the midlands. Eventually an international was arranged at The Oval in September. Unfortunately for the tourists, Spofforth was injured and W.G. celebrated his Test debut by scoring 152. Despite W.L. Murdoch's defiant century, England triumphed by five wickets, but it had been a memorable match watched by over 20,000 spectators. In defeat the Australians had proved to the British public that they were now formidable and worthy adversaries and from 1880 onwards it was clear that a match between England and Australia could rival any other in the cricket calendar.

The Australians were undoubtedly good, but surely not good enough to defeat a full-strength England team playing at home. When in 1882 Peate and Barlow combined to bowl Australia out for 63 on a tricky wicket at The Oval, England's supremacy must have seemed secure. However, on this occasion Spofforth was not injured. Bowling unchanged, he took seven for 46 as he kept Australian hopes alive by dismissing England for 101. On the second morning there was a heavy downpour and, according to the Lancastrian all-rounder, Barlow, the state of the wicket was unfit when play began, with the footholds slippery and the ball like soap. The Australian openers, Bannerman and Massie, seized their chance, quickly overhauling the deficit before the conditions improved for the bowlers. England were losing control of the match, and a measure of their desperation can be seen in the run-out of the Australian, Jones, when in partnership with Murdoch. Not for the last time there was a little 'needle' evident in an England v Australia match. Inevitably W.G. was involved. *Wisden* faithfully records the incident:

> At 114 Jones was run out in a way which gave great dissatisfaction to Murdoch and other Australians. Murdoch played a ball to leg, for which Lyttelton ran. The ball was returned, and Jones, having completed the first run, and thinking wrongly, but very naturally, that the ball was dead, went out of his ground. Grace put his wicket down, and the umpire gave him out. Several of the team spoke angrily of Grace's action.

Our chronicler adds that a gentleman in the pavilion remarked that 'Jones ought to thank the champion for teaching him something'. I doubt whether he did though.

England required 85 to win and it is recorded how Spofforth, during the ten minutes' interval, declared to his compatriots that 'this thing can be done'. However, with the score at 51 for two and

Above *Some of the 1888 Australian tourists. Back row (left to right): J.M. Blackham, J. Worrall, A.H. Jarvis, G.H.S. Trott, C.T.B. Turner, H.F. Boyle, Front row: C.W. Beal, A. Bannerman, P.S. McDonnell, G.J. Bonnor, J.J. Ferris, J.D. Edwards*

Below *The 1886 Parsee team which toured England. They payed all their own expenses on the trip, but unfortunately won only one, and lost 19, of their 28 matches*

ENGLAND v AUSTRALIA
Played at The Oval, 28, 29 August, 1882.
Result: Australia won by 7 runs.

Australia: First innings

A.C. Bannerman c Grace b Peate	9
H.H. Massie b Ulyett	1
W.L. Murdoch* b Peate	13
G.J. Bonnor b Barlow	1
T.P. Horan b Barlow	3
G. Giffen b Peate	2
J.M. Blackham† c Grace b Barlow	17
T.W. Garrett c Read b Peate	10
H.F. Boyle b Barlow	2
S.P. Jones c Barnes b Barlow	0
F.R. Spofforth not out	4
Extras (b 1)	1
Total	63

Fall of Wickets: 1/6, 2/21, 3/22, 4/26, 5/30, 6/30, 7/48, 8/53, 9/59, 10/63.
Bowling: Peate 38-24-31-4, Ulyett 9-5-11-1, Barlow 31-22-19-5, Steel 2-1-1-0.

England: First innings

R.G. Barlow c Bannerman b Spofforth	11
W.G. Grace b Spofforth	4
G. Ulyett st Blackham b Spofforth	26
A.P. Lucas c Blackham b Boyle	9
Hon A. Lyttelton† c Blackham b Spofforth	2
C.T. Studd b Spofforth	0
J.M. Read not out	19
W. Barnes b Boyle	5
A.G. Steel b Garrett	14
A.N. Hornby* b Spofforth	2
E. Peate c Boyle b Spofforth	0
Extras (b 6, lb 2, nb 1)	9
Total	101

Fall of Wickets: 1/13, 2/18, 3/57, 4/59, 5/60, 6/63, 7/70, 8/96, 9/101, 10/101.
Bowling: Spofforth 36.3-18-46-7, Garrett 16-7-22-1, Boyle 19-7-24-2.

Australia: Second innings

A.C. Bannerman c Studd b Barnes	13
H.H. Massie b Steel	55
W.L. Murdoch* (4) run out	29
G.J. Bonnor (3) b Ulyett	2
T.P. Horan c Grace b Peate	2
G. Giffen c Grace b Peate	0
J.M. Blackham† c Lyttelton b Peate	7
T.W. Garrett (10) not out	2
H.F. Boyle (11) b Steel	0
S.P. Jones (8) run out	6
F.R. Spofforth (9) b Peate	0
Extras (b 6)	6
Total	122

Fall of Wickets: 1/66, 2/70, 3/70, 4/79, 5/79, 6/99, 7/114, 8/117, 9/122, 10/112.
Bowling: Peate 21-9-40-4, Ulyett 6-2-10-1, Barlow 13-5-27-0, Steel 7-0-15-2, Barnes 12-5-15-1, Studd 4-1-9-0.

England: Second innings

R.G. Barlow (3) b Spofforth	0
W.G. Grace (1) c Bannerman b Boyle	32
G. Ulyett (4) c Blackham b Spofforth	11
A.P. Lucas (5) b Spofforth	5
Hon A. Lyttelton† (6) b Spofforth	12
C.T. Studd (10) not out	0
J.M. Read (8) b Spofforth	0
W. Barnes (9) c Murdoch b Boyle	2
A.G. Steel (7) c and b Spofforth	0
A.N. Hornby* (2) b Spofforth	9
E. Peate b Boyle	2
Extras (b 3, nb 1)	4
Total	77

Fall of Wickets: 1/15, 2/15, 3/51, 4/53, 5/66, 6/70, 7/70, 8/75, 9/75, 10/77.
Bowling: Spofforth 28-15-44-7, Garrett 7-2-10-0, Boyle 20-11-19-3.

Grace still at the wicket, it looked unlikely. But when Grace was caught at mid-off for 32 the tempo of the game changed. Spofforth and Boyle delivered twelve successive maiden overs and England's target grew more and more elusive. We can imagine the cheers when Lyttelton finally scored a single, but four more maidens followed. Spofforth was not to be denied. England's last five wickets could manage only seven runs and in his final 11 overs the Demon had conceded two runs and taken four wickets. One of the Australian players, Horan, recalled the tension of the last half hour. In the excitement one spectator 'dropped down dead' and another gnawed out pieces from his umbrella handle. The lips of one English batsman as he made his way to the wicket were 'ashen grey' and 'his throat so parched he could hardly speak'. Clearly the 'pressure' of a close Test match finish is not something restricted to the modern era. Spofforth, having taken fourteen wickets in the match, was carried shoulder-high to the pavilion.

At the end of the week *The Sporting Times* published the famous obituary notice.

In Affectionate Remembrance
OF
ENGLISH CRICKET,
WHICH DIED AT THE OVAL
ON
29th AUGUST, 1882,
Deeply lamented by a large circle of sorrowing friends and acquaintances.
R. I. P.
N.B.—The body will be cremated and the ashes taken to Australia.

England and Australia have played for the 'Ashes' ever since.

Finally a glimpse at county cricket in the Victorian era. In the 1870s the presence of the Grace brothers, supported entirely by a team of amateurs, arrested Nottinghamshire's domination for a while. Gloucestershire won the Championship three times, the last occasion being in 1877 and a feat which they have yet to repeat. However, with E.M. yielding to middle age and the untimely death of Fred, not even W.G. could sustain their success any longer. The professionals of Nottingham reasserted themselves, with Shrewsbury and William Gunn scoring most of the runs and Alfred Shaw and Morley taking most of the wickets. From 1879 to 1886 their ascendancy was threatened only by Lancashire who relied on

Opposite *Yorkshire: the 1893 Championship-winning team, as portrayed in the* Million

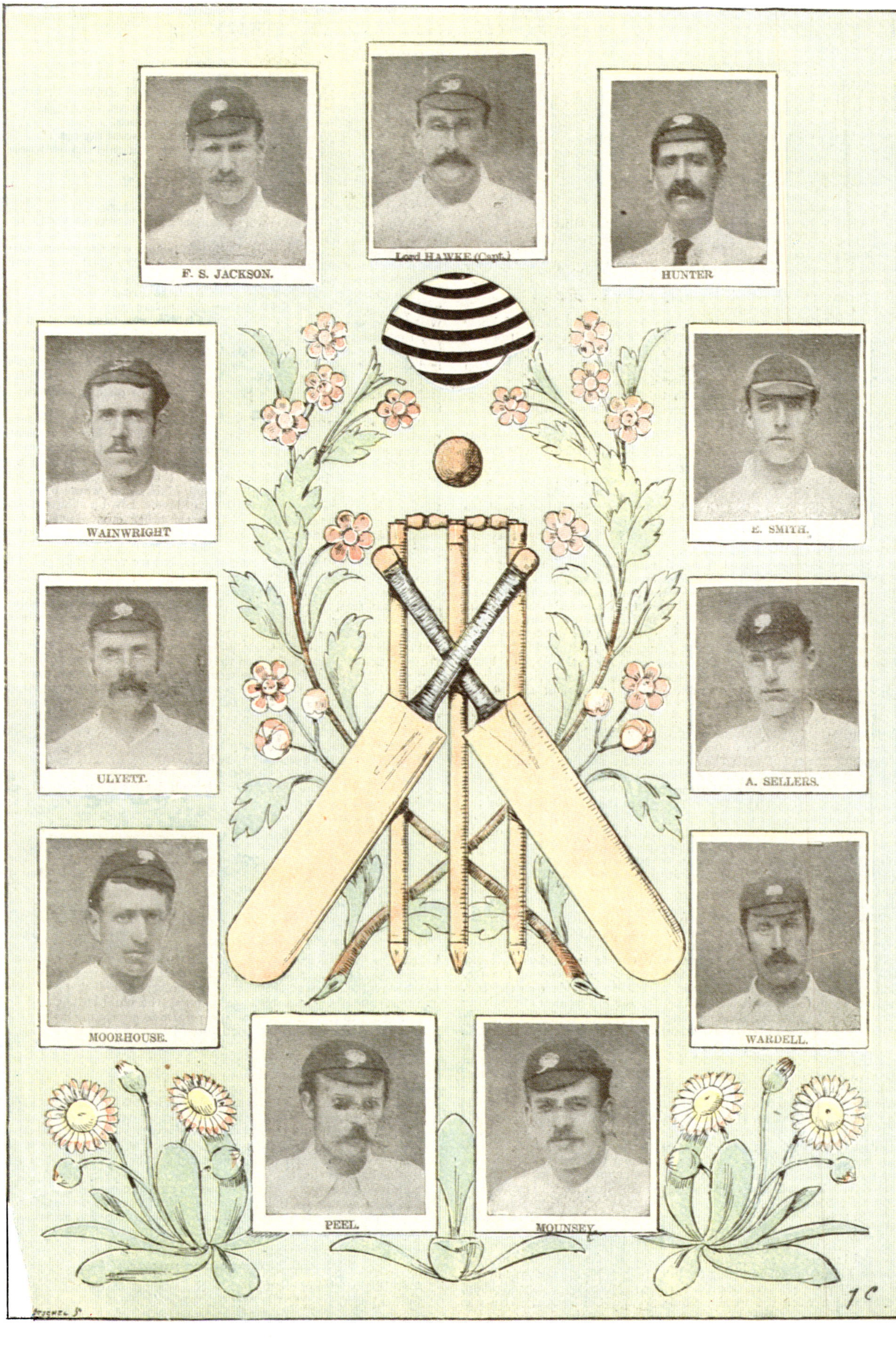
F. S. JACKSON.
Lord HAWKE (Capt.)
HUNTER
WAINWRIGHT
E. SMITH.
ULYETT.
A. SELLERS.
MOORHOUSE.
WARDELL.
PEEL.
MOUNSEY.

George Giffen, Australia's answer to W.G. He was an extremely talented all-rounder

England and Surrey's Tom Richardson. He bowled sheer pace, with a pronounced break-back

A.N. Hornby and Barlow, an outstanding amateur leg-spinner A.G. Steel and several bowlers whose actions excited considerable controversy. They were soon to be joined by a haughty Harrovian, A.C. MacLaren, who succeeded Hornby as captain. At Taunton in 1895 he surpassed all previous individual scores by notching 424 out of a total of 801. Alarmingly Lancashire's innings lasted only eight hours so that there was plenty of time for Somerset to be defeated by the remarkable margin of an innings and 452 runs.

In the 1890s Surrey and Yorkshire were the best teams. As in the 1950s Surrey's bowling attack was the envy of the other counties, and they were virtually unstoppable. Between 1887 and 1899 they were undisputed champions eight times. Tom Richardson succeeded George Lohmann as the most respected bowler in county cricket, and in harness with William Lockwood, less consistent but devastating on his day, Surrey prospered. However, up in Yorkshire Lord Hawke was cultivating a band of devoted young professionals, notably George Hirst and Wilfred Rhodes, who, alongside the brilliant amateur, F.S. Jackson, were to challenge the supremacy of Surrey at the turn of the century.

Right *C. W. Alcock's series,* Famous Cricketers and Cricket Grounds, *has furnished today's fans with many marvellous portraits of the Golden Age heroes*

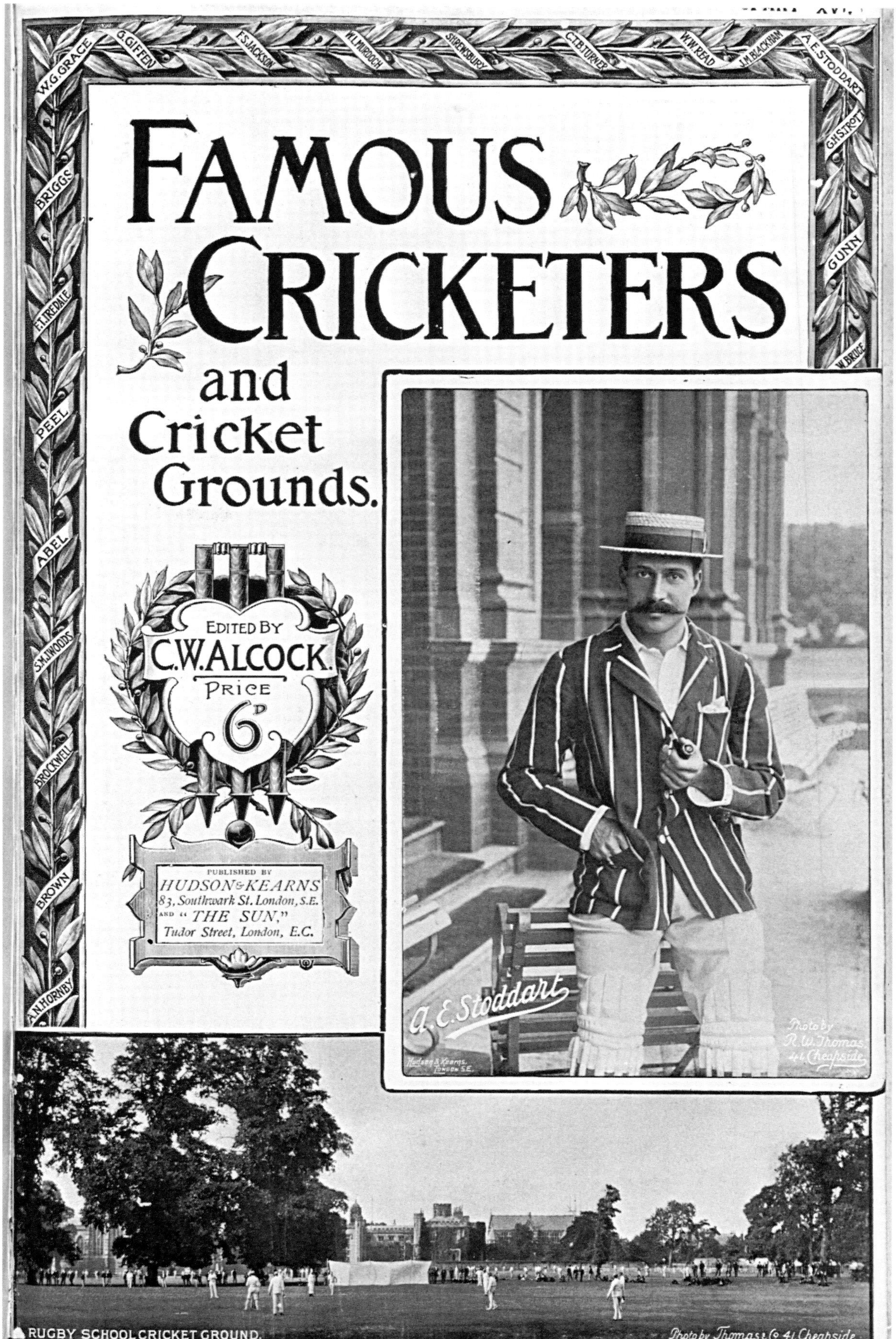
W.G.GRACE
G.GIFFEN
F.S.JACKSON
W.L.MURDOCH
SHREWSBURY
C.T.B.TURNER
W.W.READ
J.M.BLACKHAM
A.E.STODDART
G.H.S.TROTT
GUNN
W.BRUCE
BRIGGS
F.T.IREDALE
PEEL
ABEL
S.M.J.WOODS
BROCKWELL
BROWN
A.N.HORNBY
FAMOUS CRICKETERS and Cricket Grounds.
EDITED BY C.W.ALCOCK.
PRICE 6D
PUBLISHED BY HUDSON & KEARNS 83, Southwark St. London, S.E. AND "THE SUN," Tudor Street, London, E.C.
A. E. Stoddart
Photo by R. W. Thomas. 41, Cheapside.
RUGBY SCHOOL CRICKET GROUND.
Photo by Thomas & Co 41, Cheapside.

Elsewhere the likes of Ranji, Fry and Jessop were delighting spectators wherever they played, even if their counties met with little success; but we shall meet them again in the next chapter.

The Victorian era belongs to W.G. and we shall end with him – albeit on a sad note. In 1899 he played his last match for Gloucestershire, even though he could easily have held his own on the county circuit for a while longer. After a series of disputes with the committee, who had had enough of his autocratic ways and who were concerned about his plans to manage a London County team, he wrote a letter of resignation which was characteristically forthright. It ended, 'I have the greatest affection for the county of my birth, but for the committee as a body the greatest contempt'.

Fortunately his departure from the international season was less acrimonious. In 1899 he captained England in the first Test match against the powerful Australian side. He made 28 and 1 and the match was drawn, but he was now very, very heavy and he had to endure some jeering from a small section of the crowd because of his immobility in the field. It was the first time this had happened to him and it must have been hard to bear. On the way home he confided in F.S. Jackson, who was eventually to succeed him, 'It's all over, Jacker. I shan't play again'. He had, I think, done enough.

George Lohmann, taker of 112 wickets, at just 10.75, in 18 Tests

Surrey's diminutive Bobby Abel. He made over 33,000 runs in a first-class career between 1881 and 1904

William Lockwood (left) and Bobby Peel. Both were great servants of England in the 1880s and 1890s

Above left *The 1899 Australians before* ***(right)*** *their steam-trip up-river on the Thames*

Right Punch's *satirical views on the place of an Indian Prince in English cricket*

READY-MADE COATS(-OF-ARMS); OR, GIVING 'EM FITS!

PRINCE KUMAR SHRI RANJITSINHJI, DUKE OF SUSSEX.

Arms: Quarterly; 1st, sable a star of India radiant in splendour; 2nd, on a field vert several long hops volleyed and despatched proper to the boundary; 3rd, on a ground semée with centuries under an heraldic pavilion a champion of renown reguardant in envy bearded to the full and inclined to embonpoint; 4th, two canards conjoined or double duck proper collared with an eastern coronet wanting employment. *Crest:* An indian panther of agility capped and sashed azure glancing furtively to leg sinister. *Supporters:* Two umpires smocked and habited for distinction proper. *Second Motto:* "Ad ranga runem ibit rangit singe."

2

THE GOLDEN AGE

'It's grand to be an Englishman in 1910. King Edward's on the throne; it's the age of men.'

Not perhaps the most scholarly start to a chapter, since these words are uttered by Mr Banks at the beginning of the film, *Mary Poppins,* which has yet to be accepted as a work of great historical value. Yet life was pretty straightforward – at least on the cricket field – at the beginning of the twentieth century. Most of the innovations had already taken place; now was the time to lie back and enjoy the English national game at your leisure. The Empire was secure; all that was to be feared was the possibility of a wet summer.

The amateur batsmen delighted the crowds around the country, often playing with a daring, devil-may-care attitude not afforded the professionals, who needed their wage packet at the end of the week and a new contract at the end of the year. For some of the amateurs playing cricket was an indulgence that they permitted themselves until it was time to do something important. So they might as well enjoy it. For instance, F.S. Jackson, whose fag at Harrow was Winston Churchill, himself became a Tory MP. Some would go on to achieve greater things. Even the best amateurs of 'The Golden Age' like Ranji, Fry, Jackson and MacLaren would like to give the impression that their successes were achieved without any great effort, just a natural flowering of their own prodigious talent. But I'll wager they practised as hard as anybody. Certainly we know that Ranji hired professional bowlers from Surrey whilst at Cambridge so that he could make the cricketing transition from India to England.

On the pitch as well as in the nets, the professionals did most of the bowling – the labourers' job. Epitomised by Wilfred Rhodes, they were conscientious, respectful and eager to sustain their gifts for as long as possible. When batting they were more aware of the worth of a quick single than was the amateur, who disdained such methods.

It was good to win and to try hard – but not too hard. *Wisden* chastises the young Surrey wicket-keeper, Herbert Strudwick, for being a trifle over-zealous.

> Strudwick bubbles over with an energy that sometimes carries him too far. I can see no advantage in his habit of leaving his post and chasing the ball to the boundary. The practice is simply the result of over-keenness, but as it does no good it ought to be checked, and I would suggest to the Surrey captain a system of modest fines, the amount being increased for each offence.

The Australians, of course, tried very hard all the time. A.C. MacLaren had taken a team to the Antipodes in the winter of 1901–02, but despite his own superlative performances they were soundly beaten four-one. His side lacked depth in batting because none of the leading amateurs made the trip. Moreover the Yorkshire committee refused to let Hirst and Rhodes go, just in case the arduous trip should impair their performances the following summer. As long ago as 1902 Yorkshiremen took their cricket very seriously, and after all the captain did play for Lancashire. However, everyone was available when the Australians came to England in 1902 and there was every prospect of a titanic struggle between two strong sides. Despite a wet summer this proved to be the case. Indeed, by examining the series of 1902 in some detail we shall be able to become acquainted with many of the principal characters of the era.

The English side that took to the field in the first Test at Birmingham is often reckoned to be the strongest combination yet. The following were chosen: MacLaren, Fry, Ranjitsinhji, Jackson, Tyldesley, Lilley, Hirst, Jessop, Braund, Lockwood and Rhodes.

In 1902 MacLaren was the undisputed leader. His class as a batsman was beyond question. Neville Cardus wrote, 'There never was a cricketer with more than the grandeur of A.C. MacLaren'. We must of course recognise that MacLaren played for Cardus' beloved Lancashire, but there are plenty of others to support his assessment, like C.B. Fry: 'He

Opposite *The making of the Golden Age cricket ball, described in the* Graphic *of 1907*

The · First · Process · Cutting · and · Straking · the · Hides

Winding · the · Quilt ·

Hammering · Quilt · into · Mould · to · ensure · the · shape · being · correct ·

· Guaging · a · Quilt · before · being · inserted · into · the · covers ·

Paring · the · halves · before · sewing ·

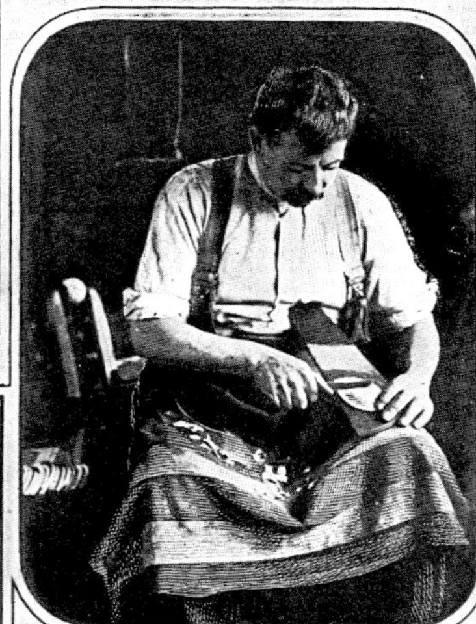

Cutting · the · Quarters · which · are · inserted · between · the · covers · & · the · quilt ·

Material · used · in · the · production · of · a · First-Class · Cricket Ball ·

Pressing · the · halves · together · They · are · placed · in · half moulds · and · screwed · up · in · a · vice ·

· The · Final · Process · Sewing · the · halves · together ·

Weighing · the · Balls · before · they · are · finally · sewn · up ·

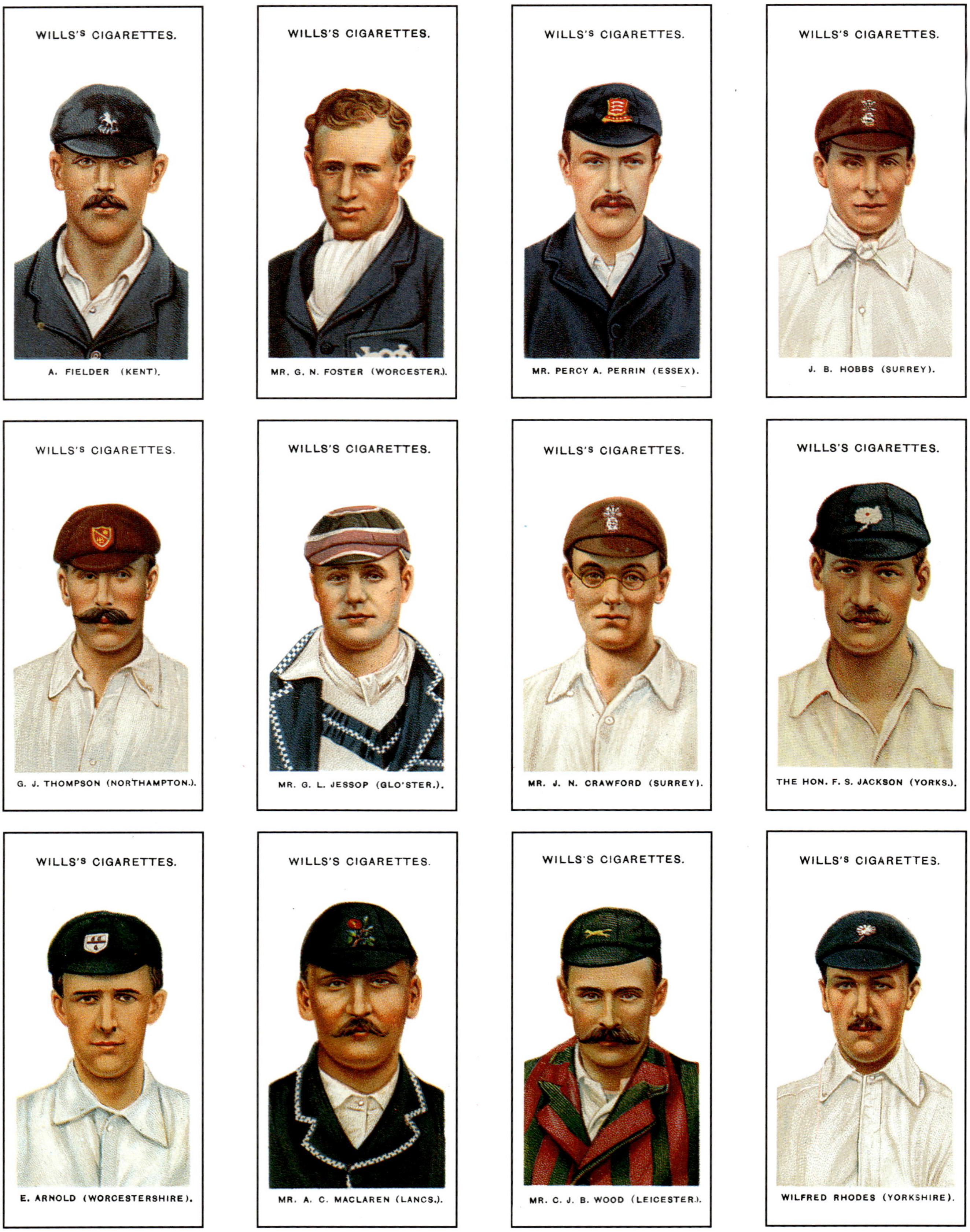

A selection of Golden Age heroes, courtesy of Wills's cigarettes

WILLS'S CIGARETTES.
LORD HAWKE (YORKSHIRE).

WILLS'S CIGARETTES.
MR. R. E. FOSTER (WORCESTER.).

WILLS'S CIGARETTES.
MR. C. B. FRY (SUSSEX).

WILLS'S CIGARETTES.
G. DENNETT (GLOUCESTERSHIRE).

WILLS'S CIGARETTES.
A. R. WARREN (DERBYSHIRE).

WILLS'S CIGARETTES.
MR. A. O. JONES (NOTTS.).

WILLS'S CIGARETTES.
L. C. BRAUND (SOMERSET).

WILLS'S CIGARETTES.
MR. C. H. B. MARSHAM (KENT).

WILLS'S CIGARETTES.
C. BLYTHE (KENT).

WILLS'S CIGARETTES.
S. F. BARNES (STAFFORDSHIRE).

WILLS'S CIGARETTES.
GEORGE H. HIRST (YORKSHIRE).

WILLS'S CIGARETTES.
MR. P. F. WARNER (MIDDLESEX).

*Gilbert Jessop (**left**) and (**below**) the aptly named 'Long' John Tunnicliffe, both captured by the pioneer of modern cricket photography, George Beldam*

stood bolt upright and swept into every stroke, even a defensive backstroke, with deliberate and dominating completeness.' It would have been a surprise if anyone else was selected to captain the English team.

And yet with the benefit of hindsight the assumption that MacLaren was the best available captain is at the very least questionable. In his career he led England 22 times; only four Test matches were won, 11 were lost. There was hardly a paucity of talent available, particularly for home Test matches, so it would be misleading to conclude that he was lumbered with a team of no-hopers throughout his career. Alan Gibson once suggested that England under MacLaren 'must have been a good side to watch, save for the passionate partisans, but an uncomfortable side in which to play'. MacLaren was a fiery character and his anger could be directed at anyone, ranging from the selectors to his own team. He was also prepared to be unconventional. For the 1901–02 tour of Australia he had plucked Sydney Barnes out of the Lancashire league, having seen him bowling at the Old Trafford nets. This seemed like a master stroke after two Test matches in which Barnes took 19 wickets, but unfortunately, Barnes' knee gave way in the third Test at Adelaide and he was of no further use to his captain on the tour. Barnes himself was a man with an independent mind and the two of them obviously had a turbulent relationship. Indeed, it was reported that during a particularly perilous sea-crossing the only consolation for MacLaren, who was by nature a pessimist, was that 'at least if we go down we'll take that bugger Barnes down with us'.

We'll come across MacLaren throughout this summer but unfortunately – and remarkably – neither Ranji nor his friend and colleague, C.B. Fry, survived the series. For both the 1902 season was an unprecedented disaster, at least at international level. For the statistically minded Ranji averaged 4.75 for the series, Fry 1.25. Just to redress the balance let me tell you that in the three seasons 1899–1901 Ranji scored 8,692 runs, Fry 7,838. They were cricketing giants who unaccountably lost form in the summer of 1902.

Of all the great batsmen of this era, I think I would have chosen to watch Ranji score a hundred ahead of any other, preferably from a deckchair at Hove. Colonel Philip Trevor, who did have the privilege of seeing him bat, refrained from actually defining his charm but simply observed that 'in the matter of charm his batting stands alone'. One imagines him to have been a totally instinctive player; once, asked about the fundamentals of batting, he gave this reply: 'First find where the ball is going to pitch; then go to it; then hit it.' Nothing too technical about that. And yet he spent as many hours improving and refining his technique as any professional.

Even C.B. Fry needed the occasional net!

Ranji could play all the shots but his trademark was the leg-glance. If the ball was pitched fast and short of a length, he would move across to the off side and play the ball off his left hip with the full face of the bat: a last-minute flick of the wrists would send the ball scurrying down to the fine-leg boundary, an area hitherto unexplored by batsmen.

Surprisingly Ranji did not win a blue at Cambridge until his last year. Thereafter his skill and temperament shone through. He scored a century on his debut for Sussex and for England. He was a master on rain-affected wickets; on one occasion after a thunderstorm he scored 202 against Middlesex in three hours; the next best contribution from the Sussex players was 17. His highest score was against Somerset at Taunton, 285 not out, which was remarkable not because he was playing Somerset (they were always eager to get into the record books somehow) but because he had spent all of the previous night fishing. Ranji was a genius but, as the 1902 season reminds us, he was also fallible, and there is no better man to watch on a cricket field than a fallible genius. Expectation is heightened by the possibility of failure.

Sussex were a good side to go and watch because if Ranji did not make runs you could be pretty sure C.B. Fry would. Today Fry's *curriculum vitae* would either terrify a potential employer or be thrown into a waste paper basket, having been dismissed as a poor practical joke. At Oxford he won blues at cricket, soccer, athletics and was deprived of a rugby blue only by a last-minute injury. He was a brilliant scholar, who gained a first in 'Mods' and honours in *Literae Humaniores*; in addition he won one of the major Oxford poetry prizes. Even worse, he was a man of striking good looks.

He was capped for England at soccer and appeared for Southampton in the FA Cup final; he set a world record, which lasted 21 years, for the long jump. He wrote a novel with his wife, called *A Mother's Son*; he edited his own magazine, and after the war he was actually offered, but declined, the throne of Albania. He stood three times for parliament and – to my latter-day amazement – was not elected; he was, however, standing as a Liberal. Yet of all his achievements he treasured most his 48 years as director in charge of the training ship 'Mercury'.

Given all the above it is surprising that he had time to notch 94 first class centuries and to play 26 Test matches for England. Though thinking about it, perhaps this is not as astonishing as at first sight. If Ranji at the crease trusted his instincts, C.B. Fry relied upon logic. In batting alone he was a scientist rather than an artist.

We must move on. F.S. Jackson was a contemporary of MacLaren's at Harrow. Indeed he was his captain in 1889. Maybe England's chances in this series would have been enhanced if he had remained as his captain for longer. In fact he led England on only five occasions – in the 1905 Ashes series, winning two and drawing the other three. He was a 'lucky' captain – he won the toss every time – but 'lucky' captains are invariably good ones. Like MacLaren – and no doubt most Harrovians – he was his own man, but he was more able to maintain a united and happy side than was his contemporary. C.B. Fry regarded the 1905 season as his happiest in Test cricket and he 'delighted in Jackson's captaincy'. Jackson was also respected by the professionals.

Ranji: the apotheosis of cricket's Golden Age

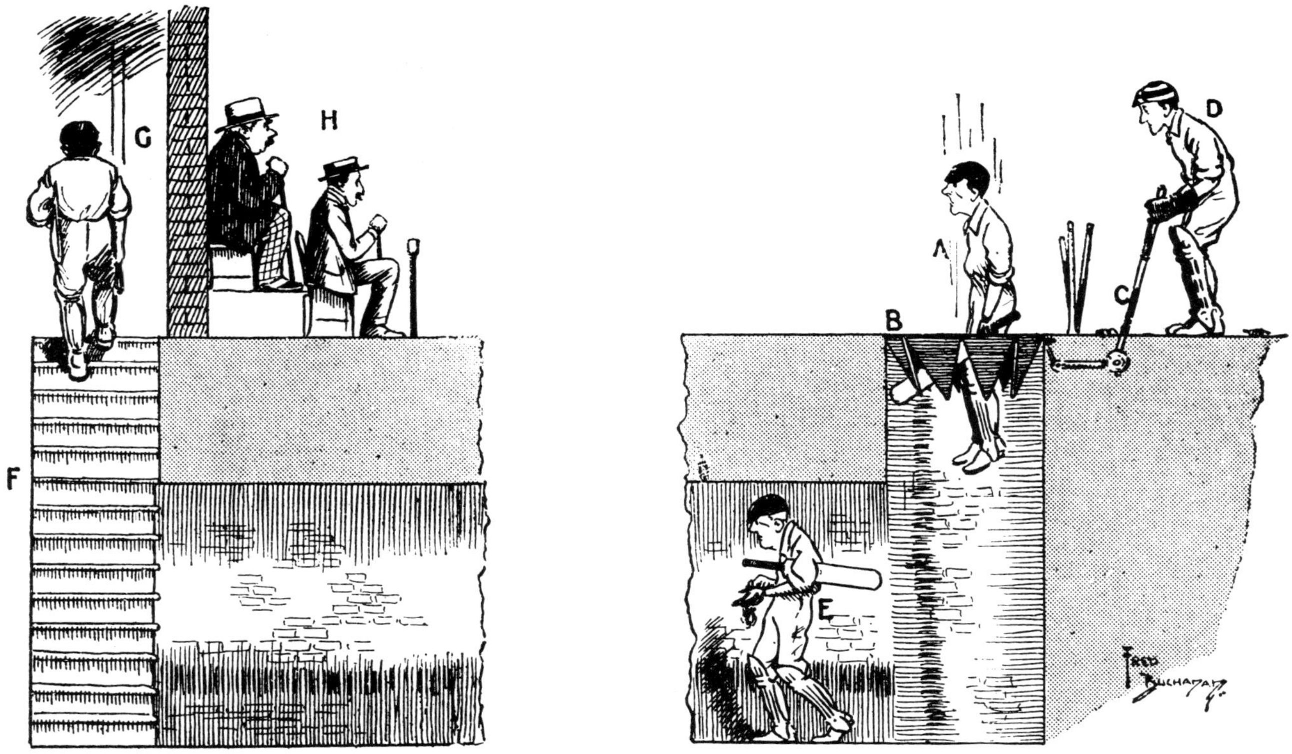

THE "TUBE" EXIT FOR UNSUCCESSFUL BATSMEN.

(A) ABASHED BATSMAN (BOWLED FOR A BLOB) DISAPPEARING THROUGH STAR TRAP (B), OPERATED AT LEVER (C), BY SYMPATHETIC WICKET-KEEPER (D).

(E) THE SAME BATSMAN PURSUING HIS INVISIBLE WAY ALONG UNDERGROUND PASSAGE TO STAIRCASE (F) LEADING TO INTERIOR OF PAVILION (G), THUS AVOIDING THE STONY STARES OF CONTEMPTUOUS SPECTATORS (H).

Below *'Dick' Lilley, courageous and calm wicketkeeper*

Above Punch's *pioneering device has, alas, never caught on*

Wilfred Rhodes, who also played with him at Yorkshire, said that 'He ... possessed the gift of a fine temperament, with plenty of confidence and pluck and always appeared at his best on great occasions, especially when fighting with his back to the wall' – the sort of qualities we expect a Yorkshire professional to admire.

In May 1902 the selectors would have pencilled in these four great amateur batsmen – Ranji, Fry, Jackson and MacLaren – with an air of confidence; the sole professional batsman in the side was J.T. Tyldesley, a fleet-footed little Lancastrian, who was also a marvellous fielder. Lilley from Warwickshire was the wicketkeeper. Despite stiff competition he was England's first choice throughout the decade, reliable with the gloves and a useful bat and – perhaps even more decisive – a shrewd 'reader' of the game. Modern wicketkeepers might take umbrage at Colonel Trevor's observation that 'it is a matter of unfortunate notoriety that the large majority of wicketkeepers, excellent as they may be and doubtless are at their technical job, are poor judges of cricket'. Lilley, he says, was the great exception to this rule.

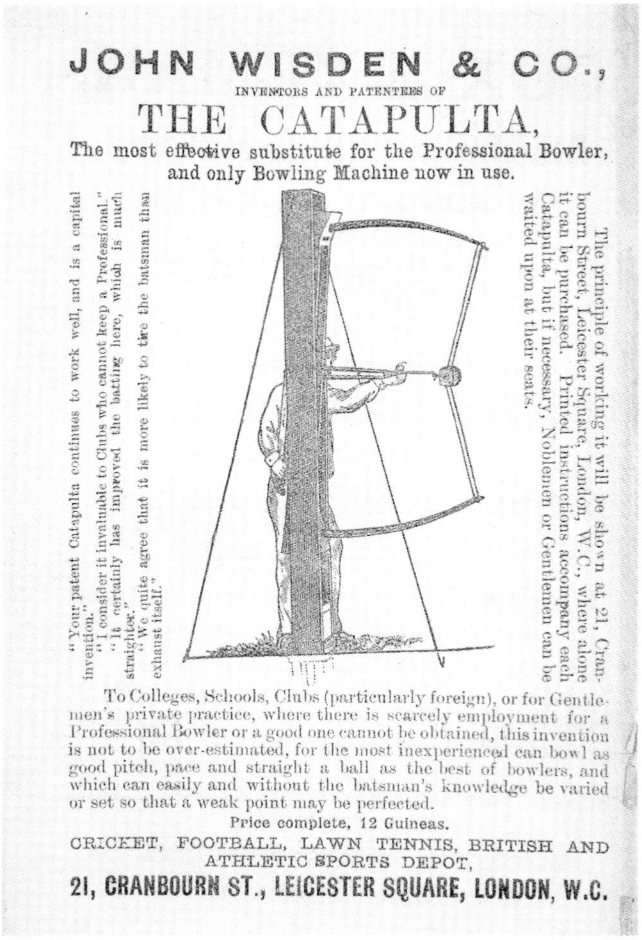

Not a piece of mediaeval siege equipment, but the Catapulta, as advertised in the 1904 Wisden

A good side has at least one all-rounder capable of turning the match with either bat or ball: this one had three. The first was George Hirst, who in 1906 was to set a standard never to be equalled in first-class cricket – the double double; to be more precise he scored 2,385 runs and took 208 wickets. A left-arm bowler, he was one of the first exponents of swing bowling, bringing the ball into the right hander 'like a boomerang'. Next came Len Braund, leg-spinner, forceful batsman, brilliant slip-fielder and one of the few professionals in the Somerset side. Good though Braund was, the west country's hero at this time was the third all-rounder, Gilbert Jessop, the 'Croucher'.

Gilbert Jessop would have been a distinctly handy limited-overs cricketer. Today I don't suppose he would enjoy that assessment any more than he liked being called the Croucher. C.B. Fry was almost Churchillian when he described the Gloucestershire captain: 'No man has ever driven a ball so hard, so high and so often in so many different directions. No man has ever made cricket so dramatic an entertainment.'

Someone – goodness knows how – has worked out that Jessop scored on average at a rate of 80 runs per hour. When he 'came off' the game was turned upside down; his style of batting won matches. To give one example, against Sussex in 1903 he scored 286 out of 355 in 175 minutes. We shall come to another one in a minute. In addition to his explosive batting he was a superb cover-point and a dangerous fast bowler. It is strange that he didn't play more than 18 times for England. Sometimes the experts questioned his technique; it was too risky. However, if selection had been left to the rank and file of cricket followers he would have played many more Tests.

There are two professional bowlers to complete the eleven, Lockwood and Rhodes. Lockwood could be lethal when everything clicked; he took three hat tricks to prove the point. He lacked the subtlety and control of Barnes, but he was fast, unpredictable and sometimes inspired. Rhodes was

Below and opposite *Illustrations – with their original captions – from the Badminton Library's* Cricket, *by A.G. Steel and the Hon R.H. Lyttelton*

Doubtful delivery

much more predictable. I don't imagine he ever bowled badly, though in a career spanning four decades he must have sent down the odd long-hop – it hasn't been recorded though. He was a devoted student of the game, capable of plotting the downfall of batsmen on the best of wickets. He possessed the humility of the truly great but also had a wry sense of humour, if this exchange is to be believed:

> 'Was there any ball that Hedley Verity bowled that you didn't bowl?'
> 'Yes, there was the ball they cut for four.'

Throughout his career his slow left-arm spinners, deadly upon rain-affected wickets, accounted for no less than 4,187 batsmen, another record that will never be threatened. You may be surprised to learn that he was England's number 11 for the first Test of 1902. Within 10 years he would be walking out with Jack Hobbs to open the batting for his country.

So the cricketing public had every right to feel confident that this combination was capable of regaining the Ashes, and after two days of the first Test at Birmingham in 1902 one victory seemed certain. MacLaren had won the toss and half-an-hour later he was striding out with C.B. Fry to open the innings. Fry was caught behind for a duck and then there was another setback, as *Wisden* records, 'a misunderstanding, for which Ranjitsinhji considered himself somewhat unjustly blamed, led to MacLaren being run out, and then Ranjitsinhji himself, quite upset by what had happened, was clean bowled'. We can only surmise what MacLaren said to his partner between being dismissed and setting off for the pavilion, but it seems unlikely that it was along the lines of 'Don't worry about it, keep going, old chap'. Ranji's 13 was his highest score of the series. Tyldesley, supported first by Jackson and then Hirst, rescued the situation, scoring a timely 138, and by the end of the first day's play England had reached 351 for nine.

Heavy overnight rain prevented play resuming until three o'clock the next day. MacLaren, taking the advice of Lilley, decided to bat on for half-an-hour to give the bowlers' footholds a chance to dry, and England declared at 376 for nine. The Yorkshire pair of Hirst and Rhodes now set to work – there were no qualms about opening the bowling with a left-arm spinner in those days – and after an

A clear case

A pokey batsman dealing with a high-dropping full-pitch

Above *Johnny Tyldesley: England stalwart*

Opposite *Victor Trumper: George Beldam's camera catches his lithe elegance to perfection*

astonishing 90 minutes of cricket Australia were dismissed for 36 with only Victor Trumper reaching double figures. Rhodes had taken seven for 17, Hirst three for 15.

Only rain could save the Australians and it did. Remember that Test matches at this time were of only three days' duration and it was not possible to restart until a quarter-past five on the last day; by the close Australia had stumbled gratefully to 46 for two and nothing, but their pride, had been lost.

This was supposed to be one of Australia's strongest sides, yet three days later they were bowled out for 23 by Yorkshire at Leeds, and Wilfred Rhodes hadn't even bowled a ball. It became an open secret that the tourists were not enjoying this dank and dismal summer, and they may well have been relieved when the second Test at Lord's was virtually washed out. However, by July the sun had finally started to shine, and when they arrived at Sheffield, which was to host its only Test match, they were in better spirits, not least because their best bowler, Hugh Trumble, who had missed the first two games, was now restored to full fitness.

There was drama even before the game began. The English selectors, chaired by the autocratic Lord Hawke, the captain of Yorkshire, had selected Lockwood and Haigh as the two fast bowlers in the twelve. The equally autocratic MacLaren decided that he wanted Barnes, and a few hours before the game he sent a telegram to summon him to Bramall Lane. Barnes duly arrived and both Lockwood and Haigh were omitted from the final eleven. In fact Barnes was to take seven wickets in the match, but he didn't appear again in the series.

England trailed by 49 runs on the first innings and then a decisive partnership between Trumper and Clem Hill put the match out of reach. *Wisden*: 'Trumper in the course of the season made many bigger scores than his 62 but on no occasion did he play a more marvellous innings. He obtained his runs out of a total of 80 in 50 minutes doing just what he liked with the English bowling.'

Trumper was the most popular Australian cricketer of the era; he was also the best. He possessed several of the lesser-known Australian characteristics; he was a teetotaller, shy and unfailingly modest. His batting statistics do not outweigh those of his contemporaries, though he was outstanding in 1902, but all those who saw him speak of 'genius' and 'style'. Indeed, C.B. Fry commented that 'He had no style and yet he was all style'.

The true enthusiast would undoubtedly have missed a family wedding to watch Trumper bat, but they might not have risked it to see Clem Hill, if only because of his ungainly stance, with the bat

gripped at the base of the handle and the body bent low. Yet he was one of Australia's greatest left-handers and he certainly did them proud at Sheffield, where his second-innings century meant that England needed a massive 339 to win. MacLaren now tried one of his favourite ploys – juggling the batting order. He decided to send Jessop in first, and this proved a partial success. By close of play on the second day England were 73 for one with Jessop, playing a 'brilliant game', 53 not out. However, there were no miracles the following morning. On a wearing pitch England were dismissed for 195 with MacLaren alone standing firm with a resolute 63, though whether this innings was sufficient to endear him to the selectors remains debatable. The Australians, who had been in disarray throughout May and June, had won by 143 runs and led one-nil in the series.

The scene now moves across the Pennines to Manchester and more selectorial shenanigans. Lord Hawke and his two colleagues took the precaution of picking 11 players only to ensure that MacLaren would lead out the team they wanted. Fry was dropped, which was quite understandable given his wretched run of failures; there was no Barnes and, even stranger, no Jessop. In the end they added one reserve, Fred Tate of Sussex, confident that not even MacLaren would pick him. 'My God, look what they've sent me', was allegedly MacLaren's famous reaction to the team. No doubt he was furious – with some justification – and maybe it was his fury that prompted him to retaliate by playing Tate instead of the most reliable all-rounder in England, George Hirst. The England players, it seems, were becoming pawns in a private argument.

There had been a lot of rain in Manchester and when Joe Darling won the toss he decided to bat. The pitch was too wet to assist the bowlers; it would be more helpful when it started to dry out in the afternoon, so England's tactics were to 'keep Victor quiet before lunch'. The tactics were sound but the execution less good. At lunch the Australians were 173 for one. Trumper, who scored 104, and his partner Duff had assessed the situation perfectly, and with a glorious display of hitting had taken their team to a seemingly impregnable position.

Clem Hill: effective, if ungainly. He remains possibly the only man to have assaulted a fellow Test selector

Joe Darling, dependable batsman and inspiring captain

Australia's captain, Monty Noble, goes out to bat in the 1909 Edgbaston Test. Many regard him as the greatest all-rounder his country ever produced

In the afternoon Rhodes and Lockwood exploited the drying wicket, dismissing Australia for 299, and by the close England had stuttered to 70 for five. The following morning F.S. Jackson was at his commanding best, no doubt following W.G.'s dictum, 'there's no such thing as a crisis, only the next ball'. He was ably supported by Len Braund, who since he played for Somerset was no stranger to adversity. Jackson finished with 128, Braund 65, and England ended just 37 runs short of Australia's score.

Now Lockwood was inspired; he dismissed Trumper, Duff and Hill for just 10 runs. When the score had reached 16, Darling skied the ball straight to deep square-leg off the bowling of Braund; it was dropped and the fielder, of course, was poor old Fred Tate. Darling and Gregory proceeded to put together the only worthwhile partnership of the innings, 54, and early on the third day the Australians were all out for 86. Incidentally, perhaps I should record Tate's bowling figures in the Australians' second innings – 5-3-7-2 – because that is the one Tate contribution to this game that no one seems to remember.

ENGLAND v AUSTRALIA

Played at Manchester, 24, 25, 26, July, 1902.
Result: Australia won by 3 runs.

Australia: First innings

V.T. Trumper c Lilley b Rhodes	104
R.A. Duff c Lilley b Lockwood	54
C. Hill c Rhodes b Lockwood	65
M.A. Noble c and b Rhodes	2
S.E. Gregory c Lilley b Rhodes	3
J. Darling* c MacLaren b Rhodes	51
A.J.Y. Hopkins c Palairet b Lockwood	0
W.W. Armstrong b Lockwood	5
J.J. Kelly† not out	4
H. Trumble c Tate b Lockwood	0
J.V. Saunders b Lockwood	3
Extras (b 5,lb 2,w 1)	8
Total	299

Fall of Wickets: 1/135, 2/175, 3/179, 4/183, 5/256, 6/256, 7/785, 8/292, 9/292, 10/299.
Bowling: Rhodes 25-3-104-4-, Jackson 11-0-58-0, Tate 11-1-44-0, Braund 9-0-37-0, Lockwood 20.1-5-48-6.

England: First innings

L.C.H. Palairet c Noble b Saunders	6
R. Abel c Armstrong b Saunders	6
J.T. Tyldesley c Hopkins b Saunders	22
A.C. MacLaren* b Trumble	1
K.S. Ranjitsinhji lbw b Trumble	2
Hon. F.S. Jackson c Duff b Trumble	128
L.C. Braund b Noble	65
A.F.A. Lilley† b Noble	7
W.H. Lockwood run out	7
W. Rhodes c and b Trumble	5
F.W. Tate not out	5
Extras (b 6,lb 2)	8
Total	262

Fall of Wickets: 1/12, 2/13, 3/14, 4/30, 5/44, 6/185, 7/203, 8/214, 9/235, 10/262.
Bowling: Trumble 43-16-75-4, Saunders 34-5-104-3, Noble 24-8-47-2, Trumper 6-4-6-0, Armstrong 5-2-19-0, Hopkins 2-0-3-0.

Australia: Second innings

V.T. Trumper c Braund b Lockwood	4
R.A. Duff b Lockwood	3
C. Hill b Lockwood	0
M.A. Noble (6) c Lilley b Lockwood	4
S.E. Gregory lbw b Tate	24
J. Darling* (4) c Palairet b Rhodes	37
A.J.Y. Hopkins c Tate b Lockwood	2
W.W. Armstrong b Rhodes	3
J.J. Kelly† not out	2
H. Trumble lbw b Tate	4
J.V. Saunders c Tyldesley b Rhodes	0
Extras (b 1,lb 1,nb 1)	3
Total	86

Fall of Wickets: 1/7, 2/9, 3/10, 4/64, 5/74, 6/76, 7/77, 8/79, 9/85, 10/86.
Bowling: Rhodes 14.4-5-26-3, Tate 5-3-7-2, Braund 11-3-22-0, Lockwood 17-5-28-5.

England: Second innings

L.C.H. Palairet b Saunders	17
R. Abel (5) b Trumble	21
J.T. Tyldesley c Armstrong b Saunders	16
A.C. MacLaren* (2) c Duff b Trumble	35
K.S. Ranjitsinhji (4) lbw b Trumble	4
Hon. F.S. Jackson c Gregory b Saunders	7
L.C. Braund st Kelly b Trumble	3
A.F.A. Lilley† c Hill b Trumble	4
W.H. Lockwood b Trumble	0
W. Rhodes not out	4
F.W. Tate b Saunders	4
Extras (b 5)	5
Total	120

Fall of Wickets: 1/44, 2/68, 3/72, 4/92, 5/97, 6/107, 7/109, 8/109, 9/116, 10/120.
Bowling: Trumble 25-9-53-6, Saunders 19.4-4-52-4, Noble 5-3-10-0.

On Saturday morning there was more rain, causing the wicket to deteriorate so that England were apprehensive about scoring the 124 runs they needed for victory. In 50 minutes before lunch MacLaren and his new partner, Palairet, took the score to 36. After lunch, with the weather threatening, England tried to accelerate, losing wickets in the process; however, they were clear favourites with the score standing at 92 for three. Now Trumble and Saunders, backed by superb fielding, brought about a collapse, six wickets falling for 24 runs. As England's last man, Fred Tate, made his way to the wicket, eight runs were needed to win the match. Before he reached the middle the heavens opened and the players scampered for cover. Who would want to be in Tate's boots now? I wonder whether he wanted the rain to stop, but stop it did after an agonising delay of three-quarters of an hour. When they resumed, Tate edged Saunders' first ball for four and England were one boundary away from a famous victory. He survived the next two balls, but the fourth kept a little low and bowled him. The match was over and Australia had won by three runs. It wasn't Tate's fault, but the game has unkindly been known as 'Tate's match' ever since. He never played for England again, though he continued to take a stack of wickets for Sussex. However, his son, Maurice, more than redeemed the family name a generation later. So the Ashes remained with the Australians. Despite that, the last game at The Oval was as gripping as the fourth Test at Manchester.

It seems that a truce was called between the selectors and the captain, as *Wisden* records that the selection committee 'restored Jessop and Hirst to the places they ought to have filled at Manchester'. Australia scored 324 in the first innings of the match; in reply England just managed to avoid the follow-on thanks to stout rearguard actions from Hirst and Lockwood, Trumble, bowling unchanged, taking eight for 65. Now England countered; Trumper was run out needlessly and Lockwood struck his best form, so that when the Australians were dismissed for 121, England needed 263 to win, a formidable target on a wicket damaged by rain, but not an impossible one. However, with half the side out for 48, England's wretched summer seemed certain to end on a humiliating note. Yet again Jackson remained calm in a crisis and Jessop reacted in the only way he knew; he blazed away before lunch, but was far from convincing; he could have been stumped and was dropped at long-off. However, after the interval any uncertainty vanished.

Opposite *The unfortunate Fred Tate*

Yorkshire and England bastions (left to right) Schofield Haigh, George Hirst and Wilfred Rhodes

The leg-spinner, Saunders, was despatched for four consecutive boundaries. Undeterred by Jackson's dismissal, Jessop continued to his second 50 in 32 minutes. Outside the ground buses pulled up so that their passengers could catch a glimpse of the drama. His innings ended when he was caught at short-leg off Armstrong for 104, and the buses moved on; he had been at the crease for 77 minutes whilst 139 runs had been added and *Wisden* observed that 'a more astonishing display has never been seen'.

With the score standing at 187 for seven, the match had been transformed, but England still needed another 76 runs for victory. Now, instead of the daring and abandon of the country's most dashing amateur, England were relying upon the grit and good sense of a Yorkshire professional, George Hirst, who was doubtless still smarting from his omission from the previous Test. Supported first by Lockwood, then by Lilley, he had advanced the score to 248 when the ninth wicket fell. The *Guardian*'s cricket correspondent describes the scene:

> Fifteen runs were wanted when Rhodes came in, and a north-countryman whispered that all was right now two Yorkshiremen were to-

gether. He was right. Rhodes looked as calm and unmoved as when he takes those few quiet steps to the wicket .... Hirst was continually busy with the pitch, and before every ball took a breathing space and twirled his bat in preparation. Darling shifted the field almost every ball, and when Rhodes was batting some of them crept very near in.

Both Hirst and Rhodes later denied that they had agreed to 'get 'em in singles', but the legend lives on. In fact Rhodes' first scoring shot was a streaky boundary off Noble; but thereafter every run, apart from one overthrow, was indeed a single. The crowd was utterly absorbed by the climax of the game. When Hirst took another single to level the scores 'one member of the crowd, a clergyman, thought it was won, and started running across the ground at full pace towards the pavilion. He was so excited that he did not notice his mistake till he was well out in the field and a policeman was in chase.' No doubt he was forgiven, especially when Rhodes had driven Trumble wide of mid-on to give England the most unexpected of victories. Now the rest of the crowd invaded the pitch and surrounded the players around the pavilion. The Ashes may have been lost but honour was restored.

George Hirst: a cool head in a crisis

ENGLAND v AUSTRALIA

Played at The Oval, 11, 12, 13 August, 1902
Result: England won by one wicket

Australia: First innings

V.T. Trumper b Hirst	42
R.A. Duff c Lilley b Hirst	23
C. Hill b Hirst	11
J. Darling* c Lilley b Hirst	3
M.A. Noble c and b Jackson	52
S.E. Gregory b Hirst	23
W.W. Armstrong b Jackson	17
A.J.Y. Hopkins c MacLaren b Lockwood	40
H. Trumble not out	64
J.J. Kelly† c Rhodes b Braund	39
J.V. Saunders lbw b Braund	0
Extras (b 5, lb 3, nb 2)	10
Total	324

Fall of Wickets: 1/47, 2/63, 3/69, 4/82, 5/126, 6/174, 7/175, 8/256, 9/324, 10/324.
Bowling: Lockwood 24-2-85-1, Rhodes 28-9-46-0, Hirst 29-5-77-5, Braund 16.5-5-29-2, Jackson 20-4-66-2, Jessop 6-2-11-0.

England: First innings

A.C. MacLaren* c Armstrong b Trumble	10
L.C.H. Palairet b Trumble	20
J.T. Tyldesley b Trumble	33
T.W. Hayward b Trumble	0
Hon F.S. Jackson c Armstrong b Saunders	2
L.C. Braund c Hill b Trumble	22
G.L. Jessop b Trumble	13
G.H. Hirst c and b Trumble	43
W.H. Lockwood c Noble b Saunders	25
A.F.A. Lilley† c Trumper b Trumble	0
W. Rhodes not out	0
Extras (b 13, lb 2)	15
Total	183

Fall of Wickets: 1/31, 2/36, 3/62, 4/67, 5/67, 6/83, 7/137, 8/179, 9/183, 10/183.
Bowling: Trumble 31-13-65-8, Saunders 23-7-79-2, Noble 7-3-24-0.

Australia: Second innings

V.T. Trumper run out	2
R.A. Duff b Lockwood	6
C. Hill c MacLaren b Hirst	34
J. Darling* c MacLaren b Lockwood	15
M.A. Noble b Braund	13
S.E. Gregory b Braund	9
W.W. Armstrong b Lockwood	21
A.J.Y. Hopkins c Lilley b Lockwood	3
H. Trumble (10) not out	7
J.J. Kelly† (11) lbw b Lockwood	0
J.V. Saunders (9) c Tyldesley b Rhodes	2
Extras (b 7, lb 2)	9
Total	121

Fall of Wickets: 1/6, 2/9, 3/31, 4/71, 5/75, 6/91, 7/99, 8/114, 9/115, 10/121.
Bowling: Lockwood 20-6-45-5, Rhodes 22-7-38-1, Hirst 5-1-7-1, Braund 9-1-15-2, Jackson 4-3-7-0.

England: Second innings

A.C. MacLaren* b Saunders	2
L.C.H. Palairet b Saunders	6
J.T. Tyldesley b Saunders	0
T.W. Hayward c Kelly b Saunders	7
Hon. F.S. Jackson c and b Trumble	49
L.C. Braund c Kelly b Trumble	2
G.L. Jessop c Noble b Armstrong	104
G.H. Hirst not out	58
W.H. Lockwood lbw b Trumble	2
A.F.A. Lilley† c Darling b Trumble	16
W. Rhodes not out	6
Extras (b 5, lb 6)	11
Total (9 wickets)	263

Fall of Wickets: 1/5, 2/5, 3/10, 4/31, 5/48, 6/157, 7/187, 8/214, 9/248.
Bowling: Trumble 33.5-4-108-4, Saunders 24-3-105-4, Noble 5-0-11-0, Armstrong 4-0-28-1.

'Plum' Warner, who captained the first side to Australia under the aegis of the MCC

Maybe if the relationship between the selectors and their captain had been more harmonious the result of the series would have been reversed. Certainly Jessop declared that the rubber was lost 'in the selection room', but those in the crowd at The Oval for the final day's play would not have been interested in a post mortem of all the conflicts surrounding the England team. They had been richly entertained by a procession of larger-than-life characters. That was enough.

The 1902 series was undoubtedly the most exciting of the period, though there were several other excellent tussles. In 1903–04 Pelham Warner – 'Plum' throughout the cricket world – captained the English team in Australia, the first under the auspices of the MCC. England won the series three-two and it was notable for a staggering Test match debut by the Worcestershire amateur, R.E. Foster, who scored 287 in Sydney, and the bowling of B.J.T. Bosanquet.

R.E. Foster, greatest of the seven Worcestershire brothers. He captained England at both soccer and cricket

Bosanquet was perhaps the last of the pioneers, for he is accepted as the inventor of the 'googly' – an off-break bowled with a leg-break action. Since the arrival of the googly no other 'new' ball has been created, unless we regard the advent of continuous short-pitched bowling as an 'innovation'.

Bosanquet developed the delivery after experiments with a tennis ball whilst playing a game called 'Twisti-Twosti'. The object of this game was to bounce the ball on a table so that your opponent sitting opposite could not catch it. It is still played in modern cricket dressing rooms on very wet days. From there he progressed to a cricket ball and to the nets. He never achieved consistent control; indeed at Lord's in 1900 an unfortunate named Coe, having scored 98 for Leicestershire, was stumped off a Bosanquet delivery which bounced four times. But if he found a length he posed new problems, which only the best could counter. His bowling won two Test matches for England, not a bad record since he

The 1903–04 MCC tourists arrive at their hotel in Tasmania

Below *The 1907-08 MCC team enjoy dinner in their honour at the Grand Hotel, Melbourne*

ENGLAND v SOUTH AFRICA
Played at Leeds, 29, 30, 31 July, 1907.
Result: England won by 53 runs.

England: First innings

T.W. Hayward st Sherwell b Faulkner	24
C.B. Fry b Vogler	2
J.T. Tyldesley b Faulkner	12
R.E. Foster* b Sinclair	0
L.C. Braund lbw b Faulkner	1
G.H. Hirst c Hathorn b Sinclair	17
G.L. Jessop c Sherwell b Faulkner	0
E.G. Arnold b Faulkner	0
A.F.A. Lilley† c Schwarz b Faulkner	3
C. Blythe not out	5
N.A. Knox c Faulkner b Sinclair	8
Extras (b 1,lb 2,nb 1)	4
Total	76

Fall of Wickets: 1/9, 2/41, 3/42, 4/42, 5/53, 6/53, 7/57, 8/63, 9/63, 10/76.
Bowling: Vogler 8-3-14-1, Schwarz 7-0-18-0, Faulkner 11-4-17-6, Sinclair 10.3-2-23-3.

South Africa: First innings

L.J. Tancred st Lilley b Blythe	0
P.W. Sherwell*† lbw Blythe	26
C.M.H. Hathorn c Lilley b Hirst	0
A.W. Nourse c Arnold b Blythe	18
G.C. White c Hirst b Blythe	3
J.H. Sinclair st Lilley b Blythe	2
G.A. Faulkner c Braund b Blythe	6
S.J. Snooke c Lilley b Knox	13
W.A. Shalders c Fry b Blythe	21
A.E.E. Vogler c Hayward b Blythe	11
R.O. Schwarz not out	5
Extras (b 3,lb 1,nb 1)	5
Total	110

Fall of Wickets: 1/6, 2/9, 3/34, 4/47, 5/49, 6/56, 7/59, 8/73, 9/102, 10/110.
Bowling: Hirst 9-3-22-1, Blythe 15.5-1-59-8, Arnold 4-1-11-0, Knox 3-0-13-1.

England: Second innings

T.W. Hayward st Sherwell b Vogler	15
C.B. Fry lbw White	54
J.T. Tyldesley c Snooke b Schwarz	30
R.E. Foster* lbw b Faulkner	22
L.C. Braund c Schwarz b White	0
G.H. Hirst b White	2
G.L. Jessop c Hathorn b Faulkner	10
E.G. Arnold c Schwarz b Faulkner	12
A.F.A. Lilley† lbw b White	0
C. Blythe not out	4
N.A. Knox run out	5
Extras (b 7,lb 1)	8
Total	162

Fall of Wickets: 1/37, 2/100, 3/106, 4/107, 5/115, 6/126, 7/151, 8/152, 9/154, 10/162.
Bowling: Vogler 4-0-18-1, Schwarz 5.4-0-18-1, Faulkner 20-3-58-3, Sinclair 4-0-13-0, White 16-3-47-4.

South Africa: Second innings

L.J. Tancred run out	0
P.W. Sherwell*† c Foster b Blythe	1
C.M.H. Hathorn b Arnold	7
A.W. Nourse lbw b Blythe	2
G.C. White c Arnold b Blythe	7
J.H. Sinclair (7) c Braund b Blythe	15
G.A. Faulkner (6) c Foster b Blythe	11
S.J. Snooke c Hirst b Blythe	14
W.A. Shalders lbw b Hirst	5
A.E.E. Vogler c Tyldesley b Blythe	9
R.O. Schwarz not out	0
Extras (b 3,nb 1)	4
Total	75

Fall of Wickets: 1/0, 2/3, 3/10, 4/16, 5/18, 6/38, 7/56, 8/66, 9/75, 10/75.
Bowling: Hirst 9-2-21-1, Blythe 22.4-9-40-7, Arnold 13-7-10-1.

played only seven times, but in between those inspired spells he could be woefully inaccurate.

Strangely Bosanquet's invention was refined not by his English contemporaries but by a quartet of South Africans. R.O. Schwarz played alongside Bosanquet in the Middlesex side for a couple of years. Bosanquet taught Schwarz, and when he returned home to South Africa Schwarz taught Messrs Vogler, Faulkner and White. Just imagine four wrist-spin bowlers in the same side. Today you need a round-the-world air ticket to discover four first-class wrist-spinners. On the fast matting wickets at the Old Wanderers ground, in Johannesburg, and at Newlands in Cape Town, they were virtually unplayable, as the English tourists in 1905 discovered. This team was also led by Plum Warner, who was proving the ideal man to carry the flag overseas, and whilst it was nowhere near the best side available, it came as a rude shock when the South Africans won the series four-one. They were rewarded with a tour to England in 1907. Each of the three matches was closely contested but the only victory was gained by England in a low-scoring match at Leeds. South Africa needed just 129 runs to win but Colin Blythe, Kent's left-arm spinner, was lethal on the rain-affected pitch. He took 15 wickets for 99 runs in the match and England won by 53 runs. However, there was no doubt that a third force in international cricket had arrived.

Above *Anywhere for cricket, in the early 1900s*

Overleaf *The 1913–14 MCC team to South Africa. Back row (left to right): A.E. Relf, H. Strudwick, I.D. Difford, M.W. Booth, C.P. Mead, S.F. Barnes, F.E. Woolley. Seated: J.B. Hobbs, M.C. Bird, J.W.H.T. Douglas (captain), Hon L.H. Tennyson, W. Rhodes. Front row: E.J. Smith, J.W. Hearne*

Above *One of 13 South African victims (L.A. Stricker, clean bowled) for S.F. Barnes in the 1912 Oval Test*

If Bosanquet was the most innovative bowler of the age, then Sydney Barnes was undoubtedly the most complete. If he had possessed the unthinking wholehearted commitment of a Tom Richardson he would definitely have played more than 27 Tests for England. Between 1902 and 1907 he didn't play any Test cricket, and the main reason for this is that Barnes could be 'difficult'. In addition he chose not to place himself on the unending treadmill of county cricket for any length of time. He played a few times for Warwickshire in the 1890s and had two full seasons for Lancashire in 1902 and 1903. Thereafter he restricted himself to playing in the Lancashire League and for his native Staffordshire, where his records are staggering. It is reckoned that he took 4,069 wickets in the League, at an average of six, and for Staffordshire 1,441 wickets at an average of eight. He was so good that it was unthinkable to omit Barnes from the best possible English eleven no matter where he played his domestic cricket. This state of affairs prompted Cardus to write: 'throughout his career he remained mysteriously aloof, appearing in the full sky of first-class cricket like a meteor – declaring the death of the most princely of batsmen.' In fact Sydney Barnes achieved what Phil Edmonds at the end of his career declared to be his goal, even though it proved elusive, namely a career combining a mixture of club and Test cricket. In his 27 Test matches he took 189 wickets, an average of seven wickets per

W.J. Burton, one of the pioneering West Indian cricketers, who toured England with the 1900 and 1906 teams

Above *The first of the Triangular Tests: Warren Bardsley during his 121 for Australia, who won against South Africa. The Australian T.J. Matthews created a world record by bagging a hat-trick in each innings*

STUDY OF A "TRIANGULAR" TEST MATCH.

Right *An ironic vision of the unsuccessful Triangular Tests by E.H. Shepard,* Winnie the Pooh's *illustrator*

match. So if he had played the same number of Test matches as Dennis Lillee (70) perhaps he would have taken 490 Test wickets. I know statistics are dangerous, but at least this gives an indication of his superiority over his rivals, as well as his domination of batsmen.

Barnes dominated three Test series. In Australia in 1911–12, once J.W.H.T. Douglas allowed him use of the new ball, he took 34 wickets on the perfect batting wickets. In harness with Frank Foster he ensured that England won the rubber four-one. Then he turned his attention towards the South Africans. In the ill-fated triangular tournament of 1912 he captured 34 wickets in three Tests against them, and on the matting of South Africa in 1913–14 he was unplayable, with 49 wickets from four Tests at an average of 10.93. Typically he refused to play in the fifth match, because he contended the South Africans had not carried out their promise of special reward if he took part in the tour. He achieved these staggering results not through excessive pace but superb command of swing and cut. He was blessed with an economical run-up, a perfect upright action and fingers of steel – 'he fingered a cricket ball sensitively like a violinist his fiddle'. Those fingers must have been crucial in imparting the spin and swing that none of his contemporaries could match. His most deadly ball was delivered from wide of the crease; the ball swung into the right-handed batsman but, on pitching, it changed direction, ideally clipping the off bail. Eighty years on batsmen have still found no answer to such a delivery. Barnes rarely smiled on a cricket pitch; perhaps in his youth he rarely smiled at all, but he mellowed in old age and Alan Ross has described in verse Barnes guiding a blind Wilfred Rhodes around one of the Test grounds in the sixties.

Right *1912: The first 'timeless' Test – won by the hosts – in England.* ***Above*** *The England team take the field and* ***(below)*** *the Australians flee from the rain*

Opposite *Frank Foster, Johnny Douglas and Plum Warner in Australia on the 1911–12 tour. Douglas captained England successfully after Warner had withdrawn through illness*

Below *The 'welcome home' menu card at the dinner in honour of the returning 1911–12 MCC team from Australia*

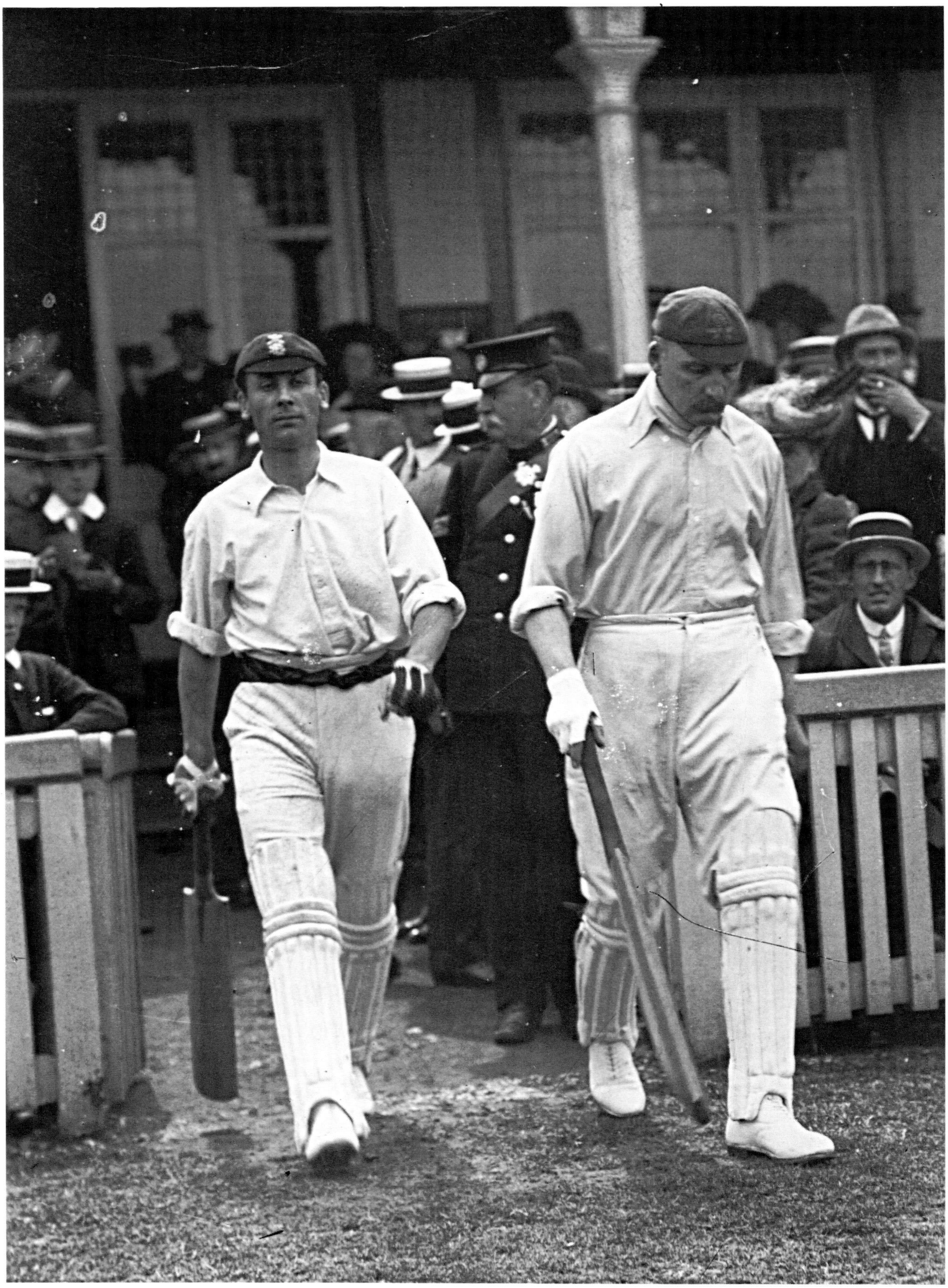

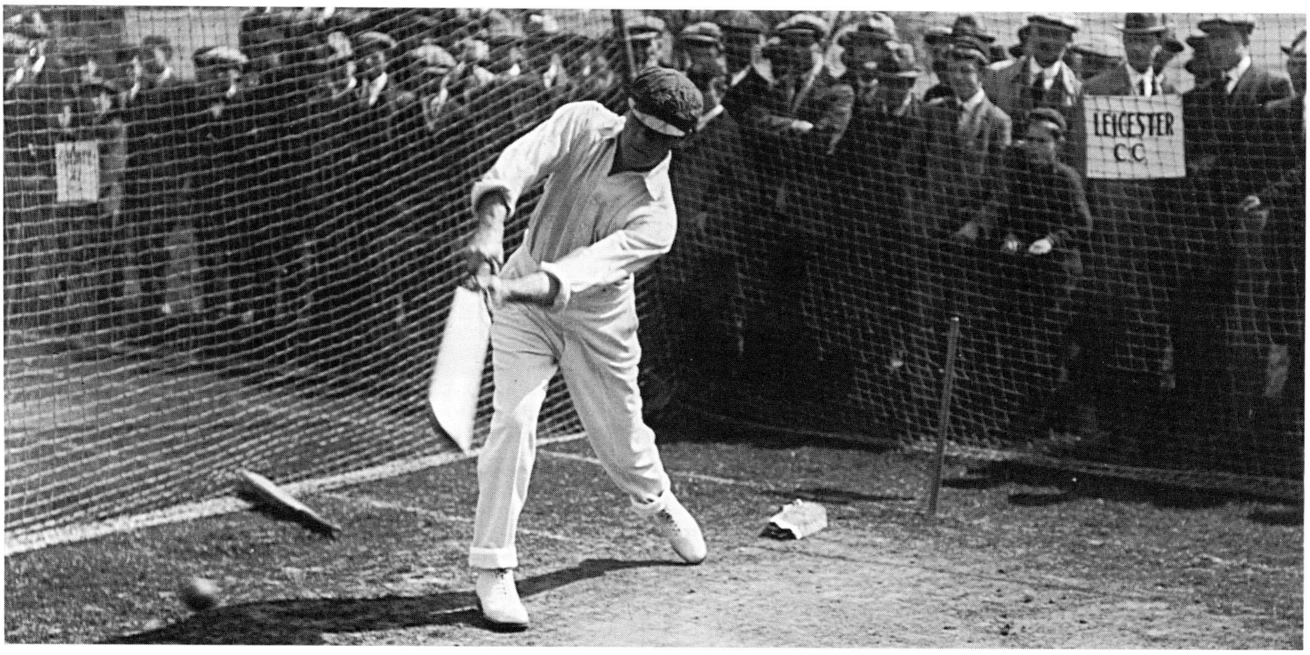

Above *Warren Bardsley enjoys a net, while an interested Leicestershire audience look on*

Right *Friends – and rivals. Three captains who contested the Triangular Test series (left to right): South Africa's Frank Mitchell, England's C.B. Fry and Australia's Syd Gregory*

Opposite *Jack Hobbs (left) and Archie MacLaren opening the innings for England on the second day of the 1909 Edgbaston Test against Australia. England won by 10 wickets*

Above *1914 saw the sad demise of Albert Trott, who successfully represented both England and Australia in Tests. He once hit a ball from Monty Noble over the top of the Lord's pavilion*

Opposite *Conquering heroes return from the South African tour of 1913–14.* ***Above*** *Mr and Mrs J.W. Hearne and (right) Mr and Mrs E.J. Smith.*
Below *Frank Woolley and friend*

Two ramrod ancients halt as Statham starts his run.
Then, elbows linked, but straight as sailors
On a tilting deck, they move. One, square-shouldered as a tailor's
Model, leans over, whispering in the other's ear:
'Go easy. Steps here. This end bowling.'
Turning, I watch Barnes guide Rhodes into fresher air,
As if to continue an innings, though Rhodes may only play by ear.

It is a picture that the batsmen of the 1900s would have found hard to imagine.

Of the cricketers we have met so far, only Rhodes would continue to represent England after the war. I must just mention two others whose career records would have been even more staggering but for the four year interruption – Jack Hobbs and Frank Woolley. Indeed, these two head the chart of the most runs scored in a first-class career. Hobbs made his debut for England on the unsuccessful tour of 1907–08 (he scored a masterful 83 on his debut); Woolley first played against Noble's victorious Australians in 1909. However, we shall meet them properly once the hostilities are over.

Away from the international scene cricket prospered. Thousands still flocked to Lord's to watch the Gentlemen play the Players, Oxford play Cambridge and Eton play Harrow. The County Championship was now firmly established, and the arrival of Northamptonshire in 1905 took the number of contestants to 16. With no television and little transport, the county matches provided the only opportunity for the majority of cricket followers to see the heroes of the Golden Age in action. Test

matches were something reported in the national newspapers, so that a cricket lover from Norton Fitzwarren would have been quite content to see Somerset lose to Sussex, provided Ranji scored a hundred.

The old counties dominated the competition. In this period Yorkshire won the title six times; they were still led by Lord Hawke, who finally retired in 1910 after 28 years at the helm. A benevolent despot, on the one hand he demanded the highest standards of dress, discipline and behaviour ('I shave twice a day so you can shave once'), on the other he fought hard to improve the professional's lot. He instituted winter pay and devised a scheme whereby two-thirds of a player's benefit money was retained and invested, rather than being handed over straightaway. No doubt the players approved of the scheme – at least after their retirement.

Spy

VISITORS FROM OUR EASTERN EMPIRE: SOME OF THE INDIAN CRICKETERS WHO ARE NOW PLAYING IN ENGLAND

PALVANKAR BALU (Mahratta) — KEKI M. MISTRI (Parsee) — SYED HUSSEIN (Mohammedan) — MAHARAJA OF PATIALA (Captain) — SHAFGNAT HUSSEIN (Mohammedan)

Bourne and Shepherd

Above *Some members of the 1911 All-Indian touring party to England.* Wisden *records that the trip was a 'complete disappointment', but that more success might have been achieved if Mistri had not had to spend all but three matches off the field, in attendance on the Maharajah of Patiala*

Opposite *'Spy's' vision of Lord Hawke*

Right *The 'tykes' at play: Lord Hawke shares a joke with his champion spinner, Wilfred Rhodes*

TWO GENTLEMEN OF WARWICKSHIRE.

MR. F. R. FOSTER (*Captain of the Warwickshire XI., who have just won the Cricket Championship*). "TELL KENT FROM ME SHE HATH LOST."—*II. Henry VI., iv. 10.*

WILLIAM SHAKSPEARE. "WARWICK, THOU ART WORTHY!"—*III. Henry VI., iv. 6.*

Kent, we can imagine, played in a more relaxed, less regimented atmosphere; none the less they were champions four times in this period. They relied upon the dashing batting of the amateur K.L. Hutchings, the fast bowling of Fielder, the emerging all-round talents of Frank Woolley and the left-arm spin of Colin Blythe.

Blythe was Rhodes' rival for the England team; he was no more accurate than the Yorkshireman – an impossible goal – but some reckoned him to be an even more difficult proposition on a rain-affected wicket. His 19 Test appearances brought him the remarkable tally of 100 wickets, and on the two occasions that he bowled England to victory he was,

by the end of each match, on the verge of a complete breakdown, for he was a sensitive soul. In all he took 2,506 wickets from 1899 to 1914; perhaps he would have added to this figure, but he was one of several notable cricketers who did not survive the war. He was killed in France in 1917.

Cricket, as well as all the other affairs of man, was brought to a stunned standstill by the turmoil in Europe. War was declared on 4 August 1914; county cricket struggled on to the end of the month but was then called to a halt. Surrey, the leaders, decided to cancel their last two matches and some people suggested that they had therefore forfeited their right to the Championship. However, the second-placed team, Middlesex, led by Plum Warner, had no objection to make, and at a meeting in November the MCC committee ruled that Surrey should be declared champions. It really didn't matter any more.

Chevallier Tayler's picture of Kent playing Lancashire at Canterbury in 1906. Blythe is bowling to Tyldesley

Opposite below *In 1911 the Championship went to Warwickshire – here immortalized by a punning* Punch

Opposite above *A match card produced to mark the Centenary of Lord's current ground in 1914*

3

BRADMAN . . . AND OTHERS

> I see them in foul dug-outs, gnawed by rats,
> And in the ruined trenches, lashed with rain,
> Dreaming of things they did with balls and bats.

Siegfried Sassoon's dreamers must have wondered whether sanity would ever return, let alone county cricket. For many it didn't. The 1920 *Wisden* records a Roll of Honour listing 77 well-known cricketers who died in action.

Nervously, county cricket resumed in 1919. It was decided that matches should be played on a two-day basis, an unsuccessful experiment that lasted just one season. None the less interest was high, if only because the resumption of competitive cricket was a symbol of a return to normality. However, apart from the long list of absentees, the four-year hiatus inevitably produced several changes during the period between the two World Wars.

Firstly the impact of the amateur declined. The Edwardian age of leisure had passed, and it was no longer possible for every aspiring amateur to allow himself the luxury of playing cricket throughout the summer months. In 1902 J.T. Tyldesley was the only professional batsman to play in the first Test match, a ratio never to be repeated after the First World War. Now the professionals would fill most of the places, though there would be at least one amateur in the team, because it remained imperative

Cricketing convalescence for soldiers and nurses, at Étaples in 1916

Above *Lord Hawke, King George V and Walter Long, MP watch England play the Dominions at Lord's in 1918*

that the England side should be led by a gentleman. For though there were fewer gentlemen on the cricket field, they still held an impenetrable monopoly in the committee rooms.

Another new feature of the period was the domination of the bat over the ball, which could be attributed to an improvement in the preparation of the wickets and the dearth of truly fast bowlers. Before 1914 three days of fine weather were usually sufficient to produce a winner in a Test match; by 1930 the large proportion of draws in England saw the duration of a Test match extended to four days. In South Africa in 1938–39 the experiment of a 'timeless Test' was tried, but of course it ended in a draw. After 10 days the match was plodding towards its climax, but the boat which was to carry the Englishmen home could wait no longer. The idea was shelved.

The advance of technology had reached the groundsman's shed, where there were new heavy rollers and mowing machines that produced wickets which refused to deteriorate. Only the intervention of rain allowed the likes of Hedley Verity to produce the most startling of bowling figures. For instance, a thunderstorm at Leeds in 1932 (allied to his superb control) enabled Verity to finish with figures of 19.4-16-10-10 against the luckless Nottinghamshire batsmen.

Hedley Verity, masterful left-arm spinner, was the greatest cricketer to lose his life in the Second World War

BATSMAN
TOTAL
BATSMAN
1
555
2
224
CAUGHT
313
WICKETS
LAST PLAYER
BOWLERS 7

Until the arrival of Harold Larwood, there were few English bowlers capable of striking terror into their contemporaries, and it was left to the broad shoulders of the medium-paced Maurice Tate to carry the burden for England and to atone for his father's misfortune. Batsmen, both English and Australian, generally made the most of the favourable conditions. Amidst all the changes one thing remained reassuringly familiar, and that was Yorkshire's domination of domestic cricket. In the 21 seasons between the wars they won the Championship no fewer than 12 times and they never finished lower than fifth. Ever present was Herbert Sutcliffe, a player who looked and behaved like a gentleman and who scored a thousand runs or more in every season between the wars. Until 1933 he was partnered by Percy Holmes, who, despite the onset of lumbago, combined with him to score 555 for the first wicket against Essex at Leyton, a new record once the scorers had retrieved an elusive no-ball. Wilfred Rhodes kept going until 1930, but his retirement merely allowed Hedley Verity to step out of his shadow, and whilst Maurice Leyland might not delight the purists, he guaranteed Yorkshire, and latterly England, a plentiful supply of runs, especially in a crisis.. The fast-bowling mantle passed smoothly from Macaulay and Emmott Robinson to the tireless Bill Bowes. In addition Yorkshire performed with a ruthless professional soundness which continued to distinguish them from their southern counterparts. They played with only one amateur and that was the captain, who was usually the overseer of their victories rather than the major contributor, though the fielding alone of A.B. Sellers set a sterling example from 1932 onwards.

Apart from Middlesex's triumphs under Pelham Warner in 1920 and 1921 the Championship rested in the north even when Yorkshire failed to win it. Between 1926 and 1930, Lancashire won the title four times, owing partly to the bowling of the ageing Australian paceman, Ted McDonald, one of the first imported players to have an impact upon county cricket. The only other intruders in the Championship were Nottinghamshire in 1929, led by A.W. Carr and spearheaded by Larwood and Voce, and Derbyshire in 1936, who surprised everyone when winning their one and only Championship. So the 'business' cricketers of the north prevailed.

In the winter there was more cricket to keep our

Above *The famous scoreboard – after readjustment!*

Kent's finest inter-war players: ***(left)*** *the cavalier Percy Chapman, 'Tich' Freeman, who took over 3,000 county wickets, and Frank Woolley.* ***Opposite*** *Les Ames, reliable wicketkeeper and scorer of 102 first-class centuries* leading professionals gainfully employed, with the arrival on the international scene of the West Indies, New Zealand and India. Indeed, in the winter of 1929–30 MCC despatched two sides abroad, one to New Zealand under A.H.H. Gilligan, the other to the West Indies under the Hon. F.S.G. Calthorpe. These sides were obviously some way short of England's best, so that a pattern emerged; the away series would be closely fought, but when the emerging countries came to England they were outgunned. For example, on their first tour of England in 1928 the West Indies lost all three Tests by an innings; however, the emergence of George Headley and the dazzling all-round skills of Learie Constantine ensured that matches during the next decade were more closely contested.

Right *The Maharajah Sir Vijaya Vizianagram, captain of the 1936 Indians in England, adopting a relaxed attitude to post-prandial fielding practice*

Above *Pressure upon the umpire is not a new phenomenon, as Tom Webster here illustrates in a 1924* Daily Mail

Opposite *The 'Grand Old Man' of South African cricket, 'Dave' Nourse. He was a powerful and dependable batsman, a useful bowler and a brilliant slip fielder*

'Manny' Martindale, Constantine's formidable fast-bowling partner, who split Hammond's chin at Old Trafford in 1933

Below *The 1933 West Indians. Back row (left to right): J.M. Kidney, H.C. Griffiths, C. Christiani, I. Barrow, E. Achong, C. Merry, E.A. Martindale, C.A. Wiles, G.A. Headley. Front row: H.C. Grant (captain), C.A. Roach, B. Sealey, V.A. Valentine, O. Dacosta*

Constantine enthralled crowds in the same way as Gilbert Jessop had in the 1900s, whether batting, bowling or fielding. Consider his performance for the West Indies against Middlesex in June 1928. Going to the crease at 79 for five he made 86 out of 107 in less than an hour, thereby saving the follow-on. Unstrapping his pads, he proceeded to take seven for 57 as Middlesex were bowled out for 136, which left the West Indies requiring 259 for victory – a lost cause, it seemed, when the score stood at 121 for five. Enter Constantine, who hit 103 out of 133 in an hour, enabling the West Indies to win the match by three wickets. No one could hit the ball more ferociously, as J.W. Hearne would witness. *Wisden* records that 'in stopping a drive from Constantine, Hearne had a finger so badly damaged that he could play no more cricket last season'. His approach to batting was refreshing, to say the least: 'When I first went in, my immediate objective was to hit the ball to each of the four corners of the field. After that I tried not to be repetitive.'

Constantine's Test figures are not a true reflection of his worth (a batting average of 19.24, a bowling average of 30.10). George Headley's are. He is one of four players (Bradman, Graeme Pollock and Sutcliffe are the others) who averaged over 60 in Test cricket. Bearing in mind that there were few other 'class' players to share the burden in the West Indies sides of the thirties, it was no surprise that he should be regarded as the 'black Bradman' outside the West Indies. In the Caribbean, of course, Bradman was known as the 'white Headley'. When the West Indies achieved their first triumph over England on the 1929–30 tour Headley, inevitably, laid the foundations of victory by scoring a century in each innings.

The New Zealanders had to wait rather longer (48 years) for their first victory over England. The Indians, who first toured England in 1932, fared a little better, recording their first win in the 1951–52 series. So the new Test countries provided a welcome distraction for cricket followers, but there is

Constantine hits hard and high against Essex at Leyton in 1928

The genius of George Headley, scorer of two centuries at Lord's in the Test of 1939

South Africa's skipper – and fine batsman – H.W. Taylor (right) and Leicestershire's Major Fawke in 1924, the year England ousted the Springboks for 30, as Tom Webster illustrates (***above***)

no question that Australia and England still possessed the best cricketers and that an Ashes series remained the pinnacle of cricket.

Which is why *Wisden*'s editor, Sydney Pardon, sounds so inconsolably gloomy in the 1922 edition: 'During all the years I have edited *Wisden* there has never been a season so disheartening as that of 1921.' The reason for his despair is not hard to find. In the 10 Tests since the war England had lost eight and drawn two. In Australia in 1920–21 the home side won every match convincingly, and of the tourists only Jack Hobbs maintained his reputation. In the dry summer of 1921 the Australians were equally invincible. England, deprived of Hobbs through ill health, lost the first three Tests and managed two draws at the end of the series. England were no doubt still hungover from the war, and the selectors became a little frantic, using 30 players throughout the summer. In addition, their opponents were exceptionally strong. The Australian side was led by Warwick Armstrong, who both in stature and demeanour could be regarded as Australia's answer to W.G. He first toured England back in 1902 as a 10-stone stripling; by 1921 his weight had doubled and he made it clear that he wasn't going to be pushed around by anyone. He was the sort of captain who ordered his team to be in bed at 11 o'clock, stayed out himself to one in the morning, and yet was certain that there would be no rumblings as a result, such were the respect and fear that he commanded from his team. I imagine that Ian Chappell would have thought him an excellent model.

Above *The 1921 Headingley Test: Warren Bardsley neatly caught by first slip, Frank Woolley, off Johnny Douglas*

Above *Charlie Macartney, the 'Governor-General', hits out during his superb century before lunch on the first day of the 1921 Headingley Test*

England and Australian captains Warwick Armstrong (left) and Johnny Douglas ponder the prospects ahead after tossing up at Trent Bridge in May 1921. Australia won the match by 10 wickets

Left *Arthur Mailey: painter, journalist, wit and – not least – leg-spin bowler.*

Below *Mailey's 1926 cartoon of Lord Harris, drawn on the back of a menu card*

Right *Jack Gregory (left) and Herbie Collins. Gregory was a superb fast bowler, as well as the scorer of a 70-minute Test century*

Armstrong was fortunate to have such a well-balanced team under his command. In Gregory and McDonald he had a pair of bowlers much faster than any Englishman. Mailey's leg-spinners dipped deceptively at the end of their flight whilst Armstrong himself bowled accurate leg-cutters in the manner of W.G. Warren Bardsley, solid rather than spectacular, proved a worthy successor to Clem Hill, whilst Charlie Macartney, the 'Governor General', was sufficiently dashing and imperious to invite comparisons with Victor Trumper.

Sydney Pardon did not like seeing an England side humiliated, and humiliated they were. As the

final Test of the series, which had been curtailed by rain, was meandering to a draw Armstrong withdrew to the outfield, picked up a wind-tossed newspaper and proceeded to read it whilst play continued. He later declared that he was simply trying to find out whom the Australians were playing. Just twisting the knife a little.

England fared little better in 1924–25, losing the series four-one, though there were a few consolations for the optimist. Herbert Sutcliffe had united with Jack Hobbs to form the most reliable of opening pairs and Maurice Tate took 38 wickets in the series, which was a record at the time for an Ashes series. Finally, after seven years of famine, the Ashes were regained in the final Test at The Oval in 1926, where for the first time England were led by the dashing Percy Chapman. The architects of victory were all giants of the game at contrasting stages of their careers. Hobbs and Sutcliffe scored 374 runs between them in the match. Wilfred Rhodes, dramatically recalled at the age of 48, took six wickets and so did Harold Larwood, playing in his second Test. A thunderstorm on the Monday evening changed the tempo of the match and the Englishmen proved that they were far better equipped on rain-affected wickets.

Tom Webster illustrates England's reliance on Herbert Sutcliffe during the 1924–25 series against Australia. On this occasion – the second Test, at Melbourne – he scored 176 and 127, but England still lost

Opposite *Arthur Gilligan (left) tosses up with the Australian Herbie Collins at the start of the 1925 Adelaide Test. Australia won by 11 runs on the seventh day of the match.*

Below *The Oval, 1926: Ponsford caught by Larwood off Rhodes and England's victory is around the corner*

ENGLAND v AUSTRALIA
Played at The Oval,
14, 16, 17, 18 August, 1926.
Result: England won by 289 runs.

England: First innings

J.B. Hobbs b Mailey	37
H. Sutcliffe b Mailey	76
F.E. Woolley b Mailey	18
E.H. Hendren b Gregory	8
A.P.F. Chapman* st Oldfield b Mailey	49
G.T.S. Stevens c Andrews b Mailey	17
W. Rhodes c Oldfield b Mailey	28
G. Geary run out	9
M.W. Tate b Grimmett	23
H. Larwood c Andrews b Grimmett	0
H. Strudwick† not out	4
Extras (b 6, lb 5)	11
Total	280

Fall of Wickets: 1/53, 2/91, 3/108, 4/189, 5/213, 6/214, 7/231, 8/266, 9/266, 10/280.
Bowling: Gregory 15-4-31-1, Grimmett 33-12-74-2, Mailey 33.5-3-138-6, Macartney 7-4-16-0, Richardson 7-2-10-0.

Australia: First innings

W.M. Woodfull b Rhodes	35
W. Bardsley c Strudwick b Larwood	2
C.G. Macartney b Stevens	25
W.H. Ponsford run out	2
T.J.E. Andrews b Larwood	3
H.L. Collins* c Stevens b Larwood	61
A.J. Richardson c Geary b Rhodes	16
J.M. Gregory c Stevens b Tate	73
W.A.S. Oldfield† not out	33
C.V. Grimmett b Tate	35
A.A. Mailey c Strudwick b Tate	0
Extras (b 5, lb 12)	17
Total	302

Fall of Wickets: 1/9, 2/44, 3/51, 4/59, 5/90, 6/122, 7/229, 8/231, 9/298, 10/302.
Bowling: Tate 37.1-17-40-3, Larwood 34-11-82-3, Geary 27-8-43-0, Stevens 29-3-85-1, Rhodes 25-15-35-2.

England: Second innings

J.B. Hobbs b Gregory	100
H. Sutcliffe b Mailey	161
F.E. Woolley lbw b Richardson	27
E.H. Hendren c Oldfield b Grimmett	15
A.P.F. Chapman* b Richardson	19
G.T.S. Stevens c Mailey b Grimmett	22
W. Rhodes lbw b Grimmett	14
G. Geary c Oldfield b Gregory	1
M.W. Tate not out	33
H. Larwood b Mailey	5
H. Strudwick† c Andrews b Mailey	2
Extras (b 19, lb 18)	37
Total	436

Fall of Wickets: 1/172, 2/220, 3/277, 4/316, 5/373, 6/375, 7/382, 8/425, 9/430, 10/436.
Bowling: Gregory 18-1-58-2, Grimmett 55-17-108-3, Mailey 42.5-6-128-3, Macartney 26-16-24-0, Richardson 41-21-81-2.

Australia: Second innings

W.M. Woodfull c Geary b Larwood	0
W. Bardsley (4) c Woolley b Rhodes	21
C.G. Macartney c Geary b Larwood	16
W.H. Ponsford (2) c Larwood b Rhodes	12
T.J.E. Andrews (6) c Tate b Larwood	15
H.L. Collins* (5) c Woolley b Rhodes	4
A.J. Richardson (8) b Rhodes	4
J.M. Gregory (7) c Sutcliffe b Tate	9
W.A.S. Oldfield† b Stevens	23
C.V. Grimmett not out	8
A.A. Mailey b Geary	6
Extras (lb 7)	7
Total	125

Fall of Wickets: 1/1, 2/31, 3/31, 4/35, 5/63, 6/83, 7/83, 8/87, 9/114, 10/125.
Bowling: Tate 9-4-12-1, Larwood 14-3-34-3, Geary 6.3-2-15-1, Stevens 3-1-13-1, Rhodes 20-9-44-4.

However, in 1928–29 they were to prove their superiority on the dry wickets of Australia. The English batting was awesome with Hobbs and Sutcliffe, supported by Hendren, Jardine and Chapman; but the discovery of the series was Walter Hammond, who amassed 905 runs in the series at an average of 113.12. For one year at least he was undoubtedly the best batsman in the world. The bowling was left in the capable hands of Maurice Tate, Harold Larwood and an unlikely hero in Australia, the phlegmatic Somerset farmer, Jack White. His left-armers depended more on flight than spin, but 'whether it was cows or batsmen, he had the treatment for the trouble'. The Australians, who lost the series four-one, were rebuilding now that Bardsley, Collins and Macartney had gone. One of the newcomers was the 20-year-old Don Bradman. He was omitted from Australia's team for the second Test, which was probably, with hindsight, a poor decision.

England's run of victories continued in the first Test at Trent Bridge in 1930, where they won by a margin of 93 runs. The second Test was played at Lord's. By any standards it was a remarkable match, in which many of the key figures of the era participated, and the result was to have far-reaching consequences. Here are the two sides.

England: Hobbs, Woolley, Hammond, Duleepsinhji, Hendren, Chapman (captain), Allen, Tate, Robins, White, Duckworth. (There were two notable absentees, Sutcliffe and Larwood, who were both injured.)
Australia: Woodfull (captain), Ponsford, Bradman, Kippax, McCabe, Richardson, Oldfield, Fairfax, Grimmett, Hornibrook, Wall.

The combined age of England's opening pair was 90, and they were the only survivors from the 'Golden Age'. Obviously they were in decline, but until the end of 1930 it was unthinkable that England should take the field without them. Hobbs and Woolley are placed first and second in the list of runscorers of all time and yet both displayed a healthy indifference to record-breaking. Wilfred Rhodes, whilst acknowledging that Hobbs was the greatest batsman of his time, added that he could have scored thousands more runs, but 'he was often content to throw away his wicket when he had reached a hundred and give someone else a chance'. I doubt whether Rhodes ever came to terms with such a philosophy.

Before the war Hobbs' partner and tutor at Surrey was Tom Hayward, who was renowned as one of the greatest defensive players of the Edwardian age. However, Hobbs did more than emulate him; before 1914 his dazzling footwork and his

Above *A memorable scene at Taunton in 1924: Jack Hobbs raises a bumper of champagne to celebrate the passing of W.G. Grace's record 126 centuries*

mastery of all the orthodox shots ensured that he scored at a cracking pace; 20 times he scored a hundred before lunch without ever appearing to be in a hurry. No one recalls his favourite shot (like Ranji's leg-glance or Boycott's forward defensive), simply because he could play all of them with equal facility. W.G. was the Champion; Hobbs was the Master.

His five years out of the game – four through war and another through illness – came when most batsmen are at the peak of their powers, the early thirties. After the war, which ended when he was almost 36, he scored 132 of his 197 centuries (naturally it was against Somerset at Taunton that he both equalled and surpassed W.G.'s record). His footwork was now less ambitious but still totally unhurried, and his ability on rain-affected wickets was the envy of everyone. He was, I suppose, the perfect model for all aspiring schoolboys, not only because of his batsmanship but also because of his bearing, for as H.S. Altham recalled, he was:

> A man of natural dignity, with at the same time an engaging twinkle that revealed a charming and constant sense of humour, utterly unspoilt by success and always prepared to help others, especially the young; he soon became and remained throughout his career an ideal support for any touring captain and the embodiment of the highest standards and values of the game.

Above *England's greatest-ever opening pair, Jack Hobbs and Herbert Sutcliffe. Together they exceeded 100 for the first wicket on 15 occasions*

Top *Frank Woolley, scorer of 145 first-class centuries, batting against the West Indies in 1939*

Above *Hammond's classic cover-drive, here in action against the West Indies in 1933*

Hobbs is the constant in several legendary opening partnerships with Hayward and Sandham at Surrey, and Rhodes and Sutcliffe for England, so it would have been a rare – and appetising – sight to see him walk out with Frank Woolley at Lord's in 1930. Whenever David Gower plays one of those effortless cover-drives, the more senior commentators often mention Frank Woolley by way of comparison. The qualities that link them must be their left-handedness, their sense of timing and their casual grace. Woolley was a little taller than Gower and I suspect a more formidable straight hitter; he was most definitely a better bowler. His left-arm slow bowling accounted for 2,068 batsmen, approximately 2,065 more than Gower, but it is his batting that still excites septuagenarians.

He batted like an amateur, with no thought for tomorrow. Fast bowlers might be dumped back over their heads and spinners would not be allowed to dominate. Perhaps his most memorable two innings were in the Lord's Test of 1921 when he defied the pace of Gregory and McDonald, scoring 95 and 93. Whilst his colleagues wilted, Woolley counter-attacked, and not only did his bold methods work, they also endeared him to all present. By the end of his career the scribes had run out of superlatives, and R.C. Robertson-Glasgow gave up searching in the most graceful manner. 'Frank Woolley was easy to watch, difficult to bowl to and impossible to write about. When you bowled to him there weren't enough fielders; when you wrote about him there weren't enough words.' And Robertson-Glasgow had plenty of good ones at his disposal.

I will mention Hammond now, even though in 1930 his career was just beginning to blossom. He succeeded Hobbs as the prime English batsman; indeed by 1930, after his triumphant tour of Australia, he had already done so. If Hobbs was masterful, then Hammond was majestic.

Once he had reached maturity he didn't bother with the hook shot and he rarely pulled; he simply didn't need to. The power of his driving off front and back foot enabled him to play with a straight bat and still dominate the best bowlers. Cricket lovers in the west country worshipped him; it was enough just to witness that regal walk to the wicket, with a blue handkerchief peeping out of his hip pocket. Like another west country hero, Viv Richards, he could undermine the bowler even before he took guard.

Arguably he was the most complete cricketer of the era, for in addition to his career aggregate of 50,551 runs he took 732 wickets. His bowling, like his batting, was based on a classical technique, a smooth flowing sideways action which could produce late away-swing. His slip-fielding was peerless. He was the complete cricketer, universally respected by his contemporaries and yet, I suspect, never completely fulfilled. For from 1930 onwards he was destined to be only the second-best batsman in the world, and as Alan Gibson suggests, he was not a man 'content to be second best'. Throughout the last 18 years of his career he was dogged by Bradman. All his achievements had to be measured against the Don, and however brilliantly he performed he could not surpass him. In 1938 he decided to play as an amateur so that he could captain England. If he couldn't outscore Bradman, perhaps he could deprive the little man of the Ashes, but the series was squared. After the war he led an ill-fated tour to Australia, at the age of 43, but it was no good. He returned heavily defeated and demoralised, and played little first-class cricket thereafter. It was a sad end.

Back in June 1930, no one yet appreciated the impact that Bradman was to have. Doubts had been expressed about his ability to play on the damper English wickets; he soon dispelled them.

On 27 June 1930, at Lord's, Percy Chapman won the toss, and despite a gem of an innings from Woolley, England's three greatest players were back in the pavilion for 105. However, England were rescued by Duleepsinhji, Ranji's nephew, who scored 173 in his first Test against Australia. The innings closed on the second morning at a total of 425, a score which would satisfy most Test captains over the years. In reply Woodfull and Ponsford added 162, so that when Ponsford's concentration lapsed after meeting the King, the English bowling was beginning to waver. In the next two-and-three-quarter hours it was ruthlessly torn apart, with Bradman finishing the day on 155 not out and the score 404 for two.

Duleepsinhji in action against the 1930 Australians, here during his half-century at The Oval

On the Monday, 325 more runs were added before the declaration at the tea interval; Bradman's final contribution was 254 and Kippax, McCabe, Richardson and Oldfield all joined in the fun. When the Australian total had reached 700 there was a moment of black comedy, as the scoreboard operators by the Tavern had to improvise a '7' in the hundreds column. No one had witnessed such devastation of a national side before. The Australian total of 729 for six meant that England required 304 to avoid an innings defeat, and at 147 for five they appeared doomed. Now Chapman, true to his image, attacked and flailed the leg-spin of Clarrie Grimmett around the ground. In two-and-a-half hours he achieved his highest Test score of 121 – and England were trying to save the game! Walter Robins, no doubt inspired by his captain, became over-excited and ran out Jack White, who at this stage of his career was not well suited to quick singles, and the England innings closed at 375. This left the Australians 72 to win in plenty of time. After they had lost three wickets for just 22 runs, Woodfull calmly guided his side to the most remarkable of Test victories.

Wisden records that 'the Englishmen lost a match, which, with a little discretion on the last day, they could probably have saved'. However, it was not in Percy Chapman's nature to be discreet. His success as an England captain had been based upon his dashing carefree style of leadership and these qualities were to bring his downfall. He was heavily criticised after this defeat and his detractors had a

Bill Woodfull was a fine batsman, but, as Tom Webster illustrated, adhesive rather than exciting

point; for an England side to score 425 and 375 and still be defeated within four days seems downright irresponsible today. It was not in his nature to set negative containing fields; he wanted to dismiss the batsman whatever the circumstances; to be fair to him his resources in this match were thin; his two young amateur bowlers Allen and Robins had yet to reach their prime, and were both temperamentally committed to a policy of all-out attack, which left the more experienced Tate and White to shake their heads, roll up their sleeves and to soldier on as best they could. Most importantly, no one had seen such clinical destruction before. The advent of Don Bradman no longer permitted an England side simply to stride out on to the field, 'give it a damn good go' and still expect to win. If England were to win a Test series, the problem of Bradman had to be solved. To emphasise the point Bradman scored 334 out of a total of 566 in the third Test at Leeds; at the close of play on the first day he was 309 not out from a total of 458 for three. Today 309 runs in a day by an entire Test team would be regarded as mayhem, at least in the popular press.

Four more to Bradman on the way to his 334 at Leeds

ENGLAND v AUSTRALIA
Played at Lord's, 27, 28, 30 June, 1 July, 1930.
Result: Australia won by seven wickets.

England: First innings

J.B. Hobbs c Oldfield b Fairfax	1
F.E. Woolley c Wall b Fairfax	41
W.R. Hammond b Grimmett	38
K.S. Duleepsinhji c Bradman b Grimmett	173
E.H. Hendren c McCabe b Fairfax	48
A.P.F. Chapman* c Oldfield b Wall	11
G.O.B. Allen b Fairfax	3
M.W. Tate c McCabe b Wall	54
R.W.V. Robins c Oldfield b Hornibrook	5
J.C. White not out	23
G. Duckworth† c Oldfield b Wall	18
Extras (b 2, lb 7, nb 1)	10
Total	425

Fall of Wickets: 1/13, 2/53, 3/105, 4/209, 5/236, 6/239, 7/337, 8/363, 9/387, 10/425.
Bowling: Wall 29.4-2-118-3, Fairfax 31-6-101-4, Grimmett 33-4-105-2, Hornibrook 26-6-62-1, McCabe 9-1-29-0.

Australia: First innings

W.M. Woodfull* st Duckworth b Robins	155
W.H. Ponsford c Hammond b White	81
D.G. Bradman c Chapman b White	254
A.F. Kippax b White	83
S.J. McCabe c Woolley b Hammond	44
V.Y. Richardson c Hobbs b Tate	30
W.A.S. Oldfield† not out	43
A.G. Fairfax not out	20
C.V. Grimmett, P.M. Hornibrook, T.W. Wall	did not bat
Extras (b 6, lb 8, w 5)	19
Total (6 wickets declared)	729

Fall of Wickets: 1/162, 2/393, 3/585, 4/588, 5/643, 6/672.
Bowling: Allen 34-7-115-0, Tate 64-16-148-1, White 51-7-158-3, Robins 42-1-172-1, Hammond 35-8-82-1, Woolley 6-0-35-0.

England: Second innings

J.B. Hobbs b Grimmett	19
F.E. Woolley hit wkt b Grimmett	28
W.R. Hammond c Fairfax b Grimmett	32
K.S. Duleepsinhji c Oldfield b Hornibrook	48
E.H. Hendren c Richardson b Grimmett	9
A.P.F. Chapman* c Oldfield b Fairfax	121
G.O.B. Allen lbw b Grimmett	57
M.W. Tate c Ponsford b Grimmett	10
R.W.V. Robins not out	11
J.C. White run out	10
G. Duckworth† lbw b Fairfax	0
Extras (b 16, lb 13, w 1)	30
Total	375

Fall of Wickets: 1/45, 2/58, 3/129, 4/141, 5/147, 6/272, 7/329, 8/354, 9/372, 10/375.
Bowling: Wall 25-2-80-0, Fairfax 12.4-2-37-2, Grimmett 53-13-167-6, Hornibrook 22-6-49-1, McCabe 3-1-11-0, Bradman 1-0-1-0.

Australia: Second innings

W.M. Woodfull* not out	26
W.H. Ponsford b Robins	14
D.G. Bradman c Chapman b Tate	1
A.F. Kippax c Duckworth b Robins	3
S.J. McCabe not out	25
V.Y. Richardson, W.A.S. Oldfield†, A.G. Fairfax, C.V. Grimmett, P.M. Hornibrook, T.W. Wall	did not bat
Extras (b 1, lb 2)	3
Total (3 wickets)	72

Fall of Wickets: 1/16, 2/17, 3/22.
Bowling: Tate 13-6-21-1, White 2-0-8-0, Robins 9-1-34-2, Hammond 4.2-1-6-0.

The crowd consider the state of a distinctly damp Headingley wicket during the 1930 Test

It is hard to avoid statistics when discussing Bradman, since they do at least demonstrate how he dwarfed every other batsman in the history of the game. In 338 first-class innings he scored 117 centuries; he reached 200 on 37 occasions, 300 on six, and against Queensland in the summer of 1929–30 he scored 452 not out. When his captain, Alan Kippax, declared New South Wales' innings closed at 761, he assured him that he felt quite fit enough to go on a little longer. In Test cricket he scored 6,996 runs at an average of 99.94; one boundary in his final appearance at The Oval in 1948 would have ensured an average of three figures. After a standing ovation he was bowled second ball for a duck by an Eric Hollies googly; apparently he was still a little watery-eyed after his reception, which at least reminds us that he was mortal and not just a run-making machine. There had been precious little evidence before. Spectators flocked to see him bat; they were awed by his presence rather than charmed; his goal was to score as many runs as possible rather than to be loved. He was super-efficient and a genius, two qualities rarely recognised in the same person – as Robertson-Glasgow put it 'an artist without the handicap of an artistic temperament, a genius with an eye for business'.

England's Maurice Leyland in action during the 1930 Old Trafford Test

Right *The two Maurices, Tate and Leyland, resume their partnership against Australia in the 1930 Old Trafford Test*

Left *A rare colour picture of 'The Don', demonstrating his style in practice at Lord's*

Above *The statue of C.K. Nayudu at Indore. He was India's first Test captain, and an admirable batsman*

Bradman captained Australia from 1936 to his retirement in 1948. I doubt whether he was adored by his team-mates – he was too withdrawn, almost aloof, for that. In *Farewell to Cricket* he explained, with typical clarity, his position.

> I was often accused of being unsociable because at the end of the day I did not think it my duty to breast the bar and engage in a beer-drinking contest. At least I made no attempt to interfere with the habits of others, and if I thought my most important need was a cup of tea I had as much right to complain of their late entry into the dining-room as they had to complain of my absence from the bar.

Surely it was enough that he should be the best batsman of all time without having to be the most gregarious, and it is worth noting that Australia lost none of the five rubbers they contested during the period of his captaincy. Meticulous preparation and his own prolific runscoring saw to that. When he retired, it came as no surprise to his contemporaries that he should become a most astute businessman.

How the Australian outback kept up with the cricket in those primitive pre-'Test Match Special' days. The occasion was The Oval game of 1930

In the 1930 series Bradman finished with an aggregate of 974 runs at an average of 139.14, figures which clearly illustrated the scale of the problem confronting the English selectors when they sat down to discuss who should lead the 1932–33 tour to Australia. Chapman's approach was now too generous and suddenly outdated, Jack White was too old, Bob Wyatt from Warwickshire was a possibility, but in the end they decided upon Douglas Jardine of Winchester, Oxford and Surrey. On the eve of departure his old cricket master, Rockley Wilson, is said to have declared that 'he will probably win back the Ashes, but he will also lose us a Dominion'. If this famous observation is an accurate quotation, it shows amazing perspicacity on Wilson's part, for few others could predict the controversy that was to surround the 1932–33 tour. After all, there was nothing new in an Oxbridge-educated amateur embarking with a band of worthy professionals in pursuit of the Ashes. Even more reassuring would be the presence of Plum Warner as manager; he had taken the MCC flag all around the globe spreading the gospel of 'play up and play the game' wherever he stopped. There was, however, one curiosity – the strange decision to take four fast bowlers – Larwood, Voce, Bowes and Allen – in addition to Maurice Tate. Such a selection is commonplace today, but in the thirties it was a remarkable decision.

The brilliant – and tragic – Archie Jackson, whom some believe was at least the equal of 'The Don'

The key to Jardine's plan: the two-pronged pace attack of Harold Larwood (left) and Bill Voce

Jardine had a plan. Even without Bradman Australia possessed a strong batting side. Woodfull and Ponsford were as resolute and well established as Hobbs and Sutcliffe had been for England, if less graceful, and Richardson and McCabe were both outstanding Test players. Add Bradman to this combination and the Australians seemed unbeatable. But if they could undermine the confidence of Bradman himself, then the Ashes might be secured.

Jardine called his tactic 'leg theory'. The Australians, once they had witnessed it, preferred the more emotive term 'bodyline'. Leg theory had been used before, but only as a defensive ploy to stop free-scoring batsmen. Jardine chose to use it as an offensive weapon; hence the proliferation of fast bowlers. Once the shine had been removed from the ball so that it would no longer swing, which didn't take many overs on the hard, dry pitches of Australia, he would move seven fielders to the leg side, and the bowler's main line of attack would be directed at leg stump and pitched short of a length. The batsman therefore had three options. He could attempt to fend the ball off or duck, which was Woodfull's response; this method ran the risk of being caught by the umbrella of fieldsmen hovering close on the leg side. He could react more aggressively by regular use of the hook and pull shots. In the first Test of the series McCabe took this course

and scored a spectacular 187 not out, but he was unable to repeat this performance; this option demanded lightning reflexes and plenty of good fortune, as the captain could position as many men as he wished on the leg-side boundary. Bradman pioneered the third method: he reacted in his own way, which was to step away to the leg side so that he could exploit the wide open spaces on the off. This created plenty of scoring opportunities, but it was fraught with danger since his stumps were left exposed. In fact, by any other standards Bradman had a successful series – he averaged 56.57 – but by his own this represented a considerable decline, enough to ensure victory for England in four of the five Tests.

The key to the plan rested with the Nottinghamshire fast bowler, Harold Larwood. Larwood's Test career was a relatively short one, even for a fast bowler, and it was fortunate, at least for Jardine, that he had reached his peak at the age of 28 when the boat set sail for Australia. In 1932 he was without doubt the fastest bowler in the world and he was accurate; in addition he possessed the qualities of perseverance and loyalty, as the tour was to prove beyond doubt. He was supported by his Nottinghamshire colleague, Bill Voce, who possessed a far better action and physique than the actor who depicted him in the highly amusing Australian dramatisation *Bodyline*, and by the gawky, bespectacled Yorkshireman, Bill Bowes, whose main contribution throughout the series was to bowl Bradman first ball at Melbourne. This delivery even prompted his taciturn captain to give an involuntary leap of delight, a most uncharacteristic reaction.

The fourth fast bowler was Gubby Allen, an amateur from Cambridge University and Middlesex. Throughout the tour he steadfastly refused to bowl leg theory and he was very successful, though whether he would have taken as many wickets in 'normal' circumstances is debatable.

The crisis – and we are justified in calling it a crisis since the ramifications of the tour were discussed at Downing Street – reached its peak in the sleepy city of Adelaide, the venue of the third Test match. The Australian captain, Woodfull, was hit over the heart by Larwood, who was bowling in his conventional style. When he had recovered from the blow, he looked up to see that the field had been rearranged in preparation for leg theory. The crowd were furious and hurled abuse at the tourists, most of which was aimed at Jardine, the one with the Harlequin cap. Beyond the boundary, mounted troops were prepared to restore order in the likely event of a pitch invasion, and the pessimists wondered what might happen if Bradman himself was hit. In the same innings the much-respected Australian wicketkeeper, Bertie Oldfield, was forced to retire hurt after having his skull fractured by a Larwood delivery. Unsurprisingly these two incidents sparked bitter exchanges between the English management and the Australian players, and between the Australian Cricket Board and the MCC.

Top *Stan McCabe pulls his final boundary during his great 187 not out in the first Test at Sydney in 1932*

Opposite *Harold Larwood in action*

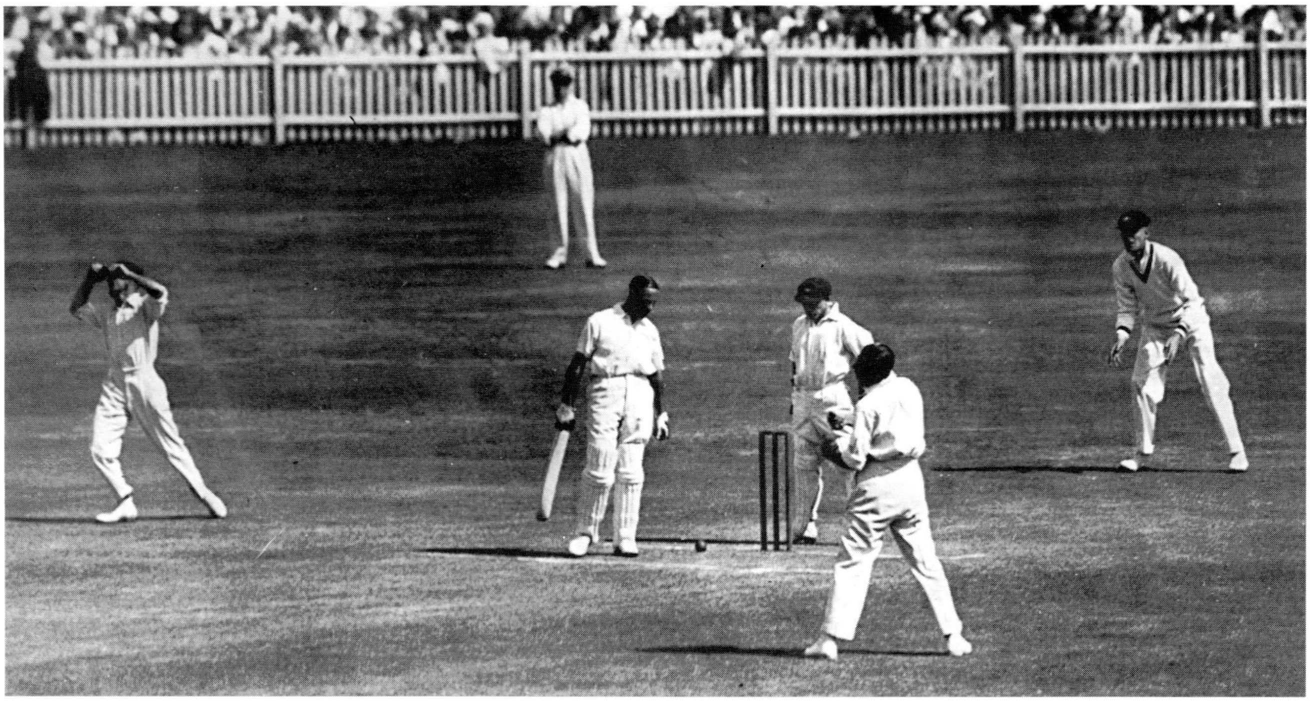

The first Test at Sydney, 1932: a narrow escape for Herbert Sutcliffe, as the ball fails to dislodge the bails. The Australians are suitably disgusted!

At the end of the day's play the England manager, Warner, went to the Australian dressing room to inquire about the well-being of Oldfield and Woodfull. This was one of the more unpleasant tasks of what was becoming a nightmarish tour for Warner; for he found himself in an impossible position. Certainly his concern for the injured Australians would have been genuine, and we know from his later writings that he wholeheartedly disapproved of Jardine's methods; yet he felt duty-bound to remain outwardly loyal to the captain whom he himself had helped select. We can be sure that he tried desperately hard to persuade Jardine to modify his tactics during the tour, but Jardine was not a man to be swayed off course by mere rhetoric. By the end of the tour the relationship between captain and manager must have reached an all-time low, as this extract from a Warner letter of January 1934 indicates.

> He is a queer fellow. When he sees a cricket ground with an Australian on it he goes mad! He rose to his present position on my shoulders and of his attitude to me I do not care to speak . . . in many quarters here – where they do not know the truth – he is a bit of a hero.

Woodfull's reaction to Warner's inquiry was, by his standards, a fierce one for he was a man of quiet dignity, deeply respected by his peers. 'I do not want to speak to you Mr Warner. There are two teams out there; one is playing cricket and the other is not. It is too great a game to spoil. The matter is in your hands.'

There was now an exchange of cables between the two cricket boards, another battle which, at least in the short term, the MCC won. The Australian cable objected to the use of bodyline, which was reasonable in the circumstances, but it added, 'In our opinion it is unsportsmanlike'. Such a suggestion inflamed the MCC committee men back in London.

We must remember that those in England had very little idea what was going on. They were deprived of the half-an-hour of edited highlights that Richie Benaud sends us each winter evening, and there were only three journalists in Australia to interpret proceedings. One was a ghosted Jack Hobbs, who didn't condemn bodyline until the tour had been completed, another was Bruce Harris, who was not a cricket specialist and who supported Jardine, while the other was Warwick Armstrong, and no one had yet forgotten his attitude towards the English on a cricket field. So it is not surprising that the MCC resented the allegations.

The MCC's return cable was more expertly drafted. It deplored the suggestion of unsportsmanlike play, expressed complete confidence in the captain, team and managers. It ended thus:

> We hope the situation is not now as serious as your cable would seem to indicate, but if it is such as to jeopardise the good relations between English and Australian cricketers and you consider it desirable to cancel the remainder of programme we would consent, but with great reluctance.

The idea of cancelling the tour did not appeal to the Australians. Apart from everything else the series was proving to be an enormous financial success. So the last two matches were played and the Australians, clearly demoralised, lost them both. In the final game at Sydney, Larwood, batting as a night-watchman, scored 98 and was cheered back to the pavilion. It was Jardine they hated.

No one quite knew how to react when the tourists returned home. Larwood was never to play for England again. A combination of a serious foot injury, acquired in that final Test at Sydney, and some unplacatory newspaper articles saw to that. However, Jardine retained the England captaincy, and when the West Indian combination of Constantine and Martindale bowled bodyline in the Old Trafford Test of 1933 he defied them without flinching, scoring 127. For many this was the first glimpse of bodyline, and the majority, from Ranji downwards, didn't like it. In the winter Jardine led a successful trip to India, but on his return in March 1934 he declared that he had no intention of playing against Australia in the summer of 1934. Instead he took to the press box. This decision must have come as a great relief to the MCC, since there had been some doubt whether the Australians would come at all. Without Jardine and Larwood there was every possibility that 'normal' cricket would resume – except that Bradman would start scoring double centuries again, which he did.

Above *Douglas Jardine partaking of refreshment from Tom, The Oval's resident butler in the 1930s*

The leg-trap set for Jack Fingleton during the first Sydney Test of 1932. This time he was lucky

A future master craftsman: the teenage Len Hutton at work in Pudsey in the early 1930s

Below *'Tiger' Bill O'Reilly, who had a fast bowler's temperament, in action* ***(left)*** *and obliging an admirer* ***(right)***

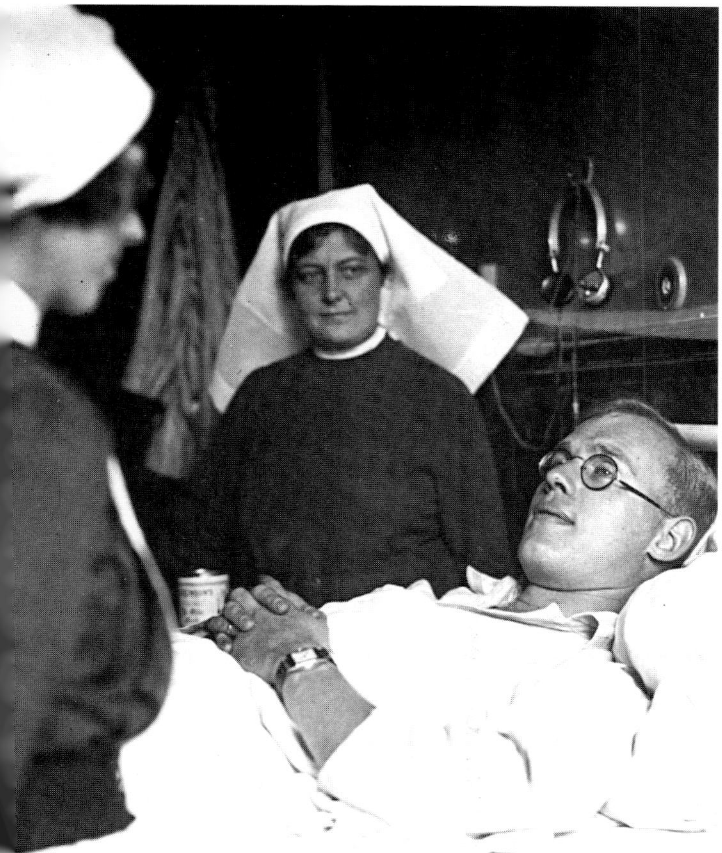

Apart from a hiccup at Trent Bridge when Bill Voce bowled bodyline for Nottinghamshire against the tourists, the 1934 summer helped to heal the wounds. The Australians regained the Ashes by winning the series two-one, and by way of contrast it was their two leg-spinners, Clarrie Grimmett and Bill O'Reilly, who undermined the English batting. Between them they bowled 730 overs throughout the series, taking 53 of the 71 wickets that fell. England yet had something to cheer about when they won by an innings at Lord's, Verity achieving match figures of 15 for 104.

However, one hurdle still remained before cricketing relations between Australia and England could be completely restored, and that was the 1936–37 tour of Australia. The selectors came up with a happy choice as captain, namely Gubby Allen. It may have helped that he was born in Australia, but more important was the fact that he was remembered as the one English fast bowler who refused to bowl bodyline in 1932–33. When Allen was appointed, he insisted that if Voce was picked he would have to express in writing his regret over

Left *Bill Bowes, back in his sick bed having heroically discharged himself to take five Australian wickets in the second innings of the 1934 Oval Test, including that of Bill Woodfull (**below**).*

bodyline, something he had refused to do in the intervening three years. So Bill Voce finally relented. The tour proved to be a diplomatic success, and for a while it seemed that England would be triumphant on the field as well, for they won the first two Test matches. Bradman was captaining the Australians for the first time and many began to question whether the added responsibility was affecting their prized runmaker. He answered the doubters by scoring 270, 212 and 169 in consecutive Tests, and Australia won the last three matches of this closely contested series, Bradman thereby entering the record books once again as the only captain whose side has rallied to win a Test series after being two-nil down. So the final Australian tour before the war ended on a more tranquil note than its predecessor, albeit in defeat for England, and it is interesting to note Arthur Mailey's assessment of the two England captains involved.

> Allowing for the relative skills of both sides, Allen got more out of his team than did Douglas Jardine. Allen was a keen student, so was Jardine, but where Jardine belonged to the atomic bomb era, Gubby fought his battles with pike and spears. When Gubby's battle ended, the noise and strife ended with it, but in the tough Scot's case, the 'death dust' lingered for a considerable time.

Ken Farnes, Larwood's successor as England's spearhead, who was tragically killed on active service in 1941

Below *The 1930s saw the emergence of another young lion, Denis Compton, for whom the future seemed golden*

To which Jardine's retort might have been, 'But who won the Ashes?'

The final series of the period was in 1938, when Hammond turned amateur so that he could captain England. The tourists were not a vintage side, as they depended too much on Bradman for their runs and O'Reilly for their wickets, but victory on a dusty wicket at Headingley ensured that they retained the Ashes in a series where prodigious totals were commonplace. England did manage to win the final Test of the series at The Oval by a reasonably clear-cut margin – an innings and 579 runs. Hammond declared the English first innings closed at 903 for seven, only after he had received assurances that an injury to Bradman would prevent him batting. The young Len Hutton batted himself into the record books by occupying the crease for 13 hours and 17 minutes whilst scoring 364, thereby surpassing the opposing captain's 334, then the highest score in Tests between England and Australia. The Australian spinner, Fleetwood-Smith, achieved a less enviable record – his final bowling figures in that innings were 87-11-298-1.

England had found another magnificent opener, but as with Hobbs before him, many of his best years were stolen by the onset of war in Europe, the appointment of Hitler in 1932 proving even more disruptive than that of Jardine.

Cricketing chic: a thirties batswoman applies the finishing touches to her pre-match preparation

ENGLAND v AUSTRALIA

Played at The Oval,
20, 22, 23, 24 August, 1938.
Result: England won by an innings and 579 runs.

England: First innings

L. Hutton c Hassett b O'Reilly	364
W.J. Edrich lbw b O'Reilly	12
M. Leyland run out	187
W.R. Hammond* lbw b Fleetwood-Smith	59
E. Paynter lbw b O'Reilly	0
D.C.S. Compton b Waite	1
J. Hardstaff, jr not out	169
A. Wood† c and b Barnes	53
H. Verity not out	8
K. Farnes, W.E. Bowes } did not bat	
Extras (b 22, lb 19, w 1, nb 8)	50
Total (7 wickets declared)	903

Fall of Wickets: 1/29, 2/411, 3/546, 4/547, 5/555, 6/770, 7/876.
Bowling: Waite 72-16-150-1, McCabe 38-8-85-0, O'Reilly 85-26-178-3, Fleetwood-Smith 87-11-298-1, Barnes 38-3-84-1, Hassett 13-2-52-0, Bradman 2.2-1-6-0.

Australia: First innings

W.A. Brown c Hammond b Leyland	69
C.L. Badcock c Hardstaff b Bowes	0
S.J. McCabe c Edrich b Farnes	14
A.L. Hassett c Compton b Edrich	42
S.G. Barnes b Bowes	41
B.A. Barnett† c Wood b Bowes	2
M.G. Waite b Bowes	8
W.J. O'Reilly c Wood b Bowes	0
L.O'B. Fleetwood-Smith not out	16
D.G. Bradman* absent hurt	
J.H.W. Fingleton absent hurt	
Extras (b 4, lb 2, nb 3)	9
Total	201

Fall of Wickets: 1/0, 2/19, 3/70, 4/145, 5/147, 6/160, 7/160, 8/201.
Bowling: Farnes 13-2-54-1, Bowes 19-3-49-5, Edrich 10-2-55-1, Verity 5-1-15-0, Leyland 3.1-0-11-1, Hammond 2-0-8-0.

Australia: Second innings

W.A. Brown c Edrich b Farnes	15
C.L. Badcock b Bowes	9
S.J. McCabe c Wood b Farnes	2
A.L. Hassett lbw b Bowes	10
S.G. Barnes lbw b Verity	33
B.A. Barnett† b Farnes	46
M.G. Waite c Edrich b Verity	0
W.J. O'Reilly not out	7
L.O'B. Fleetwood-Smith c Leyland b Barnes	0
D.G. Bradman* absent hurt	
J.H.W. Fingleton absent hurt	
Extras (b 1)	1
Total	123

Fall of Wickets: 1/15, 2/18, 3/35, 4/41, 5/115, 6/115, 7/117, 8/123.
Bowling: Farnes 12.1-1-63-4, Bowes 10-3-25-2, Verity 7-3-15-2, Leyland 5-0-19-0.

Above *The team that really tamed the Aussies at The Oval in 1938: 'Bosser' Martin and his 'pet' – the heaviest of heavy rollers*

Below *A relaxed trio – Paynter, Hutton and Hardstaff – embarking for the second day's play at The Oval in 1938. The England score was already 347 for 1*

The two record-breakers (Hutton and Fleetwood-Smith) battle for the stumps at the end of the historic match

Below *Soaking up the culture: the 1938 Aussies enjoying a visit to Pompeii on their way to England*

4

POST-WAR BOOM

War naturally brought an end to county and international cricket, but there were still fixtures for *Wisden* to report. Indeed, the 1944 edition tells us that the Adjutant-General of the forces and Mr Ernest Bevin, the Minister of Labour, both desired that the first-class game be encouraged in every way. Matches such as the London Counties XI against the British Empire XI were designed to raise funds, which they undoubtedly did, to raise morale for both players and spectators, which they may well have done, and to give the impression that life was going on as normal, which was asking a bit much, even of a cricket match.

On 31 August 1940 the Buccaneers played a British Empire XI at Lord's, and *Wisden* records that '"The Battle of Britain", interfered with the match, causing late arrivals, which necessitated an altered batting order and bringing about an early cessation when the Buccaneers seemed within sight of victory'. How thoughtless of the German Luftwaffe to interrupt proceedings. In 1943, 38,000 spectators watched an exciting two-day match between England and the Dominions. During the two days 950 runs were scored, 35 wickets fell and the match ended in the last over. In the war years there wasn't much incentive to play dourly for a draw.

Business as usual for this bat-making factory in 1940

This spirit of enterprise was maintained throughout the hastily arranged Victory Tests between England and Australia in 1945, a series which ended happily with two victories each. Whilst the *Wisden* reporter relates these matches with all the solemnity of a normal Test, certain snippets of information remind us of the unusual circumstances in which they were played. For example, we learn that at Old Trafford, the venue of the fifth match, German prisoners of war were paid three farthings an hour for putting certain parts of the bomb-scarred ground in a safe condition. They must have been a little confused about the Englishman's sense of priorities. Our correspondent also notes that 'Hassett surprised many people by not having the wicket rolled between the innings', though he adds, by way of explanation, that 'the heavy roller was not available, as it was requisitioned during the war and used to lay out airfields in the Middle East'.

For a while the game flourished as never before. Post-war euphoria, coupled with its attendant austerity, meant that county cricket was an attractive source of entertainment. It was cheap; it was convenient and it provided a welcome escape from food and petrol rationing and the aftermath of German bombs. Capacity crowds filled Lord's and The Oval to watch county games between Middlesex and Surrey, and all around the country county treasurers wore an unaccustomed smile. Even better, in 1947 the sun shone and Compton

Above *Italy, 1944: missionaries from the Gunners introducing some bemused locals to cricket*

Below *Furniture moves out and cricket moves in: life gets back to normal at The Oval in 1945*

Above *The toppers and tails return to Lord's for the 1947 Eton v Harrow match*

Lord's, 1947: Bill Edrich drives Eric Rowan to the boundary during his 370-run stand with Denis Compton for the third wicket against South Africa

and Edrich commanded the stage for Middlesex, for England against the South Africans, indeed wherever they played. First some statistics. Denis Compton scored 3,816 runs with 18 centuries; Bill Edrich 3,539 runs and 12 centuries. Less well publicised is the fact that between them they also took 140 wickets, Edrich taking 67 with his vigorous fast bowling and Comp-ton 73 with his mischievous left-arm wrist-spin – 'he can bowl in a Test as if he were trying things out on a friend in the nets'.

However, the crowds did not flock to the grounds to witness records being broken. Both Compton and Edrich gave the impression that they played cricket for fun and that they were glad – and relieved – to be alive; and there were plenty who could identify with that. Robertson-Glasgow, in an essay for the 1948 *Wisden,* wrote:

> They seem to be playing not only in front of us and for us, but almost literally with us. Their cricket is communicative. We are almost out of breath at the end of an over by Edrich. We scratch our heads perplexedly at a googly from Compton which refuses to work. We smile with something near to self-satisfaction when, with easy vehemence, he persuades a length-ball from the leg stump to the extra-cover boundary.

Everyone respected Hutton's class and dedication, but they adored Compton simply for being Compton. Even his weaknesses were endearing. He was not by all accounts a dreadfully good time-keeper, and like his friend and Australian counterpart, Keith Miller, he might turn up at the ground still dressed in his dinner-jacket; his fielding could range between the brilliant and the absent-minded; he advertised Brylcreem; he persisted with that precarious sweep shot and his running between the wickets became legendary for its indecision. Compton's first call could be used only as a basis for negotiation, we are always told.

Yet he was not simply a fair-weather cricketer, as his courage against the pace of Lindwall and Miller testifies. In 1948 at Manchester a Lindwall bumper struck his head and he had to leave the field so that stitches could be inserted. He returned to complete an undefeated 145, the only Englishman to pass 50 in the innings, and as *Wisden* records, 'For five hours twenty minutes he carried his side's responsibilities and nothing earned more admiration than the manner in which he withstood some lightning overs of extreme hostility by Lindwall'.

The 'Brylcreem Boy'

Compton's knee passes another fitness test

Compton, whether fending off the Australians, running riot for Middlesex, or darting down the left wing for the Arsenal, was a national hero. After he had incurred a knee injury in the winter of 1948–49, the nation awaited the latest bulletin on Denis' fitness with as much interest as we now, curiously, devote to Royal pregnancies.

In 1947 the batting of Compton and Edrich, aided by Robertson and Brown, ensured that Middlesex scored so many runs so quickly that they ended the monopoly of the northern counties in the County Championship for the first time since 1921. Scoring at 80 runs per hour enabled their bowling attack, which was not the strongest in the country, sufficient time to dismiss the opposition. Walter Robins, their captain, refused to let any game dawdle to a meaningless draw.

In 1948 and 1951 two new counties were added to the list of champions: Glamorgan, under the forthright leadership of Wilfred Wooller, who conducted his side in the manner that we would expect of an uncompromising Welsh rugby international, and Warwickshire, who were led by H.E. Dollery, a professional, whose success must have irked those who steadfastly held that only those with an amateur background had the wherewithal to lead. Thereafter the traditional strongholds took control.

Above Three key members of the successful Surrey side of the 1950s: (left to right) Alec Bedser, Peter Loader and Peter May

For the next seven years Surrey maintained a stranglehold in domestic cricket. In contrast to Middlesex, their strength was their bowling attack, which was formidable in any conditions – Alec Bedser, Peter Loader, Tony Lock and Jim Laker, supported, when needed, by Eric Bedser and the captain, Stuart Surridge.

Alec Bedser's career has several parallels with that of Maurice Tate. Both carried the burden of England's bowling after the ravages of war, holding the fort until the advent of some genuine speedsters to spearhead the attack. Tate had to wait for Larwood, Bedser for a combination of Statham, Trueman and Tyson. Both pounded away on the unresponsive wickets of the sub-continent without complaint or support, becoming masters of their craft in the process.

Bedser was medium fast but accurate enough to allow Godfrey Evans or Arthur McIntyre to stand up at the wicket, which was where he preferred them to be. His stock delivery was the inswinger, which would be interspersed with the leg-cutter. On good wickets he commanded respect from Bradman downwards; on bad ones – and there were several of those at The Oval throughout this period – his accuracy and his appetite for hard work made him a match-winner.

Jim Laker, master off-spinner

Tony Lock, Jim Laker's spinning partner

He was proud of being a professional, and after his retirement in 1960 he became one of the rare professionals to serve regularly on the England selection committee. Indeed, for 12 years he was chairman, devoting himself to the task with the same wholehearted commitment that he had shown on the field, his only flaw being that he sometimes suffered from an unfortunate lapse of memory when being introduced to some of his new selections.

Jim Laker also remained in the public eye after his retirement, as a dry, almost lugubrious commentator for BBC Television. Laker was one of the first off-spinners to make an impact on the international scene. Before 1939, England's spin department was generally left in the hands of bowlers who turned the ball away from the right-handed batsmen, either left-armers like Rhodes and Verity or leg-spinners like Braund and Robins. However, when the lbw law was amended to allow batsmen to be given out to balls pitching outside the off stump, the lot of the off-spinner improved dramatically, and they suddenly began to proliferate in county cricket.

Laker possessed all the necessary qualities – a classical action, superb control of flight and spin, and the ability to assess swiftly his opponent's strengths and weaknesses, which was to become a valuable asset in his commentator's role. During his

ENGLAND v AUSTRALIA

Played at Manchester,
26, 27, 28, 30, 31 July, 1956.
Result: England won by an innings and 170 runs.

England: First innings

P.E. Richardson c Maddocks b Benaud	104
M.C. Cowdrey c Maddocks b Lindwall	80
Rev D.S. Sheppard b Archer	113
P.B.H. May* c Archer b Benaud	43
T.E. Bailey b Johnson	20
C. Washbrook lbw b Johnson	6
A.S.M. Oakman c Archer b Johnson	10
T.G. Evans† st Maddocks b Johnson	47
J.C. Laker run out	3
G.A.R. Lock not out	25
J.B. Statham c Maddocks b Lindwall	0
Extras (b 2, lb 5, w 1)	8
Total	459

Fall of Wickets: 1/174, 2/195, 3/288, 4/321, 5/327, 6/339, 7/401, 8/417, 9/458, 10/459.
Bowling: Lindwall 21.3-6-63-2, Miller 21-6-41-0, Archer 22-6-73-1, Johnson 47-10-151-4, Benaud 47-17-123-2.

Australia: First innings

C.C. McDonald c Lock b Laker	32
J.W. Burke c Cowdrey b Lock	22
R.N. Harvey b Laker	0
I.D. Craig lbw b Laker	8
K.R. Miller c Oakman b Laker	6
K.D. Mackay c Oakman b Laker	0
R.G. Archer st Evans b Laker	6
R. Benaud c Statham b Laker	0
R.R. Lindwall not out	6
L.V. Maddocks† b Laker	4
I.W. Johnson* b Laker	0
Extras	0
Total	84

Fall of Wickets: 1/48, 2/48, 3/62, 4/62, 5/62, 6/73, 7/73, 8/78, 9/84, 10/84.
Bowling: Statham 6-3-6-0, Bailey 4-3-4-0, Laker 16.4-4-37-9, Lock 14-3-37-1.

Australia: Second innings

C.C. McDonald c Oakman b Laker	89
J.W. Burke c Lock b Laker	33
R.N. Harvey c Cowdrey b Laker	0
I.D. Craig lbw b Laker	38
K.R. Miller (6) b Laker	0
K.D. Mackay (5) c Oakman b Laker	0
R.G. Archer c Oakman b Laker	0
R. Benaud b Laker	18
R.R. Lindwall c Lock b Laker	8
L.V. Maddocks† (11) lbw b Laker	2
I.W. Johnson* (10) not out	1
Extras (b 12, lb 4)	16
Total	205

Fall of Wickets: 1/28, 2/55, 3/114, 4/124, 5/130, 6/130, 7/181, 8/198, 9/203, 10/205.
Bowling: Statham 16-10-15-0, Bailey 20-8-31-0, Laker 51.2-23-53-10, Lock 55-30-69-0, Oakman 8-3-21-0.

Above *Lancashire chairman T.E. Burrows presents Jim Laker with the weapons he used in his record spell while (**right**) the 1956 Aussies, in less hostile conditions, play the Duke of Norfolk's XI at Arundel*

13 years at Surrey he was consistently successful, but it was not until 1956 that he established himself as an international force. In that year he mesmerised the touring Australians to such an extent that Don Bradman, in his coaching book *The Art of Cricket*, devoted an entire chapter to the best way to combat off-spin generally and Laker in particular. In May at The Oval, playing for Surrey, he took all 10 wickets in the Australian first innings, and in the fourth Test match at Manchester he ended the match with figures of 19 for 90, a staggering performance even if the wicket was helpful.

At the other end on both occasions, no doubt tearing out what was left of his hair, was Tony Lock. Where Laker remained totally unemotional and phlegmatic as he quietly led the batsmen to their downfall, Lock was brimful of aggression and venom. Up until 1959 Lock bowled his left-arm spinners faster than normal; the wickets at The Oval turned, but turned slowly, and he realised that the quicker he bowled the ball the less time the batsman had to adjust to the spin. With Laker he soon formed the most devastating spin attack in the country; however, throughout his early career there were constant murmurings about the legality of his action, particularly when he bowled his fastest ball.

Doug Insole, having been bowled by Lock, at The Oval, was once prompted to inquire of the umpire as he left the field, 'How was that – run out?'

By the end of the 1958–59 tour of Australia, 'throwing' had become a sensitive issue. The England tourists felt that they had been 'thrown out' by Meckiff, an assertion that the camera supports, and it was clear that a controversy was looming. Tony Lock saw some film of himself bowling in New Zealand at the end of the tour and he had to agree that his action looked very dubious. To his credit he decided of his own volition, to remodel it, and after toiling in the indoor nets he reverted to slower, more classical left-arm spin. In this new style he was still good enough to be picked for England.

He left Surrey in 1963 to captain Leicestershire and Western Australia, where he finally settled, taking up Australian citizenship. I saw him coaching in Perth, aged 58, still looping the ball perfectly off two paces and bellowing instructions to his young charges. Stuart Surridge discovered that the best way to motivate him was by a constant stream of well-intentioned insults, a ploy that Lock himself emulated when he became a successful captain. A raw Dennis Lillee, of all people, was subjected to the unlikely situation of being harangued by this

The 1948 Australians. Back row (left to right): D.T. Ring, D. Tallon, A.R. Morris, C.L. McCool, R.A. Saggers, R.R. Lindwall, W.A. Johnston, S.J.E. Loxton, K.R. Miller, E.R.H. Toshack. Front row: R.N. Harvey, I.W. Johnson, A.L. Hassett, D.G. Bradman, W.A. Brown, S.G. Barnes, R.A. Hamence

balding old Englishman, and does not seem to have suffered as a result. Anyway, he soon redressed the balance.

Surrey's fourth and quickest front-line bowler was Peter Loader. He played just 13 times for England, his opportunities being limited by the advent of Trueman, Statham and Tyson, but his county record matches those of the other three. This quartet were goaded into action by Stuart Surridge, the captain from 1952 to 1956. During his reign Surrey played 157 matches, winning 101, drawing 32 and losing just 25. His philosophy was straightforward – attack at all times – and in the 1955 season Surrey's record was unique; they played 28 games in the Championship, winning 23 and losing five, with no draws at all. One example of Surridge's forthright approach was a game against Worcestershire in August 1954, a match they needed to win to clinch the Championship. Having dismissed the opposition for 25, Surrey declared their first innings at 92 for three, a decision which must have astounded any young professional not accustomed to Surridge's methods. In their second innings Worcestershire mustered 40 and the match, which admittedly had been played on a rain-affected wicket, was finished in a little over five hours.

Surrey's domination was finally ended by Yorkshire in 1959; by anyone else's standards, they had been successful throughout the fifties, usually finishing second to Surrey, but by the exacting demands of their own supporters this was regarded as failure. Towards the end of the fifties there were rumours of dressing room unrest, culminating in a series of revelatory newspaper articles by Johnny Wardle or, to be more precise, the *Daily Mail* ghost writer. Wardle was promptly withdrawn from the England tour party to Australia and his county career came to a premature end, but the public purge didn't seem to do them any harm because they won three Championships in four years. It is interesting to note that scandal and controversy were as prevalent in the fifties as they are in the eighties. In addition to the throwing controversy and the Wardle affair, Jim Laker, ostensibly a pillar of the establishment was for a time no longer welcome at The Oval or Lord's after the publication of his autobiography *Over to Me*.

Hampshire briefly broke the monopoly of the old guard by becoming the champions in 1961, led by Colin Ingleby-Mackenzie; with a name like that he could hardly be expected to be a dour, attritional captain, and he wasn't. He delighted in telling reporters, after Hampshire's, success that the only rule was, 'I absolutely insist that all my boys should be in bed before breakfast'. Lord Hawke in his grave must have squirmed at the injustice of it all.

Although domestic cricket prospered in those immediate post-war years, the Ashes remained firmly in the hands of Bradman and a new breed of Australians, forming a close parallel with results after the first war. An English side in the field could do no more than toss the ball to the ever-willing Bedser, whereas Bradman possessed a powerful all-round attack, spearheaded by Lindwall and Miller.

Like all great partnerships they complemented rather than duplicated one another. Lindwall possessed the smooth rhythmical run-up and the classical action; indeed, during the controversial 1958–59 series he described himself as the 'last of the straight-arm bowlers'. In 1948 he proved that he was fast – the scars on Denis Compton's head bore eloquent testimony to that – but he was also cunning, developing variations of pace and swing. Like most Antipodean pacemen, he liked the occasional glass of beer, but I imagine that he was a quiet drinker – he shunned the limelight – whereas his partner was renowned as a *bon viveur*.

If Lindwall relied upon technique allied to extreme physical fitness, Miller's performances depended on flair and a favourable moon. His run-up might be 15 yards long or five, according to his mood. On one occasion, when he dropped the ball in the middle of his approach, he simply picked it

Above *A melancholy Wally Hammond. He captained the first England side to Australia after the war and they were soundly beaten by Bradman's men*

Below *Ray Lindwall, bowling against England at The Oval in 1953*

Above *Miller captures another wicket, as he has Washbrook caught by Tallon, at Trent Bridge in 1948*

Below *Old Trafford, 1948: the only draw England managed against the Australians that summer*

Above *Miller, the batsman, hits out powerfully*

ENGLAND v AUSTRALIA

Played at Leeds,
22, 23, 24, 26, 27 July, 1948.
Result: Australia won by seven wickets.

England: First innings

L. Hutton b Lindwall	81
C. Washbrook c Lindwall b Johnston	143
W.J. Edrich c Morris b Johnson	111
A.V. Bedser c and b Johnson	79
D.C.S. Compton c Saggers b Lindwall	23
J.F. Crapp b Toshack	5
N.W.D. Yardley* b Miller	25
K. Cranston b Loxton	10
T.G. Evans† c Hassett b Loxton	3
J.C. Laker c Saggers b Loxton	4
R. Pollard not out	0
Extras (b 2, lb 8, w 1, nb 1)	12
Total	496

Fall of Wickets: 1/168, 2/268, 3/423, 4/426, 5/447, 6/473, 7/486, 8/490, 9/496, 10/496.
Bowling: Lindwall 38-10-79-2, Miller 17.1-2-43-1, Johnston 38-12-86-1, Toshack 35-6-112-1, Loxton 26-4-55-3, Johnson 33-9-89-2, Morris 5-0-20-0.

Australia: First innings

A.R. Morris c Cranston b Bedser	6
A.L. Hassett c Crapp b Pollard	13
D.G. Bradman* b Pollard	33
K.R. Miller c Edrich b Yardley	58
R.N. Harvey b Laker	112
S.J.E. Loxton b Yardley	93
I.W. Johnson c Cranston b Laker	10
R.R. Lindwall c Crapp b Bedser	77
R.A. Saggers† st Evans b Laker	5
W.A. Johnston c Edrich b Bedser	13
E.R.H. Toshack not out	12
Extras (b 9, lb 14, nb 3)	26
Total	458

Fall of Wickets: 1/13, 2/65, 3/68, 4/189, 5/294, 6/329, 7/344, 8/355, 9/403, 10/458.
Bowling: Bedser 31.2-4-92-3, Pollard 38-6-104-2, Cranston 14-1-51-0, Edrich 3-0-19-0, Laker 30-8-113-3, Yardley 17-6-38-2, Compton 3-0-15-0.

England: Second innings

L. Hutton c Bradman b Johnson	57
C. Washbrook c Harvey b Johnston	65
W.J. Edrich lbw b Lindwall	54
A.V. Bedser (9) c Hassett b Miller	17
D.C.S. Compton (4) c Miller b Johnston	66
J.F. Crapp (5) b Lindwall	18
N.W.D. Yardley* (6) c Harvey b Johnston	7
K. Cranston (7) c Saggers b Johnston	0
T.G. Evans† (8) not out	47
J.C. Laker not out	15
R. Pollard did not bat	
Extras (b 4, lb 12, nb 3)	19
Total (8 wickets declared)	365

Fall of Wickets: 1/129, 2/129, 3/232, 4/260, 5/277, 6/278, 7/293, 8/330.
Bowling: Lindwall 26-6-84-2, Miller 21-5-53-1, Johnston 29-5-95-4, Loxton 10-2-29-0, Johnson 21-2-85-1.

Australia: Second innings

A.R. Morris c Pollard b Yardley	182
A.L. Hassett c and b Compton	17
D.G. Bradman* not out	173
K.R. Miller lbw b Cranston	12
R.N. Harvey not out	4
Extras (b 6, lb 9, nb 1)	16
Total (3 wickets)	404

S.J.E. Loxton, I.W. Johnson, R.R. Lindwall, R.A. Saggers†, W.A. Johnston and E.R.H. Toshack did not bat.

Fall of Wickets: 1/57, 2/358, 3/396.
Bowling: Bedser 21-2-56-0, Pollard 22-6-55-0, Cranston 7.1-0-28-1, Laker 32-11-93-0, Yardley 13-1-44-1, Compton 15-3-82-1, Hutton 4-1-30-0.

up on the way to the wicket and hurled it down regardless; a Lindwall or a Hadlee would have stopped, gone back to his mark and started again. On the spur of the moment he might bowl a googly or an outrageous slower ball, in the manner of Botham; alternatively he might stir himself to bowl at extreme pace, for no other reason than that he wanted to work up a good thirst for the evening, or maybe he wanted to sweat out the previous night's intake. His batting was as cavalier as his bowling and he would have made the Test team as a specialist batsman if necessary. He was also a successful captain of New South Wales, no doubt in the Ingleby-Mackenzie mould. On one occasion, taking the field at Sydney, he was informed that there were 12 men on the pitch, which prompted the typically uncomplicated response, 'One of you bugger off and the rest scatter!' His approach to cricket was, if anything, slightly less analytical than that of Compton, and massively removed from that of his 1948 touring captain.

The bowling of Lindwall and Miller was crucial to the side's success, along with the batting of Bradman, which showed no sign of deterioration; he just scored a little slower. The 1948 Australians overwhelmed all opposition, and the pundits entered into the futile debate as to whether they were stronger than Armstrong's in 1921. Only in the fourth Test at Leeds did an England victory seem a possibility when Norman Yardley was able to declare, leaving the Australians 404 to win in 344 minutes on a turning wicket. Bradman and Arthur Morris both scored centuries and Australia won by seven wickets with 15 minutes to spare – a crushing defeat which emphasised, with piercing clarity, the gulf between the two sides.

The 1950–51 tour to Australia didn't alter the disparity between the two teams, even though Bradman had retired. England, led by Freddie Brown, lost the series four-one. Brown, despite his age – he was 40 – performed creditably throughout the series, in which Hutton was by far the most successful batsman, whilst Compton had a disastrous tour. However, it was unrealistic to expect Brown to continue much longer as captain, which left the selectors in a quandary, for there wasn't an amateur around who was well qualified for the job. In the 1950 series against the West Indies, the selectors had flirted with two former Cambridge blues, Hubert Doggart and Doug Insole, no doubt with an eye to the succession. But because both were inexperienced, and neither could not be regarded as automatic choices as batsmen, their claims receded. On the 1950–51 tour, Brown had been impressed by Hutton's tactical acumen, and he consulted him as frequently as the official vice-

Neil Harvey is run out during the exciting second Test – won by Australia by 28 runs – of the 1950-51 series against England

A triumphant Freddie Brown, after England had won the final Test of the 1950-51 series

Godfrey Evans (left) and Denis Compton, keeping in trim on board their ship to Australia in 1950

Reg Simpson, whose 156 not out was the cornerstone of England's victory in the final Test of the 1950-51 series

Below *Doug Wright, taker of a record seven first-class hat-tricks, bowling for Kent in 1950. Don Bradman regarded him particularly highly*

Len Hutton: always the perfectly balanced stylist

captain, Denis Compton, whose approach to the game set little store upon detailed strategic thinking.

So Hutton was the obvious choice to succeed Brown; but he was a professional, and there was no chance that he would him take amateur status as Hammond had in order to captain England. Today it seems ridiculous that anyone should be concerned about the prospect of a professional captaining England, but in the fifties there were still those who felt a gut reaction that this was an undesirable state of affairs, whatever the credentials of the candidate. Despite misgivings in some quarters, Hutton was duly appointed.

Given the circumstances, it is not surprising that Hutton was a cautious captain. If he failed, the doubters would be quick to point to his professional status as the reason, a convenient, though illogical argument. In addition, Hutton was born in Pudsey and had learnt his cricket in the most uncompromising nursery of Yorkshire CCC, where unnecessary risks were more than frowned upon. Before the war he sometimes played irresponsibly, by Yorkshire's standards; he was not content simply to wear down the opposition; he liked to tear them apart. Alan Gibson records how his captain, Brian Sellers, used to chide his young protégé, 'All very well, scoring your seventies and eighties before lunch, but remember you're opening for Yorkshire and don't be bloody silly'. Once proper cricket resumed in 1945, Hutton was rarely 'silly'.

During the war he sustained a nasty injury whilst in the army, albeit in a gymnasium, and after several operations, his left arm was shortened by an inch. This injury, coupled with a deep sense of his own responsibility as a batsman, caused him to be a less enterprising player in the post-war years. Against the rampaging Lindwall and Miller he seemed to be carrying alone the burden of England's batting. True, Compton was there, but he never gave the impression of being overwhelmed by the burden of responsibility. Hutton had endured years of humiliation against the Australians, which made him doubly determined to recover the Ashes; for England to be an 'attractive side to watch' was very low on his list of priorities.

He began by leading England to a straightforward

The captaincy crisis, highlighted by Lee of the Evening Standard. ***(Below left)*** *A response to the dilemma over who was to take the side to Australia in 1950.* ***(Below right)*** *Rumours reach Lord's that a professional might captain England in 1952*

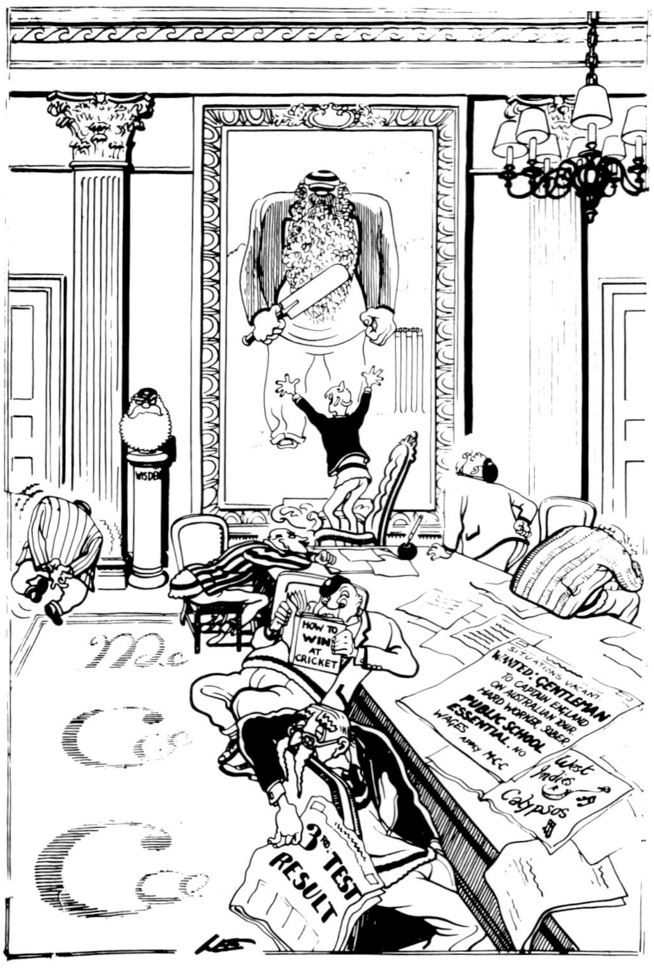

'Vinoo' Mankad, well protected from an English May. He is arguably the finest all-rounder India has ever produced

three-nil victory against the Indians in 1952. In the previous winter India had recorded their first-ever win against England in Madras, by an innings and eight runs, but as usual the tourists were far short of being a full-strength team, even though the young Brian Statham and Tom Graveney were there. However, the Indians were no match for the full side in English conditions. Trueman, in his first Test series, terrorised their batsmen, and most importantly, Hutton scored plenty of runs, as well as captaining the side with aplomb, thus ensuring that he would retain the job when the Australians came in 1953.

This series enthralled the public, not because of scintillating strokeplay or a succession of last-minute victories as in 1902, but because the struggle was so intense and so even. England had been deprived of the Ashes since 1934, and in Coronation year, with Everest conquered, the entire nation seemed to be wrapped up in the struggle for that insignificant little urn. Norman Preston, *Wisden's* editor, records that 'No other series of Tests captured such public attention. What with day-by-day front page newspaper articles and radio and television broadcasts there were times when industry almost stood still while the man in the street followed the tense battle between bat and ball'. I wonder whether the Minister of Labour was still so concerned about the survival of first-class cricket.

Australia were no longer invincible. For the first time since 1930 Bradman no longer appeared on the team sheet of the touring side, and Hutton himself considered that he was worth three men to any team. The parallel with events after the first war was maintained, with the first four Tests being drawn, just as they were in 1926; so everything hinged on the final match at The Oval.

Hutton lost the toss for the fifth time in succession – no doubt the traditionalists averred that this had never happened to an amateur captain – and Lindsay Hassett elected to bat. England's opening bowlers were Bedser, who had already taken 36 wickets in the series, and Fred Trueman, playing in his first Test against Australia, and these two were largely responsible for bowling Australia out for 275 just before the close on the first day. There was time for just two overs from Lindwall and Miller. Lindwall, who had scored a vital 62, was obviously loose, and his fourth and fifth balls were vicious bouncers at Hutton. *Wisden* reports that the 'fifth flew off the handle of Hutton's bat and five slips surged forward for the catch which unexpectedly

Right *Cricketing glamour in the 1950s was not confined to Compton. Here Anthony Asquith directs a number of the England team in his film* The Final Test, *starring Jack Warner (centre) and Robert Morley*

Below *A preoccupied Len Hutton, flanked by Alec Bedser, leads the England team out at The Oval in 1953*

never arrived. The ball dropped short because it lost its pace in transit through striking Hutton's cap which it removed.' The cap just missed the stumps so that the England captain had survived two close calls in the space of one delivery. The whereabouts of the Ashes and Hutton's tenure as England captain may well have depended on that moment of good fortune, for he went on to score 82 as England crept to a first-innings lead of 31.

When Australia batted again, Hutton took off Trueman after he had bowled just two overs and Bedser after three so that he could bowl Laker and Lock in tandem. *Wisden*, in an uncharacteristically melodramatic mood, declares: 'That was the move that brought home the Ashes.' Laker trapped Hassett leg-before-wicket and then the Australians slumped from the relative comfort of 59 for one to 61 for five. Archer and Davidson counter-attacked boldly, but the Australian score of 162 meant that a total of 132 was sufficient to retrieve the Ashes.

Hutton ran himself out for 17 and 'looked terribly disappointed as he walked slowly back to the pavilion', which was hardly surprising as he was jeopardising a life's ambition. On the fourth morning, May and Edrich took the score to 88 before May succumbed to Miller bowling off-spin, an indication that the Australians were a spinner short in this match (they had omitted Benaud from their twelve). Who better than Compton and Edrich to guide England to victory? At seven minutes to three Compton made the winning hit and the crowd swarmed on to the pitch as the players fought desperately to make their way back to the pavilion. Hutton, I suspect, had got over his disappointment by now.

The nation, in the grip of patriotic fervour, rejoiced and the sports writers went to town. 'After nineteen years of frustration, war, humiliation and near misses, we've got those old Ashes back where they belong – in England, where we have taught the best part of the world how to play cricket ... and what it means', bellowed the *Daily Mirror*. Now Hutton appeared unrivalled as England captain and he was the automatic choice to take England to the West Indies the following winter. England drew the series two-all, a creditable performance considering that they had trailed two-nil. However, critics of England's professional captain did have some ammunition when the side returned, for there were plenty of the controversies that have bedevilled tours more recently.

The English players were unhappy about the standard of umpiring and on several occasions showed their dissent openly. At Georgetown bottles were thrown on to the field, and Hutton had to persuade the umpires to stay where they were ('we

ENGLAND v AUSTRALIA

Played at The Oval,
15, 17, 18, 19 August, 1953.
Result: England won by eight wickets.

Australia: First innings

A.L. Hassett* c Evans b Bedser	53
A.R. Morris lbw b Bedser	16
K.R. Miller lbw b Bailey	1
R.N. Harvey c Hutton b Trueman	36
G.B. Hole c Evans b Trueman	37
J.H. de Courcy c Evans b Trueman	5
R.G. Archer c and b Bedser	10
A.K. Davidson c Edrich b Laker	22
R.R. Lindwall c Evans b Trueman	62
G.R.A. Langley† c Edrich b Lock	18
W.A. Johnston not out	9
Extras (b 4, nb 2)	6
Total	275

Fall of Wickets: 1/38, 2/41, 3/107, 4/107, 5/118, 6/160, 7/160, 8/207, 9/245, 10/275.
Bowling: Bedser 29-3-88-3, Trueman 24.3-3-86-4, Bailey 14-3-42-1, Lock 9-2-19-1, Laker 5-0-34-1.

England: First innings

L. Hutton* b Johnston	82
W.J. Edrich lbw b Lindwall	21
P.B.H. May c Archer b Johnston	39
D.C.S. Compton c Langley b Lindwall	16
T.W. Graveney c Miller b Lindwall	4
T.E. Bailey b Archer	64
T.G. Evans† run out	28
J.C. Laker c Langley b Miller	1
G.A.R. Lock c Davidson b Lindwall	4
F.S. Trueman b Johnston	10
A.V. Bedser not out	22
Extras (b 9, lb 5, w 1)	15
Total	306

Fall of Wickets: 1/37, 2/137, 3/154, 4/167, 5/170, 6/210, 7/225, 8/237, 9/262, 10/306.
Bowling: Lindwall 32-7-70-4, Miller 34-12-65-1, Johnston 45-16-94-3, Davidson 10-1-26-0, Archer 10.3-2-25-1, Hole 11-6-11-0.

Australia: Second innings

A.L. Hassett* lbw b Laker	10
A.R. Morris lbw b Lock	26
K.R. Miller (5) c Trueman b Laker	0
R.N. Harvey b Lock	1
G.B. Hole (3) lbw b Laker	17
J.H. de Courcy run out	4
R.G. Archer c Edrich b Lock	49
A.K. Davidson b Lock	21
R.R. Lindwall c Compton b Laker	12
G.R.A. Langley† c Trueman b Lock	2
W.A. Johnston not out	6
Extras (b 11, lb 3)	14
Total	162

Fall of Wickets: 1/23, 2/59, 3/60, 4/61, 5/61, 6/85, 7/135, 8/140, 9/144, 10/162.
Bowling: Bedser 11-2-24-0, Trueman 2-1-4-0, Lock 21-9-45-5, Laker 16.5-2-75-4.

England: Second innings

L. Hutton* run out	17
W.J. Edrich not out	55
P.B.H. May c Davidson b Miller	37
D.C.S. Compton not out	22
T.W. Graveney, T.E. Bailey, T.G. Evans†, J.C. Laker, G.A.R. Lock, F.S. Trueman, A.V. Bedser	did not bat
Extras (lb 1)	1
Total (2 wickets)	132

Fall of Wickets: 1/24, 2/88.
Bowling: Lindwall 21-5-46-0, Miller 11-3-24-1, Johnston 29-14-52-0, Archer 1-1-0-0, Hassett 1-0-4-0, Morris 0.5-0-5-0.

needed another wicket or two that evening'). Even worse, some English ladies complained about the behaviour of some of the English touring party, which led to Trueman's good-conduct allowance being withdrawn. I had assumed that this sort of thing happened only in the decadent eighties.

Of course, all these incidents were not the fault of Hutton, but he was deemed to be responsible for the team and the tour. The manager was the admirable but inexperienced C.H. Palmer, the captain of Leicestershire, who doubled as an auxiliary player, which meant that at one moment he was the boss and the next a subordinate of Hutton – an unsatisfactory state of affairs which left Hutton carrying the can. Moreover, in the aftermath of the Ashes win, this series was dubbed 'The World Championship of Cricket' and therefore attracted great media attention; perhaps for the first time the newspapers were anxious to write about rifts between the team and off-field shenanigans, thereby creating a strained relationship between press and players, which has surfaced many times since. All of which must have come as a rude shock to Hutton, who was

Fazal Mahmood comes in after taking six for 53 in England's first innings of the 1954 Oval Test

ENGLAND v PAKISTAN

Played at The Oval, 12, 13, 14, 16, 17 August, 1954.
Result: Pakistan won by 24 runs.

Pakistan: First innings

Hanif Mohammad lbw b Statham	0
Alimuddin b Tyson	10
Waqar Hasan b Loader	7
Maqsood Ahmed b Tyson	0
Imtiaz Ahmed† c Evans b Tyson	23
A.H. Kardar* c Evans b Statham	36
Wazir Mohammad run out	0
Fazal Mahmood c Evans b Loader	0
Shujauddin not out	16
Zulfiqar Ahmed c Compton b Loader	16
Mahmood Hussain b Tyson	23
Extras (nb 2)	2
Total	133

Fall of Wickets: 1/0, 2/10, 3/10, 4/26, 5/51, 6/51, 7/51, 8/77, 9/106, 10/133.
Bowling: Statham 11-5-26-2, Tyson 13.4-3-35-4, Loader 18-5-35-3, McConnon 9-2-35-0.

England: First innings

L. Hutton* c Imtiaz b Fazal	14
R.T. Simpson c Kardar b Mahmood	2
P.B.H. May c Kardar b Fazal	26
D.C.S. Compton c Imtiaz b Fazal	53
T.W. Graveney c Hanif b Fazal	1
T.G. Evans† c Maqsood b Mahmood	0
J.H. Wardle c Imtiaz b Fazal	8
F.H. Tyson c Imtiaz b Fazal	3
J.E. McConnon c Fazal b Mahmood	11
J.B. Statham c Shujauddin b Mahmood	1
P.J. Loader not out	8
Extras (lb 1,w 1,nb 1)	3
Total	130

Fall of Wickets: 1/6, 2/26, 3/56, 4/63, 5/69, 6/92, 7/106, 8/115, 9/116, 10/130.
Bowling: Fazal 30-16-53-6, Mahmood Hussain 21.3-6-58-4, Zulfiqar 5-2-8-0, Shujauddin 3-0-8-0.

Pakistan: Second innings

Hanif Mohammad c Graveney b Wardle	19
Alimuddin (7) lbw b Wardle	0
Waqar Hasan run out	9
Maqsood Ahmed c Wardle b McConnon	4
Imtiaz Ahmed† c Wardle b Tyson	12
A.H. Kardar* c and b Wardle	17
Wazir Mohammad (8) not out	42
Fazal Mahmood (9) b Wardle	6
Shujauddin (2) c May b Wardle	12
Zulfiqar Ahmed c May b Wardle	34
Mahmood Hussain c Statham b Wardle	6
Extras (b 3)	3
Total	164

Fall of Wickets: 1/19, 2/38, 3/43, 4/54, 5/63, 6/73, 7/76, 8/82, 9/140, 10/164.
Bowling: Statham 18-7-37-0, Tyson 9-2-22-1, Loader 16-6-26-0, McConnon 14-5-20-1, Wardle 35-16-56-7.

England: Second innings

L. Hutton* c Imtiaz b Fazal	5
R.T. Simpson c and b Zulfiqar	27
P.B.H. May c Kardar b Fazal	53
D.C.S. Compton c Imtiaz b Fazal	29
T.W. Graveney (6) lbw b Shujauddin	0
T.G. Evans† (5) b Fazal	3
J.H. Wardle c Shujauddin b Fazal	9
F.H. Tyson c Imtiaz b Fazal	3
J.E. McConnon (10) run out	2
J.B. Statham (11) not out	2
P.J. Loader (9) c Waqar b Mahmood	5
Extras (lb 2,nb 3)	5
Total	143

Fall of Wickets: 1/15, 2/66, 3/109, 4/115, 5/116, 6/121, 7/131, 8/138, 9/138, 10/143.
Bowling: Fazal 30-11-46-6, Mahmood Hussain 14-4-32-1, Zulfiqar 14-2-35-1, Shujauddin 10-1-25-1.

One of New Zealand's finest post-war batsmen, Bert Sutcliffe, here reaching his century against England at The Oval in 1949

acknowledged as a master cricket tactician, but who possessed no experience or special flair for diplomacy and man-management. It is to his credit that he survived the whole ordeal.

In 1954 Pakistan made their first tour of England. Hutton was appointed captain, but illness prevented him playing in the second and third Tests, when David Sheppard deputised. In a wet summer England won the second Test at Trent Bridge by an innings, but Pakistan contrived to square the series with a remarkable win in the final Test at The Oval. Needing 168 to win, England appeared to be in command with the score at 109 for two and May and Compton in control to guide them to a standard victory against one of the 'lesser' Test playing countries. When May was dismissed Evans was promoted, apparently in an attempt to finish the match that evening. The plan backfired; Evans failed and so did Graveney, and on the following morning Pakistan won the game by 24 runs, Fazal Mahmood taking 12 for 99 in the match. So in the first series between the two countries, Pakistan had achieved a treasured first victory against England; it had taken India 20 years and New Zealand were still trying.

By the time of England's defeat, Hutton had already been chosen to take the side to Australia the following winter, though his selection had still caused surprising controversy and debate. Mindful of the problems encountered in the West Indies, there were still those, probably including Test selector Walter Robins, who felt that an overseas tour could be entrusted only to an amateur captain, and David Sheppard was approached, not for the last time in his career. He was prepared to delay his training for the ministry if he was summoned to captain England in Australia. Unfortunately this private debate somehow found its way on to the back pages of the national newspapers, so that when David Sheppard went into the common room of the theological college, Ridley Hall, he was astounded to be presented by his bewildered colleagues with banner headlines proclaiming that moves were being made to persuade him to come back into cricket and captain England. No doubt Len Hutton was equally bemused, not to mention disappointed that he should still be on trial. The newspapers conducted polls, asking their readers to choose the right man, and there was a plethora of stories about the Establishment's attitude to the professional and the rivalry between north and south. Both Hutton and Sheppard maintained a dignified silence throughout and in the end the logical decision to reinstate Hutton was reached, but it was a messy appointment, enjoyed only by the newspaper editors.

Hutton, from bitter personal experience, knew how most Test series were won and lost – through the quality of the fast bowlers. The ascendancy of Lindwall and Miller had demonstrated that to him at first hand, and if he consulted the history books he could point to Barnes and Foster, Gregory and

Frank Tyson: on his day he was simply unplayable

Colin Cowdrey drives Lindwall during his hundred in the Melbourne Test of 1954-55

McDonald, Larwood and Voce. However, Trueman was still in detention after misbehaving in the West Indies; instead the selectors picked Statham, Loader and Frank Tyson, augmented by Alec Bedser and Trevor Bailey. The selection of Tyson was a gamble; he had played just one full season for Northamptonshire and one Test match against Pakistan; he was raw, but he was fast. The other gamble was Colin Cowdrey, who had just come down from Oxford University; he was only 22 and he looked much younger. These two were to prove inspired selections, which to some extent redeemed the selectors after their mishandling of the captaincy issue.

The series began inauspiciously for England, to say the least. At Brisbane Hutton won the toss and put Australia in; they scored 601 for eight declared, Tyson taking one for 160 from 29 eight-ball overs, and England lost by an innings and 154 runs. Food for thought for the England captain. His response was to omit Alec Bedser from the next Test, bringing in Wardle and Appleyard to augment the pace attack. With hindsight, this was a masterstroke, though at the time it aroused considerable consternation; Bedser had been the backbone of the English attack since the war and even though he had suffered a nasty bout of shingles at the beginning of the tour, he was still regarded as England's most reliable bowler. It was a brave decision, though not very well executed; the first Bedser knew of his omission was when he looked at the teamsheet half-an-hour before the game. Hutton was so immersed in something, maybe his overall strategic plan or his imminent innings, that he overlooked his duties as a man-manager, a weakness that had first surfaced in the West Indies.

However, his faith in Tyson was fully justified. In the final innings of the match, when Australia needed 223 to win, Tyson, using a remodelled, shorter run, tore in downwind whilst Statham tirelessly persisted upwind. England won the match by 38 runs and in the process had discovered a winning formula, which was to ensure the retention of the Ashes.

At Melbourne in the third Test, England were rescued by Cowdrey's maiden Test century – a masterful 102 out of a total of 191. When Australia required 240 to win, the *Wisden* reporter, no doubt warming to his task down under, tells us that 'Tyson blazed through them like a bush fire', finishing the innings with figures of seven for 27. A mixture of Tyson's sheer speed, Statham's accuracy and the unusually unreliable nature of the Australian wickets were combining to undermine the confidence of the home side in this low-scoring series.

The destination of the Ashes was sealed at Adelaide, though not without a few hiccups. England needed just 94 runs in the final innings, but

Two of England's brightest batting stars of the 1950s: Peter May (left) and Colin Cowdrey

with Miller in full flight and the score 18 for three, anything could happen. Hutton was out and by now was mentally and physically exhausted by the strain of the series – captaining England drained him completely – and at the fall of the third wicket he turned to one of his colleagues in apparent despair:

> 'The beggars have done us'.

Within earshot was Denis Compton, who was pulling on his gloves and who still retained a shred of optimism:

> 'Steady on, Len, I haven't been in yet'.

In *The Cricket Captains of England* Alan Gibson has suggested that Hutton's remark was consciously designed to spur Compton to his best, another shrewd tactical ploy. I think Hutton was exhausted. Anyway Compton and May thwarted Miller, England won the match by five wickets and the series three-one, and everyone could afford to chuckle about the exchange.

At least this series finally convinced everyone of the viability of a professional captain, and in 1955 the selectors rewarded Hutton by taking the unusual step of appointing him for all five Tests against the South Africans. In fact he was a spent force after that Australian tour and he withdrew from the series; in January he announced his retirement from first-class cricket, a graceful, self-imposed departure.

His record bears comparison with any English captain; he was in charge for six series, four of which were won and two drawn. England's first professional captain had led the side very professionally. On occasions his approach had offended the idealist; he was, for instance, quite prepared to slow the over-rate if it suited him, and he was happy for his batsmen to adopt a no-risk policy. However, his goal was not to keep the members of I Zingari content but to win cricket matches for England, and in that he was successful; his success was soon to be acknowledged by a rare cricketing knighthood. J.M. Kilburn assessed his captaincy thus in the *Cricketer* in 1956:

> The outstanding characteristic of his captaincy was shrewdness. He made no romantic gestures; he lit no fires of inspiration. He invited admiration rather than affection and would have exchanged both for effective obedience. A Test match rubber played under Hutton's captaincy became a business undertaking .... Hutton did not expect his players to enjoy their Test matches until the scoreboard showed victory.

I expect Hutton himself would have been happy with that.

His successor, Peter May, came to the England captaincy via a more conventional route, a leading

public school (Charterhouse), Cambridge University and Surrey. Since 1951 he had been a regular in the England team, and as age had begun to take its toll on Hutton and Compton, he was soon regarded as the mainstay of England's batting, along with Colin Cowdrey.

Clean cut and fresh-faced, he appeared to be a typical product of the English public-school system; he was – and is – scrupulously polite and reserved, betraying little of what goes on inside. Yet it is misleading to regard his accession to the captaincy as a return to the days of the swashbuckling amateur. For a start it is widely held, however erroneously, that public schoolboys were taught to play the cover-drive, the most beautiful of cricket shots, almost to the exclusion of anything else. Peter May could cover-drive with the best of them, but the hallmark of his batting was his on-side play; he could pummel the ball off the back foot between mid-wicket and mid-on with surprising power – and the on side was meant to be the domain of the professionals. Also, his approach to captaincy owed more to Hutton than Charterhouse; he was a logical and, if necessary, ruthless leader, who shunned risking a strong position by any reckless gamble. Like Hutton, he was not captain of his county side when he took over the captaincy of England. There are advantages here, for it must ease the burden of the leader of our national side if he is removed from

Above *An anxious crowd watch England's progress against South Africa at Old Trafford in 1955, in a Piccadilly shop window. South Africa won the match by three wickets*

Below *The indefatigable Brian Statham*

the day-to-day grind of leading a county team. Maybe the mortality rate of modern England captains might be reduced as a result.

Both at Surrey, where he took over in 1957, and at Test level May succeeded to two winning sides, which are not always the ideal circumstances for succession. Both continued to prosper for a while. Surrey won two more Championships and England were on the crest of a wave.

In 1955 Jack Cheetham's South Africans were defeated three-two in an excellent series; in 1956 the Australians couldn't come to terms with Laker; in 1957 the West Indies were beaten three-nil and in 1958 New Zealand were thrashed four-nil. During this period England could be considered the best side in the world; they certainly had the most complete bowling attack. Tyson was the fastest bowler in the world, a title coveted by Fred Trueman, and at the other end, into the wind, if there was one, was Brian Statham.

Tyson did not last long and he could never surpass his performances in Australia in 1954–55; for him pace was everything, the ultimate goal. When he realised that his body could no longer permit him to bowl at full blast he withdrew from the scene. Perhaps he could have adjusted his style, in the manner of Dennis Lillee in the eighties, to have become an effective fast-medium bowler, but that challenge didn't interest him. In his autobiography he wrote that the 'coming of guile to a quick bowler can be like the advance of creeping paralysis of the body'. He was content to flicker briefly like a meteor. He would bowl fast or not at all.

Statham and Trueman were more durable, though they had little else in common. Statham was phlegmatic, reliable and remarkably gentlemanly for a fast bowler. He would bowl as many bouncers in a season as current fast bowlers attempt in a day. He would even warn the batsmen when they were coming. Once, in Jamaica, Easton McMorris was combating Statham by thrusting his front foot down the wicket. Statham quietly informed him that he would have to bowl a couple bouncers if he continued with this policy. McMorris ignored the warning and was soon hit painfully in the ribs and taken to hospital, regretting his error of judgement.

Trueman, we can be sure, would not have bothered with such niceties. He was – and is – a larger-than-life character; indeed at birth he weighed 14 lbs 1 oz, and he has made his presence felt ever since as a rebel, a raconteur, a journalist, a cabaret act and a member of the Yorkshire committee, though these last two are not mutually exclusive. He was, however, at his best as a fast bowler. He played in 67 Tests and took 307 wickets, becoming the first man to pass the 300 mark. He could have played in many more Tests, but he was viewed with great suspicion after his first unhappy tour of the West Indies, and he didn't become a regular until 1957. He was fast, he could swing the ball; he was aggressive and supremely confident. Before a county match, he would meander into the opposition dressing room and terrify his more timorous opponents simply by outlining how he was going to get them out. Plenty believed him.

A benevolent-looking Fred Trueman – not an aspect of him often seen by batsmen

To support these three there was Trevor Bailey, a lively medium-pacer and a batsman who relished a crisis. Even if there wasn't one he gained a reputation, not entirely deserved, as a man who batted as if disaster was looming just around the corner. Laker and Lock were the spinners. So in 1958, when England set off for Australia, it is no wonder that confidence was high. England's recent record under May was untarnished, and they had this galaxy of quality bowlers to call upon. The Ashes, everyone agreed, were secure for a while longer.

Above *Trevor Bailey, in contemplative mood*

Right *Trueman – the 'ball of fire'*

ENGLAND v AUSTRALIA

Played at Manchester, 27, 28, 29, 31 July, 1 August, 1961.
Result: Australia won by 54 runs

Australia First innings

W. M. Lawry lbw b Statham	74
R.B. Simpson c Murray b Statham	4
R.N. Harvey c Subba Row b Statham	19
N.C. O'Neill hit wkt b Trueman	11
P.J.P. Burge b Flavell	15
B.C. Booth c Close b Statham	46
K.D. Mackay c Murray b Statham	11
A.K. Davidson c Barrington b Dexter	0
R. Benaud* b Dexter	2
A.T.W. Grout† c Murray b Dexter	2
G.D. McKenzie not out	1
Extras (b 4, lb 1)	5
Total	190

Fall of Wickets: 1/8, 2/51, 3/89, 4/106, 5/150, 6/174, 7/185, 8/185, 9/189, 10/190
Bowling: Trueman 14-1-55-1, Statham 21-3-53-5, Flavell 22-8-61-1, Dexter 6.4-2-16-3

England: First innings

G. Pullar b Davidson	63
R. Subba Row c Simpson b Davidson	2
E.R. Dexter c Davidson b McKenzie	16
P.B.H. May* c Simpson b Davidson	95
D.B. Close lbw b McKenzie	33
K.F. Barrington c O'Neill b Simpson	78
J.T. Murray† c Grout b Mackay	24
D.A. Allen c Booth b Simpson	42
F.S. Trueman c Harvey b Simpson	3
J.B. Statham c Mackay b Simpson	4
J.A. Flavell not out	0
Extras (b 2, lb 4, w 1)	7
Total	367

Fall of Wickets: 1/3, 2/43, 3/154, 4/212, 5/212, 6/272, 7/358, 8/362, 9/367, 10/367.
Bowling: Davidson 39-11-70-3, McKenzie 38-11-106-2, Mackay 40-9-81-1, Benaud 35-15-80-0, Simpson 11.4-4-23-4.

Australia: Second innings

W.M. Lawry c Trueman b Allen	102
R.B. Simpson c Murray b Flavell	51
R.N. Harvey c Murray b Dexter	35
N.C. O'Neill c Murray b Statham	67
P.J.P. Burge c Murray b Dexter	23
B.C. Booth lbw b Dexter	9
K.D. Mackay c Close b Allen	18
A.K. Davidson not out	77
R. Benaud* lbw b Allen	1
A.T.W. Grout† c Statham b Allen	0
G.D. McKenzie b Flavell	32
Extras (b 6, lb 9, w 2)	17
Total	432

Fall of Wickets: 1/113, 2/175, 3/210, 4/274, 5/290, 6/296, 7/332, 8/334, 9/334, 10/432.
Bowling: Trueman 32-6-92-0, Statham 44-9-106-1, Flavell 29.4-4-65-2, Dexter 20-4-61-3, Allen 38-25-58-4, Close 8-1-33-0.

England: Second innings

G. Pullar c O'Neill b Davidson	26
R. Subba Row b Benaud	49
E.R. Dexter c Grout b Benaud	76
P.B.H. May* b Benaud	0
D.B. Close c O'Neill b Benaud	8
K.F. Barrington lbw b Mackay	5
J.T. Murray† c Simpson b Benaud	4
D.A. Allen c Simpson b Benaud	10
F.S. Trueman c Benaud b Simpson	8
J.B. Statham b Davidson	8
J.A. Flavell not out	0
Extras (b 5, w 2)	7
Total	201

Fall of Wickets: 1/40, 2/150, 3/150, 4/158, 5/163, 6/171, 7/171, 8/189, 9/193, 10/201.
Bowling: Davidson 14.4-1-50-2, McKenzie 4-1-20-0, Mackay 13-7-33-1, Benaud 32-11-70-6, Simpson 8-4-21-1.

England duly lost the series four-nil. Not once could the England side manage more than 300 in an innings, and the side became increasingly demoralised by the conviction that they were being 'thrown out' by Meckiff. For the first time May was subjected to severe criticism, not only for his captaincy but also because his fiancée accompanied him on the tour, and it was alleged that he didn't spend enough time with the team. The press, anxious for an easy and entertaining reason for England's surprising humiliation, made a lot of this and I suspect that the tour possibly hastened May's departure from first-class cricket. A more logical explanation for the English defeat was the brittleness of the batting, the dubious technique of some of the Australian bowlers, and the fact that the Australians were rather better than England thought they were.

Australia, purged of their chuckers and draggers, retained the Ashes in 1961. The crucial match of the series was the fourth Test at Manchester. England needed 256 to win in three hours and 50 minutes. Today such a target would be scorned, except perhaps by the West Indies, but England probably felt that they had earned victory until a last-wicket stand of 98 between Davidson and McKenzie had put the match back in the balance. Dexter, aided by Subba Row, gave England – and indeed Australia – a good chance of victory, cracking 76 in just 84 minutes. Australia's captain was Richie Benaud, and his final desperate ploy was to bowl his leg-spinners from around the wicket into the bowlers' footmarks. He had Dexter caught behind, May was bowled around his legs second ball attempting to sweep, and Brian Close played a much criticised sweep shot – people still talk about it – and the ball landed in the hands of Norman O'Neill at backward square-leg. Benaud finished with six for 70 and England, who at one stage had been 150 for one, were bowled out for 201, losing the match by 54 runs. Benaud had effected one of the most astounding escapes in Test history and was entitled to laugh over his beer, which apparently he did every time he caught a glimpse of Neil Harvey on the other side of the dressing room. They just couldn't believe the outcome of the Test.

That match, indeed the entire tour, crowned the career of Richie Benaud. The 1962 *Wisden* editor made him one of the five Cricketers of the Year and the author of his potted biography in that year's edition of the almanack was fulsome in his praise: 'If one player, more than any other, has deserved well of cricket for lifting the game out of the doldrums, that man is [Richie] Benaud.' It is worth noting here that cricket was reckoned to be 'in the doldrums' – a perennial complaint.

Above *Peter Burge, one of Australia's successes of the 1960s, batting at Lord's in 1961*

Below *Richie Benaud's around-the-wicket attack in the Old Trafford Test of 1961*

Benaud was clearly an inspirational captain, shrewd, but also prepared to gamble, and he led Australia in five successive victorious series. He was also a wonderful PR man for cricket in general and the Australian team in particular. He handled the press brilliantly, which was hardly surprising for he was already an accomplished journalist. This aspect of captaincy has come to the fore only in the post-war period. Newspapers have allowed cricket more and more space over the years, and they have increasingly relied upon the comments of the respective Test captains to fill it, either on rest days or after the game. Neither Hutton nor May would have enjoyed this task, but Benaud was one of the first to exploit this opportunity to his advantage. Jack Fingleton covered the 1961 tour and made this observation: 'I often smiled at the exodus from the press box when Benaud came from the field. He was always available for questioning and, one surmised, helped many with suggestions for angles and stories.' Well, if the Australian captain was shaping many of the news reports, there was little chance of much detrimental to the Australian team appearing in print. In modern times only Mike Brearley has rivalled him in this regard.

After his retirement Benaud devoted himself full-time to journalism and television commentating, where he has had a chance to mull over the old days with many of his contemporaries. However, once in front of the microphone he refuses to make endless and pointless references to the past, but concentrates on giving an objective assessment of the present that is respected by players and viewers alike. He is as well known now as in 1961.

*Four of Australia's finest, pictured on the 1961 tour of England. (**Opposite left**) the elegant Norman O'Neill; (**opposite right**) Neil Harvey, who scored 112, aged 19, on his 1948 debut against England; (**above**) Alan Davidson, wholehearted all-rounder; (**right**) the canny skipper, Richie Benaud*

Benaud was one of the captains in arguably the best series of the period – Australia v West Indies in the winter of 1960–61. By now the West Indies were challenging the supremacy of the oldest two cricketing countries. In 1950 they had signalled their advance most spectacularly by beating England on English soil three-one, with a first Test victory at Lord's tasting particularly sweet. Rumours had already filtered back to England of three Barbadians of astounding talent, all born within three miles and 18 months of each other – namely Walcott, Weekes and Worrell – but no one had ever heard of Ramadhin and Valentine until that summer. Whilst the formidable three Ws piled up the runs in their contrasting styles, the two little spinners undermined the English batsmen, taking 59 of the 77 wickets to fall in the series.

Three of the 1950 West Indies team enjoy the sights of Cambridge. (Left to right) C.B. Williams, H.H.H. Johnson, A.F. Rae

Spinners, the sages tell us, do not reach full maturity until after their 30th birthday – and I hope they are right – yet both these two were under 22 when they won the 1950 series for the West Indies; they could never touch such heights again.

Valentine didn't look like a cricketer unless he was bowling; a lean bespectacled man, he never managed to score double figures in his three tours of England, but that didn't matter too much, for his orthodox left-arm spinners fizzed down the wicket with unerring accuracy and plenty of spin. His speed through the air made it difficult for the batsmen to use their feet to him, and in 1950 there were not many English batsmen prepared to try anyway (Compton's knee was starting to give him problems and he missed three of the four Tests).

The unorthodox Sonny Ramadhin

Ramadhin posed different problems; the batsmen, as well as his own wicketkeeper, Walcott, were not sure which way the ball would spin after bouncing. Compton's analysis was illuminating, though not over-technical: 'All you see is a blur of black hand, a white shirt with sleeves buttoned down to the wrist and a red blur.' Throughout the series he mystified the English batsmen and delighted those who enjoy seeing unorthodoxy prosper.

It wasn't until the first Test of the 1957 series at Edgbaston, which has become a notorious graveyard for spinners, that Ramadhin was mastered, or at least blunted by English batsmen. In the first innings he took seven for 49 from 31 overs. In the second he took two for 179 from 98 overs. May (285 not out) and Cowdrey (154) added 411 for the fourth wicket. Both decided to play him as an off-spin bowler. Cowdrey, no doubt relishing the technical challenge, used his front pad as much as his bat when playing defensively as Ramadhin wheeled away, bowling a record 588 balls in the innings. Unsurprisingly Ramadhin was never again the same force in international cricket, and unfortunately Cowdrey's solution encouraged excessive pad play by batsmen far less gifted than himself. England went on to win the series three-nil and West Indian cricket appeared to be on the decline.

Sir Learie Constantine has pointed out, in the pages of *Wisden*, some of the unusual problems that confronted West Indian cricket before the sixties

Opposite *Alf Valentine at the nets in 1950*

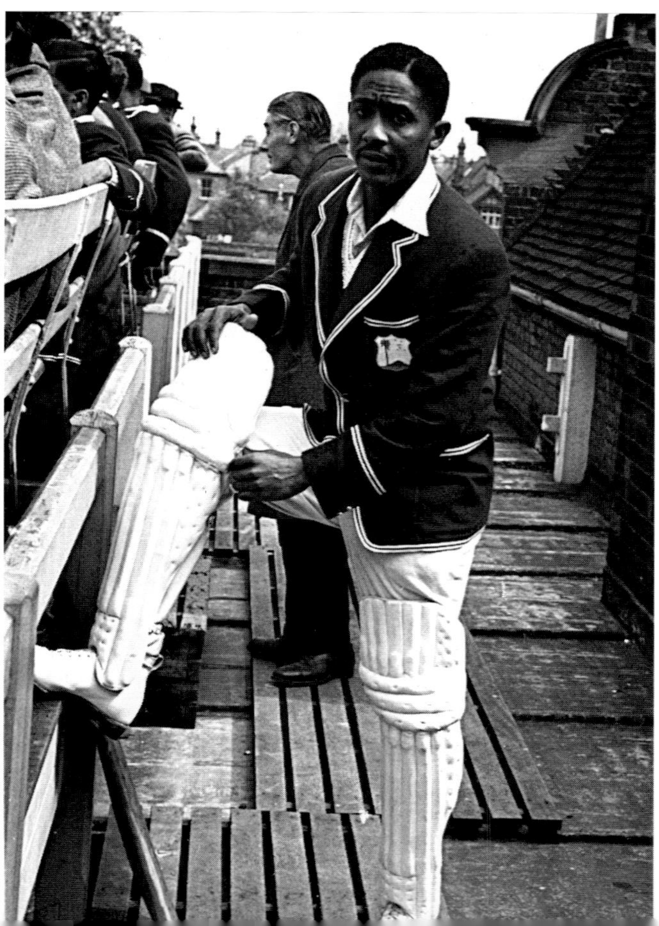

because of the geography of the Caribbean and the inter-island rivalries. For example, Jamaica is 1,300 miles from Barbados, which is nearly 500 miles from Guyana. Selecting the right side both to satisfy the home crowd and to win the match was an impossible task, and it was no easier for the captain to create one identity for the players to cling to. Constantine thought that the 1950 side was so talented that it could almost captain itself. However, he regarded the appointment of Frank Worrell, the first official black captain, as the watershed of West Indian cricket. 'Before that wonderful tour of Australia in 1960–61 Barbadians would tend to stick together and so would the Trinidadians, Jamaicans and Guyanans. Worrell cut across all that. Soon there were no groups. Just one team.'

Worrell was the most graceful of the three Ws.

Opposite *Tom Graveney, one of England's most elegant batsmen in the 1950s and 1960s. (**Above**) The end of his 258 against West Indies at Trent Bridge in 1957*

Left *Frank Worrell at Fenner's in 1950*

Clyde Walcott displays his power

'While Walcott bludgeoned the bowlers and Weekes dominated them, the stylist Worrell waved them away' (Constantine). However, his greatest contribution to West Indian cricket was to prove that a black captain was capable of captaining the West Indian team as well as, or rather better than, any of his white predecessors. There was, prior to his appointment, still the feeling that the coloured man was not capable of such a task, and it was said that 'no coloured player would play happily under him'. Worrell soon settled that argument beyond any doubt, far more swiftly and convincingly than Hutton silenced those critics who still pined for the amateur captain in England. Within four years the West Indies were regarded as champions of the world. They still played their cricket with a greater sense of freedom and enjoyment than any other nation, but under Worrell's paternal care they became a more disciplined and cohesive side. He had plenty of talent at his disposal, even though Walcott and Weekes had retired. From Guyana came Rohan Kanhai and Lance Gibbs, who was to take over the spinner's mantle from Ramadhin and Valentine. From Barbados came Garfield Sobers, who at the age of 21 had surpassed Hutton's 364, and Wes Hall, a fast bowler of immense enthusiasm and considerable pace.

In 1960 the West Indies, with Worrell as captain for the first time, slipped into Australia almost unnoticed. There were what were taken to be the usual clichés – 'the series should be fun and the West Indies would try to play attractive cricket at all times' – but for once these were not mere platitudes.

The series began at Brisbane on 9 December. This match had already been earmarked as one of the great Test matches before it reached its amazing climax. Sobers' two-hour century and the all-round performance of Alan Davidson were memorable in their own right, yet all that went before was overshadowed by the final two hours. Australia, needing 233 to win, slumped to 92 for six, which would normally be the time to start playing for a draw. Benaud and Davidson had other ideas; they hooked the fast bowlers and scurried between the wickets, taking Australia to the brink of victory. In a flurry of excitement the final (eight-ball) over brought the wicket of Benaud and two run-outs, as well as five runs. Everyone was in a state of exhaustion, jubilation and confusion, or a strange mixture of all three. The West Indians enveloped little Joe Solomon, who had contrived two direct hits from mid-wicket during the final 15 minutes. Hall was exhausted, mentally and physically, and Australia's last man out, Ian Meckiff, was confused, thinking that West Indies had won the match by one run. When the dust settled everyone began to savour the first tie in the history of Test cricket.

The cavalier Everton Weekes

AUSTRALIA v WEST INDIES

Played at Brisbane,
9, 10, 12, 13, 14 December, 1960.
Result: Match tied.

West Indies: First innings

C.C. Hunte c Benaud b Davidson	24
C.W. Smith c Grout b Davidson	7
R.B. Kanhai c Grout b Davidson	15
G. St A. Sobers c Kline b Meckiff	132
F.M.M. Worrell* c Grout b Davidson	65
J.S. Solomon hit wkt b Simpson	65
P.D. Lashley c Grout b Kline	19
F.C.M. Alexander† c Davidson b Kline	60
S. Ramadhin c Harvey b Davidson	12
W.W. Hall st Grout b Kline	50
A.L. Valentine not out	0
Extras (lb 3, w 1)	4
Total	453

Fall of Wickets: 1/23, 2/42, 3/65, 4/239, 5/243, 6/283, 7/347, 8/366, 9/452, 10/453.
Bowling: Davidson 30-2-135-5, Meckiff 18-0-129-1, Mackay 3-0-15-0, Benaud 24-3-93-0, Simpson 8-0-25-1, Kline 17.6-6-52-3.

Australia: First innings

C.C. McDonald c Hunte b Sobers	57
R.B. Simpson b Ramadhin	92
R.N. Harvey b Valentine	15
N.C. O'Neill c Valentine b Hall	181
L.E. Favell run out	45
K.D. Mackay b Sobers	35
A.K. Davidson c Alexander b Hall	44
R. Benaud* lbw b Hall	10
A.T.W. Grout† lbw b Hall	4
I. Meckiff run out	4
L.F. Kline not out	3
Extras (b 2, lb 8, w 1, nb 4)	15
Total	505

Fall of Wickets: 1/84, 2/138, 3/194, 4/278, 5/381, 6/469, 7/484, 8/489, 9/496, 10/505.
Bowling: Hall 29.3-1-140-4, Worrell 30-0-93-0, Sobers 32-0-115-2, Valentine 24-6-82-1, Ramadhin 15-1-60-1.

West Indies: Second innings

C.C. Hunte c Simpson b Mackay	39
C.W. Smith c O'Neill b Davidson	6
R.B. Kanhai c Grout b Davidson	54
G. St A. Sobers b Davidson	14
F.M.M. Worrell* c Grout b Davidson	65
J.S. Solomon lbw b Simpson	47
P.D. Lashley b Davidson	0
F.C.M. Alexander† b Benaud	5
S. Ramadhin c Harvey b Simpson	6
W.W. Hall b Davidson	18
A.L. Valentine not out	7
Extras (b 14, lb 7, w 2)	23
Total	284

Fall of Wickets: 1/13, 2/88, 3/114, 4/127, 5/210, 6/210, 7/241, 8/250, 9/253, 10/284.
Bowling: Davidson 24.6-4-87-6, Meckiff 4-1-19-0, Mackay 21-7-52-1, Benaud 31-6-69-1, Simpson 7-2-18-2, Kline 4-0-14-0, O'Neill 1-0-2-0.

Australia: Second innings

C.C. McDonald b Worrell	16
R.B. Simpson c sub (L.R. Gibbs) b Hall	0
R.N. Harvey c Sobers b Hall	5
N.C. O'Neill c Alexander b Hall	26
L.E. Favell c Solomon b Hall	7
K.D. Mackay b Ramadhin	28
A.K. Davidson run out	80
R. Benaud* c Alexander b Hall	52
A.T.W. Grout† run out	2
I. Meckiff run out	2
L.F. Kline not out	0
Extras (b 2, lb 9, nb 3)	14
Total	232

Fall of Wickets: 1/1, 2/7, 3/49, 4/49, 5/57, 6/92, 7/226, 8/228, 9/232, 10/232.
Bowling: Hall 17.7-3-65-5, Worrell 16-3-41-1, Sobers 8-0-30-0, Valentine 10-4-29-0, Ramadhin 17-3-57-1.

One of cricket's most famous moments – and photographs: the first Test to be tied ends with Ian Meckiff's run out

Amazingly the rest of the series was able to sustain this pitch of excitment. Only 4,100 people attended that last day at Brisbane, but by the time the West Indies reached Melbourne and the final Test there were record crowds, sometimes exceeding 90,000, and even the cynics hailed the renaissance of Test cricket.

Five months after their anonymous arrival at Sydney Airport, half a million Australians lined the streets of Melbourne to give a ticker-tape farewell to Worrell and his team. The Australians had won the series two-one, but that was almost an irrelevance. *Wisden* reports:

> Never has it been more apparent that the game is greater than the result than in Melbourne on 17 February 1961. Commerce in this Australian city stood stood almost still as the smiling cricketers from the West Indies, the vanquished not the victors, were given a send-off the like of which is normally reserved for Royalty and national heroes.

The tour and the tied Test in particular highlighted two trends that will surface again in the next chapter. The first is the emergence of the West Indies as a cricketing nation, capable of dominating world cricket. No longer would an Ashes series be the unrivalled pinnacle of the game. Secondly the quality of the cricket and the approach of the two captains served to underline how sterile and unappealing much of the cricket played elsewhere had become. Now the commentators had an example to hold up for everyone to follow. E.M. Wellings was fortunate to watch every ball of the Brisbane match and he drew these conclusions for *Wisden's* editor.

> Test cricket had come to a sorry pass. Unpalatable though it is to admit, England developed the tight, restrictive tactics. Having then superior forces, they proved victorious for a time. It is not therefore surprising that others followed their lead and, in particular, sought to play England at their own game. Hence the tedium of many recent matches. Now Australia and West Indies have given a new lead, which England can neglect to follow only at the risk of grave loss of prestige.

The approach of Benaud and Worrell and their teams had given a new lease of life to an ailing game. However, in the years that followed it became clear that repeated calls for 'brighter cricket' from various committee rooms were not sufficient. Dramatic changes, at least in the structure of English cricket, were required.

5

THE DEATH OF THE AMATEUR

In 1950, on a fine Saturday, Fred Titmus made his first appearance for Middlesex at Lord's. As the teams entered the arena the public address system crackled into life.

> Ladies and Gentlemen, a correction to your scorecards: for F.J. Titmus read Titmus F.J.

Titmus, of course, was a professional, and therefore his initials belonged after his surname – especially at Lord's. The distinction between the amateur and the professional was still deemed to be important. The amateurs changed in different rooms, entered the field through different gates, stayed at different hotels and received expenses rather than wages. With rare exceptions like Hutton and Dollery, the amateurs continued to captain the team. Cricket was slow to move with the times. As late as 1968 Lord Monckton made this observation: 'I have been a member of the committee of the MCC and of the Conservative Cabinet and by comparison with the cricketers the Tories seemed like a bunch of Commies.' For various reasons the gap has closed a little since then. However, it wasn't just the amateurs who cherished the maintenance of the old ways. In the fifties a Somerset captain suggested that both gentlemen and players should use the same gate at Taunton when entering the field. The professionals were aghast at such a proposal and rejected it out of hand. They wanted to retain their identity.

In 1962, though, the distinction was abolished. *Wisden's* editor was not very enthusiastic about the decision: 'By doing away with the amateur, cricket is in danger of losing the spirit of freedom and gaiety which the best amateur players brought to the game.' He was concerned, too, that the passing of the amateur 'could have a detrimental effect in the vital matter of captaincy both at County and Test level'. Hutton's success had not convinced everybody. But the simple fact remained that fewer amateurs could afford the luxury of playing first-class cricket regularly. Several of the best ones, like Trevor Bailey at Essex and M.J.K. Smith at Warwickshire, had been employed by their respective clubs as secretaries so that they could continue their cricketing careers. So even if amateur status had not been abolished, it would have faded away.

Tom Webster's 1920s view of the Gentlemen versus Players match

More pressing problems confronted the MCC during this period. In the early sixties English domestic cricket was in a crisis. The public either lacked the time or the inclination to watch it. In 1947, admittedly a bumper year, the number who paid admission to county matches was 2,200,910. By 1957 this figure had dropped to 1,174,079 and in 1965 it had slumped to 659,560. There were plaintive cries from the administrators for players to perform 'enterprisingly', and the England selectors twice took the remarkable decision to drop century-makers because of slow play. Ken Barrington's 137 against New Zealand in 1965 clearly did not endear him to the selectors, even though England won the match by nine wickets, and in 1967 Geoff Boycott scored no less than 246 not out in England's six-wicket victory over India; he was duly left out of the next match, no doubt a little perplexed and confused by the decision. These omissions reflect two things: the deep concern at HQ about the survival of the game as a spectacle and a money-spinner, and the standing of India and New Zealand in world cricket. If Barrington and Boycott had scored their centuries against Australia or the West Indies, they would have been fêted as national heroes; but against the lesser Test-playing countries it was still deemed imperative for England to win with style, a luxury which was not afforded to the England side for very much longer.

However, exhortations from Lord's were insufficient to stem the decline, and throughout the sixties major changes to the structure of domestic cricket were introduced. One-day or limited-overs cricket was to be the panacea. In 1963 the Gillette Cup began. In its first year the matches were 65 overs per side, although they were subsequently reduced to 60. *Wisden* had its reservations, noting that the final at Lord's in September resembled 'an Association Football Cup Final more than the game of cricket and many thousands invaded the pitch at the finish', forgetting perhaps that the crowd had reacted in exactly the same way in, for example, 1902, 1926 and 1953. Yet the public flocked to the matches and the innovation was an immediate success. Twenty-five years later a ticket for the final remains a valuable commodity.

In 1969 the Sunday League was introduced, featuring 40-over matches with the bowler's run-up limited to 15 yards and his ration of overs to eight. Again the public responded enthusiastically. In the preceding years the counties had experimented with the idea of Sunday play in the Championship without any dramatic improvement in gates. It was the format of the competition that appealed. In one afternoon spectators were guaranteed a result as well

The making of a great bowler: Keith Miller (right) passes on some advice to the teenage Derek Underwood in 1963

as the helter-skelter of catches, run-outs and six-hitting. *Wisden's* understandable concern about what all this would do to the slow bowler was, to an extent, countered by the performances of Ray East of Essex, Derek Underwood of Kent and Brian Langford of Somerset, who, the editor, Norman Preston, noted with a rare tautology, 'bowled eight economical maiden overs to Essex'. The editor was bound to welcome the competition, but he expressed the hope in the 1969 edition that there would be no more tinkering with county cricket for 10 years. It was a forlorn hope, for in 1972, a third one-day competition was unveiled, the Benson and Hedges Cup.

Whatever the misgivings of the purists, it had to be admitted that these new competitions were rescuing the game. In 1973 Norman Preston noted that 'The presence of the Australians [in 1972] coupled with generous endowment from sponsorship brought beaming smiles from the county treasurers . . . county cricket is back on its feet again financially'. By the end of the 1972 season there was £600,000 to share out between the counties, Preston continued, 'So in this age of National and Social Security, cricket has found its own financial security.' The administrators had contrived an escape route, and since 1972 the structure of English domestic cricket has remained largely unaltered.

Whilst one-day matches injected new life into county cricket, attracting sponsors as well as spectators – a modern cricket club is far more concerned about sponsors than massive gates – it has also been blamed frequently for a general lowering of standards. Certainly limited-overs cricket has brought changes, some, but not all of which are an adornment to the game. For instance, the overall standard of fielding has improved dramatically over the last 20 years. Anyone who is incapable of throwing, running or catching can be mercilessly exposed on a Sunday afternoon. In an earlier era he would have grazed happily at third man, his ineptitude merely a source of mild amusement to both his colleagues and the crowd; now he is a villain who cannot be tolerated if one-day trophies are to be won.

Batsmen have been forced to improvise and hit 'over the top' to step up the run-rate, which is not altogether a bad thing. Sometimes now we attribute a Test match dismissal to the player concerned misguidedly playing a 'one-day shot'. Yet enterprising batting at Test match level will do no harm, and I suspect that Trumper and Woolley played quite a few 'one-day' shots in their time. Some notable players of this era clearly benefited from the changed structure. The best example is Glenn Turner of New Zealand and Worcestershire. In the sixties he was the dourest opening batsmen imaginable, capable of defending his wicket for hours on end, yet never dominating. Playing one-day cricket at Worcestershire forced him to discover new uncharted talents, and in 1982 he achieved the remarkable feat of scoring over 300 runs in a day against Warwickshire.

However, on the debit side, the advent of limited-overs cricket has hastened the demise of the leg-spinner in English cricket. In the sixties there were half-a-dozen survivors of varying ability; by the eighties there was not one serious leg-spinner remaining on the county circuit. Captains became as concerned about the number of runs conceded in an over as they were about taking wickets. Certainly in a Sunday League match figures of nought for 14 were usually preferable to four for 50: hence the proliferation of medium-pacers over the last two decades.

Indeed, the standard and the variety of first-class bowling has suffered the most from one-day cricket. In the fifties and early sixties the great English bowlers such as Bedser, Laker and Shackleton, of Hampshire, presumably rediscovered their optimum line and length in a net every April and persevered with it until the Scarborough Festival in September. Whilst they were quite capable of making minor adjustments for individual players, basically there was just one place to bowl – a good length at off-stump – and they became superb bowling machines, programmed solely for Test and Championship cricket. Suddenly every Sunday evening at about half-past-five, captains around the country were beseeching their bowlers to bowl anything but a good-length ball at off-stump, because such deliveries gave the batsmen too much room to swing their bats as they searched for that match-winning swat over mid-wicket at the end of the innings. On occasions good-length bowling became a liability. Spinners were expected to attack leg-stump as quickly as possible, in complete contrast to the requirements of Saturday and Monday. As a result there began a slow decline in the art of spin-bowling. It became much easier to get into the the side if you could bowl a few economical overs of medium pace and smash a quick 30 at the end of the innings. The specialist had to be very good to survive.

In 1968 one other innovation enlivened county cricket: the decision to permit each county to engage overseas cricketers. *Wisden*, along with everyone else (except Yorkshire), welcomed the influx of so many established Test players: 'For too long county cricket had been stifled by dour, safety-first methods. The overseas players by their enterprise and natural approach brought a breath of life into the three-day match'. Gary Sobers made the greatest

New Zealand and Worcestershire's Glenn Turner, whose batting style was transformed by the advent of one-day cricket

impact that year, not just because he managed to hit Malcolm Nash of Glamorgan for six sixes in one over at Swansea; he rejuvenated an ailing Nottinghamshire and drew crowds wherever he played. Elsewhere the standard of county cricket was inevitably raised with Barry Richards at Hampshire, Mike Procter at Gloucestershire, Rohan Kanhai at Warwickshire, Majid Khan at Glamorgan and Greg Chappell at Somerset, all players worth crossing a dual carriageway to watch.

Despite sticking to the policy of picking only players born in the county, Yorkshire still managed to carry off the Championship in 1968. However, they haven't won the title since, which is an indication of the impact that overseas players have had in English cricket, notwithstanding Yorkshire's ability to shoot themselves in the foot. In fact Yorkshire were champions five times between 1962 and 1968, their domination being interrupted by Worcestershire in 1964 and 1965.

From 1963 they were led by Brian Close, a man of remarkable self-confidence – he once declared, quite seriously, that he could last 15 rounds with Mohammed Ali – a fearless short-leg fieldsman and a captain inclined to trust his instincts, however ridiculous they seemed to his team-mates. He was at his best prowling at short-leg, driving his side to victory in the Championship; he was not too enamoured of all this new one-day stuff and he irritated his club by saying so in public. If any of his plans were too eccentric, Ray Illingworth was at hand to impart some shrewd common sense. On the rain-affected wickets of the sixties Close would consult Illingworth as to the appropriate moment to introduce the spinners. Illingworth would survey the pitch and might mutter 'another 20 minutes', and sure enough at the appointed time the wicket would begin to take spin and Illingworth, aided by Don Wilson, would bowl the opposition out.

Fred Trueman was by now the complete fast bowler, and a combination of Boycott, Sharpe and Hampshire, as well as Close himself, usually provided enough runs to give their bowlers scope to bowl Yorkshire to victory. There were plenty of strong characters in that team and no doubt plenty of arguments, but they knew how to win.

After 1968, however, the club's domination disintegrated, not just because of the advent of overseas players. At the end of this season Trueman retired; Illingworth was unable to secure the long-term contract that he desired and left for Leicestershire, which was an inspired decision on his part. Two years later Close was not re-engaged, to the consternation of many, and Geoffrey Boycott was appointed captain. Whilst Close enjoyed six tranquil years at Somerset, the Yorkshire committee rooms, and at times the dressing room, were full of acrimony rather than trophies.

Boycott's ability as a batsman remained unquestioned throughout the seventies, but his powers of captaincy remained a constant topic of heated debate in Yorkshire as the county's performances declined. By the end of this period, with four trophies available each year, the pressure on county teams to win something had intensified. Young players were expected to match the performances of their more experienced colleagues as soon as they arrived in the first team; they no longer had the luxury of a slow and gentle baptism in a series of three-day games. Instant cricket created a demand for instant success, with so many spoils to share. Indeed, by 1977 it was easier to chart those counties yet to win any sort of competition throughout their history, rather than list the winners. The two 'Cinderella' counties were Somerset and Essex, both of which have earned reputations as highly entertaining losers.

On the international scene the West Indies were the dominant force at the beginning and end of this period, with a lull in the middle for rebuilding. The Ashes series of the sixties were all closely fought, but Australia managed to retain them until 1970–71 when Illingworth's side won the Test series two-nil. However, a combination of Lillee and Thomson and some bouncy wickets ensured an emphatic Australian victory in 1974–75. The 'lesser' countries, meanwhile, were gradually closing the gap. In 1971 India beat England one-nil to record their first win on English soil, and contrary to the modern trend the architects of their victory were three spinners, Chandrasekhar, Bedi and Venkataraghavan. By the end of the period Pakistan's batting, headed by Mushtaq Mohammad, Majid Khan and Zaheer Abbas, was the equal of any country, but their bowling lacked depth and penetration. New Zealand became harder to beat, though they were still short of the resources or self-belief to gain victory, despite the herculean efforts of their captains, John Reid and Bevan Congdon.

Below *Ajit Wadekar, captain of the first Indian team to win a Test in England and* ***(right)*** *one of the architects of that first victory, the guileful Bishen Bedi*

However, arguably the best side in the world in the late sixties was South Africa – we will never know for sure. In 1965 they beat England one-nil and in two series in South Africa in 1966–67 and 1969–70 they trounced the Australians. A glimpse of the side selected to tour England in 1970 reflects their strength. Eddie Barlow, Barry Richards, Graeme Pollock and wicketkeeper Denis Lindsay had scored prolifically against the Australians, and the bowling attack was led by Peter Pollock and Mike Procter, two of the fastest bowlers in the world. Of course, that tour never took place as two years of bitter dispute proved that politics and sport cannot be neatly compartmentalised.

The innocent catalyst in the conflict was Basil D'Oliveira. D'Oliveira was born in Cape Town, where he dominated cricket in the coloured community – he once hit 225 in 70 minutes, and 46 runs from an eight-ball over. In 1960 several journalists, headed by John Arlott, managed to persuade Middleton, a Lancashire League club, to engage him as their professional for a modest sum. Back in South Africa raffles, fêtes and matches were organised to

Two of Pakistan's heroes in the 1970s: ***(left)*** *the graceful Zaheer Abbas, on the way to his 240 against England at The Oval in 1974;* ***(below)*** *Majid Khan, whose batting bore the stamp of a Golden Age elegance*

raise the money for his fare to England. After a hesitant start in the League, his first-year performances rivalled those of Gary Sobers and, no doubt, he looked forward to playing out his cricket career in the relative comfort and the unaccustomed freedom that Middleton provided. However, three years later he toured with a team of county cricketers; he scored some runs and deeply impressed Tom Graveney, who convinced him that he was good enough to play for Worcestershire. Following a year's qualification in 1964, he played regularly for the county in 1965, scoring 1,500 runs and taking 35 wickets. The fairly tale continued in 1966 when he was selected to play for England against the West Indies. Three scores of over 50 established that his self-taught technique and his cool temperament were equal to the rigours of Test cricket, and for the next six years he was a regular member of the England team – more or less.

In 1967–68 he toured the West Indies and suffered the first setback in his career: 'His batting was no more than useful, his fielding surprisingly faulty . . . and his bowling became of less and less consequence.' None the less he was selected for each of the five Tests in the series and kept his place for the first Test against Australia in 1968.

England lost this match by 159 runs and D'Oliveira, despite scoring 87 not out and taking two for 45 from the 30 overs he bowled in the game, was dropped. In his autobiography Colin Cowdrey, England's captain in the 1968 series, explains that D'Oliveira's bowling was not sufficiently penetrating to fill the 'first change' role. With an MCC tour to South Africa scheduled for the following winter, D'Oliveira's hopes of playing for England in his native South Africa seemed to be fading fast.

There now followed a remarkable sequence of events. D'Oliveira returned to county cricket and performed only moderately – at least by his standards. However, during the fourth Test he took 11 Hampshire wickets for 68 runs at Portsmouth. He was not picked for the final Test, but when Roger Prideaux, a batsman, was forced to withdraw from the Test side through illness, D'Oliveira was called into the squad, and on the Thursday morning he was chosen in the eleven. He had been given a last-minute chance to fulfil his ambition. Seldom can a player have gone to the crease with so much hanging upon his performance. D'Oliveira proceeded to score 158, which was a remarkable testament to his temperament (he is one of the few players whose Test average exceeds his county average), and in Australia's last innings he broke a stubborn partnership by bowling Barry Jarman, allowing Underwood to bowl England to a last-minute win. In the aftermath of this exciting victory everyone assumed that D'Oliveira would be selected for the winter tour. He wasn't. In *MCC* Cowdrey affirms that the decision was based purely on cricketing merit with no outside influence being brought to bear.

There was a public outcry; some members of the MCC resigned, MPs protested and the correspondence pages of the national newspapers were dominated by the 'D'Oliveira Affair'. From a distance it was hard to comprehend D'Oliveira's omission on cricketing grounds, and deep suspicions were aroused. Spare a thought, too, for Colin Milburn, another surprise omission; no one apparently cared a jot about his fate in the ensuing hullabaloo.

The doughty Bevan Congdon, batting during his 175 against England at Lord's in 1973. New Zealand were forced to wait another 10 years for victory in England

When, however, the selectors learnt that Tom Cartwright, the Warwickshire medium-pacer, was unable to tour because of a shoulder injury, Basil D'Oliveira was drafted into the touring party. Within 24 hours Dr Vorster, speaking in Bloemfontein, deplored the selection – 'it is not the MCC team. It's the team of the anti-apartheid movement. We are not prepared to have a team thrust upon us' – and summarily cancelled the tour. So in the space of a week the MCC had contrived to enrage both the liberals in England and the die-hard supporters of apartheid in South Africa. Throughout the entire sorry episode, the one person who was universally regarded to have conducted himself with complete dignity was Basil D'Oliveira himself.

The inclusion of D'Oliveira probably hastened the inevitable. In 1970 the South Africans were due to tour England. However, there was massive opposition to the tour from such eminent men as David Sheppard, Lord Learie Constantine and Fr Trevor Huddleston. In a much-discussed television interview the Prime Minister, Harold Wilson, considered that the MCC had made a 'big mistake' in inviting the South African team – 'a very ill-judged decision'. He said, with the proviso that any protests must not be violent: 'Everyone should be free to demonstrate against apartheid – I hope people will feel free to do so.' The administrators of the

Test grounds began investing in vast quantities of barbed wire.

The situation became sufficiently grave for it to be the subject of an emergency debate in the House of Commons. Finally on 21 May, less than two weeks before the tour was scheduled to start, the Home Secretary, James Callaghan, requested that the tour be cancelled 'on the grounds of broad public policy'. Since this amounted to a government directive, the Cricket Council had little choice but to agree. Within a week the TCCB had arranged an alternative series of matches between England and a Rest of the World side, which included the Pollock brothers, Eddie Barlow, Mike Procter and Barry Richards. Since then South Africa has remained ostracised from official world cricket, despite their strenuous attempts to regain admission.

Yet all was not complete gloom and despondency during the sixties – thanks mainly to the calypso cricketers of the Caribbean. The visit of the 1963 West Indians was eagerly awaited, especially after the excitement of the tied Test. Once they had arrived, the public were not disappointed. They won the series three-one and no one could begrudge them their victory. Rohan Kanhai's batting seduced everyone – especially when he played his falling sweep, a stroke which culminated in the batsman being prostrate on the ground and the ball racing to

Opposite *Mike Procter, great all-rounder*

Below *The Pollock brothers, Graeme (left) and Peter, in 1965. Graeme's 125 and Peter's 10 for 87 combined to beat England convincingly at Trent Bridge that summer and South Africa won the series one-nil*

Below *Barry Richards, whose Test career was limited to a mere four matches*

MANNS

the long-leg boundary. (Recently John Emburey has unveiled his own, rather less elegant version of the shot.) Gary Sobers confirmed to English critics what they had already heard – that he was the finest all-rounder in the world. At the top of the order Conrad Hunte displayed sufficient discipline and restraint to allow the strokemakers lower down freedom to play all their shots. Wes Hall charged in all day, shirt-tails flapping, white teeth grinning. Once, at Taunton, he hit a Somerset man on the inside of the thigh, an unprotected area, and unsurprisingly it hurt. Our hero didn't know whether or not he should ignore the blow stoically in a grand display of bravery, despite his obvious pain; big Wes solved his dilemma by bellowing down the wicket, 'Rub it, man, 'cos I know it hurts!' At the other end was the menacing Charlie Griffith of the lethal bouncer and yorker and occasionally dubious action. Frank Worrell's contributions with bat and ball were more modest, but his calm, dignified leadership remained vital to the team's success.

The most memorable match of the series was the one drawn game, at Lord's, where Trueman took 11 wickets in the match. Dexter's 70 in 81 minutes in England's first innings was, according to E.W. Swanton, one of the finest exhibitions of batting ever seen: 'We will talk of this batting for weeks, and many years on cricketers will say to one another: "But did you see Dexter that day at Lord's?"'

England needed 234 to win; in that second innings Cowdrey's left arm was broken by a Wes Hall delivery. Brian Close then played an astonishing innings. As the required rate of scoring increased, he opted to advance down the wicket to the nonplussed West Indian fast bowlers. Twice Hall

Above *Colin Milburn, hooking 'Garth' McKenzie at Lord's in 1968. Milburn's Test career was tragically finished after he lost the sight of an eye in a car crash*

Opposite above *The Oval after lunch on the last day of the 1968 Test against Australia. (**Opposite below**) Miraculously play resumed at 4.45 pm and England went on to win. Here Underwood bowls Gleeson*

Basil D'Oliveira, with his wife Naomi and son Damian, on the way to Buckingham Palace to receive the OBE in 1969

Below *1970: An anti-apartheid demonstrator makes his point on the windows of Gloucestershire's Jessop Tavern*

Ray Illingworth is bowled by Gary Sobers in the Trent Bridge Test – won by England – versus the Rest of the World in 1970

Below *The star-studded 1970 Rest of the World side. Back row (left to right): S.B. Hassan, Intikhab Alam, M.J. Procter, R.G. Pollock, C.H. Lloyd, G.D. McKenzie, B.A. Richards, F.M. Engineer. Front row: R.B. Kanhai, E.J. Barlow, G.S. Sobers, L.R. Gibbs*

Above *Harold Macmillan entertaining Ted Dexter and Frank Worrell, at Chequers in 1963*

Below *West Indies supporters ecstatic after victory in the final Test at The Oval in 1963*

pulled up before releasing the ball in sheer disbelief. Close's 70, in its own way as inspired as Dexter's first-innings effort, took England to the brink of victory. Hall, after an unbroken spell of three hours and 20 minutes, bowled the last over with eight wickets down and eight runs needed for an England victory. Off the fourth ball Derek Shackleton was run out, leaving England still needing six to win. For the previous hour Colin Cowdrey, his left arm now in plaster, had been practising batting left-handed – and one-handed – in front of the mirror in the dressing room. Out he strode to the non-striker's end. He recalls Worrell bellowing over to Hall, 'for God's sake don't bowl a no-ball'. However, that was the last of the heroics. David Allen sedately played out the last two deliveries and the game was over. Even *Wisden* records that 'It was a game to remember'.

The tour had been such a success that the administrators, as well as the general public, were alarmed that the West Indies were not due to tour England again until 1971. That was madness, so it was arranged that they would return in 1966; to accommodate them the authorities decided that the 'lesser' countries, that is everyone except Australia and the West Indies, should come to England on 'dual' tours, playing three Test matches each, a system which was maintained until the five-Test series against Pakistan in 1987.

When the West Indies returned in 1966 they confirmed their status as 'Champions of the World', this time under the leadership of Gary Sobers. No captain, apart from Bradman, can have dominated a series so comprehensively. In the Tests he scored 722 runs at an average of 103.14, he took 20 wickets and for good measure held 10 catches. Even Neville Cardus suggested that he might be the greatest all-rounder of all time. He would go no further than that for, characteristically, he retained a soft spot for the heroes of his youth, Wilfred Rhodes and Frank Woolley. The statistics can make a good case for Sobers, but Cardus quite rightly wasn't too bothered about them. Cricket appeared to be such an easy game when Sobers was playing it: 'Nobody has seen Sobers obviously in labour. He makes a stroke with moments to spare. His fastest ball – and it can be very fast – is bowled as though he could, with physical pressure, have bowled it a shade faster. He can, in the slips, catch the lightning snick with the grace and nonchalance of Hammond himself. The sure sign of mastery, of genius of any order, is absence of strain, natural freedom of rhythm.' Cardus was happy to rank him with anyone from the Golden Age, even though he was playing in humdrum surroundings and with ordinary players: 'He has generally maintained the *art* of

ENGLAND v WEST INDIES

Played at Lord's,
20, 21, 22, 24, 25 June, 1963.
Result: Match drawn.

West Indies: First innings

C.C. Hunte c Close b Trueman	44
E.D.A. St J. McMorris lbw b Trueman	16
G. St A. Sobers c Cowdrey b Allen	42
R.B. Kanhai c Edrich b Trueman	73
B.F. Butcher c Barrington b Trueman	14
J.S. Solomon lbw b Shackleton	56
F.M.M. Worrell* b Trueman	0
D.L. Murray† c Cowdrey b Shackleton	20
W.W. Hall not out	25
C.C. Griffith c Cowdrey b Shackleton	0
L.R. Gibbs c Stewart b Shackleton	0
Extras (b 10, lb 1)	11
Total	301

Fall of Wickets: 1/51, 2/64, 3/127, 4/145, 5/219, 6/219, 7/263, 8/297, 9/297, 10/301.
Bowling: Trueman 44-16-100-6, Shackleton 50.2-22-93-3, Dexter 20-6-41-0, Close 9-3-21-0, Allen 10-3-35-1.

England: First innings

M.J. Stewart c Kanhai b Griffith	2
J.H. Edrich c Murray b Griffith	0
E.R. Dexter* lbw b Sobers	70
K.F. Barrington c Sobers b Worrell	80
M.C. Cowdrey b Gibbs	4
D.B. Close c Murray b Griffith	9
J.M. Parks† b Worrell	35
F.J. Titmus not out	52
F.S. Trueman b Hall	10
D.A. Allen lbw b Griffith	2
D. Shackleton b Griffith	8
Extras (b 8, lb 8, nb 9)	25
Total	297

Fall of Wickets: 1/2, 2/20, 3/102, 4/115, 5/151, 6/206, 7/235, 8/271, 9/274, 10/297.
Bowling: Hall 18-2-65-1, Griffith 26-6-91-5, Sobers 18-4-45-1, Gibbs 27-9-59-1, Worrell 13-6-12-2.

West Indies: Second innings

C.C. Hunte c Cowdrey b Shackleton	7
E.D.A. St J. McMorris c Cowdrey b Trueman	8
G. St A. Sobers (5) c Parks b Trueman	8
R.B. Kanhai (3) c Cowdrey b Shackleton	21
B.F. Butcher (4) lbw b Shackleton	133
J.S. Solomon c Stewart b Allen	5
F.M.M. Worrell* c Stewart b Trueman	33
D.L. Murray† c Parks b Trueman	2
W.W. Hall c Parks b Trueman	2
C.C. Griffith b Shackleton	1
L.R. Gibbs not out	1
Extras (b 5, lb 2, nb 1)	8
Total	229

Fall of Wickets: 1/15, 2/15, 3/64, 4/84, 5/104, 6/214, 7/224, 8/226, 9/228, 10/229.
Bowling: Trueman 26-9-52-5, Shackleton 34-14-72-4, Allen 21-7-50-1, Titmus 17-3-47-0.

England: Second innings

M.J. Stewart c Solomon b Hall	17
J.H. Edrich c Murray b Hall	8
E.R. Dexter* b Gibbs	2
K.F. Barrington c Murray b Griffith	60
M.C. Cowdrey not out	19
D.B. Close c Murray b Griffith	70
J.M. Parks† lbw b Griffith	17
F.J. Titmus c McMorris b Hall	11
F.S. Trueman c Murray b Hall	0
D.A. Allen not out	4
D. Shackleton run out	4
Extras (b 5, lb 8, nb 3)	16
Total (9 wickets)	228

Fall of Wickets: 1/15, 2/27, 3/31, 4/130, 5/158, 6/203, 7/203, 8/219, 9/228.
Bowling: Hall 40-9-93-4, Griffith 30-7-59-3, Sobers 4-1-4-0, Gibbs 17-7-56-1.

Above *Charlie Griffith, one of the most feared fast bowlers of the 1960s. Richie Benaud accused him of 'chucking' on the Australian tour of the West Indies in 1965*

Rohan Kanhai, a great servant of West Indies cricket, who scored 15 Test centuries for his country

cricket at a time which day by day – especially in England – threatens to change the game into (a) real industry or (b) a sort of out-of-door "Bingo" cup jousting.' This was written before the advent of the Sunday League. Goodness knows what Sir Neville thought of that.

In 1966, when I was 11, it was Sobers who created the greatest impression; he was the man to emulate, even though my attempts, in the back yard, to imitate the languid run-up and delivery of Sobers the fast bowler were somewhat handicapped by my physique, hue and the fact that I'm right-handed. Even then I was quite happy to see him trap Boycott lbw.

After 1966 the West Indies faded. In Sobers' last 26 Tests as captain the West Indies won just two. His own performances scarcely deteriorated, but Hall and Griffith were ageing and there were not yet any obvious replacements. Nor was Sobers as natural a captain as he was a cricketer, though he displayed a welcome and surprising determination to keep any game, no matter how important, alive. In the fourth Test at Port-of-Spain in 1968, he declared the West Indian second innings closed at 92 for two, leaving England to get 215 in two-and-three-quarter hours, a decision which surprised the

*Gary Sobers: (**left**) He demonstrates his elegance on the 1973 West Indies tour of England. (**Below**) He scores another four of his 8,032 Test runs*

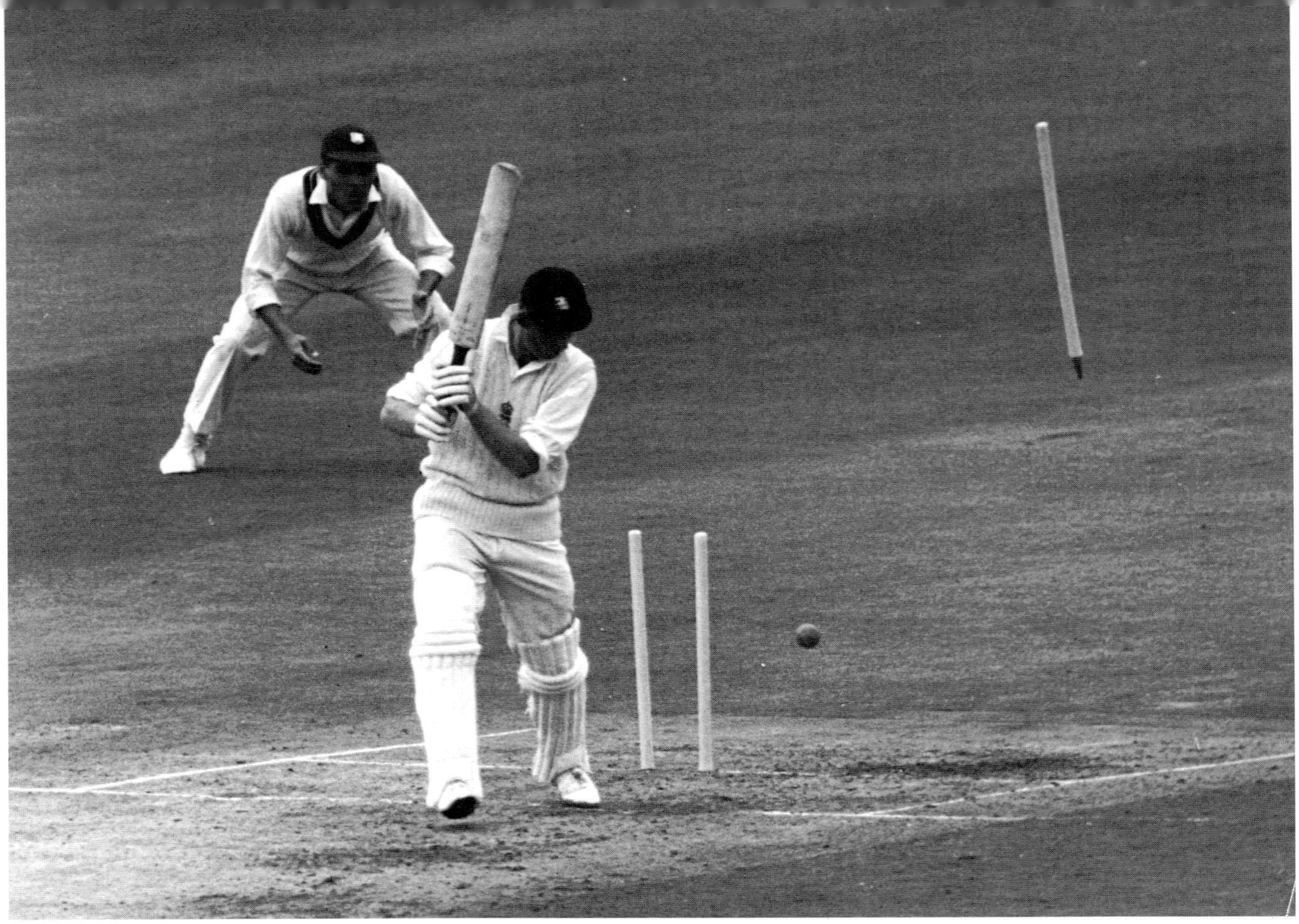

Above *Sobers could bowl fast-medium, finger and wrist-spin. Here he clean bowls England's Bob Barber*

Below *Viv Richards drives Derek Underwood for four during his peerless 291 at The Oval in 1976*

members of both sides. Cowdrey and Boycott guided England to victory, one of the very few in the history of Text cricket that have come as the result of a run-chase following a declaration, and Sobers was castigated by his own press. A lesser man would not have contemplated a declaration; a shrewder captain would have done his sums a little better.

By the end of this period, the West Indies had been reinstated as the best team in the world. In the scorching summer of 1976 they crushed England three-nil and Tony Greig, England's captain, must have wondered about the wisdom of his assertion that he would 'make them grovel'. With Greig's South African connections, nothing could have inspired Clive Lloyd's team to greater effort. A new breed of West Indian batsmen, who loved to hit the ball, ensured plenty of runs in the sun – Greenidge and Fredericks, Rowe, Kallicharran and Lloyd all had their moments of glory but were all consistently overshadowed by the young Antiguan, Vivian Richards, who in his first series against England scored 829 runs in four Tests at an average of 118.42. At the age of 24 he was unquestionably the best batsman in the world.

So the West Indies established themselves as a major force, if not the major force – Australia were to beat them convincingly in 1975–76 – in world cricket during this period. None the less an England/Australia series still retained its special mystique. For more than a decade the Ashes remained with Australia, a fact which is still a little bewildering when one considers the players available to England. At the start of the sixties Trueman and Statham were still near their prime and there were plenty of formidable, if contrasting batsmen around.

Supporters invade the Lord's wicket in 1973 during a bomb-scare. Thankfully the bomb did not materialise

Two great bowlers for West Indies in this era: ***(Below)*** *Lance Gibbs, taker of 309 Test wickets.* ***(Left)*** *Andy Roberts, quick and capable of great variety*

The end of two Test careers at Old Trafford in 1976, at the hands of the West Indians: ***(Below)*** *John Edrich is bowled by Wayne Daniel and (****right****) Brian Close loses his off-stump to Andy Roberts. They had earlier both endured a terrible barrage of bouncers at the start of the second England innings*

Above *Lord's, 1976: Tony Greig introduces the Queen to veteran campaigner Brian Close*

Left *Gordon Greenidge – on the West Indies tour of 1976 – licks his lips at the prospect of the England bowling. He made masterly centuries in each innings of the Old Trafford Test that summer*

The best to watch was Ted Dexter; he possessed an upright, classical style and a healthy desire to attack the bowling, slow or fast. On or off the field he had charisma. Whether counter-attacking West Indian fast bowlers or standing against Jim Callaghan for parliament, on both occasions no doubt relishing the enormity of the challenge, he was entertaining. His retirement from regular first-class cricket in 1965 occurred in suitably dramatic circumstances. Driving home after a day at the races, he ran out of petrol, pushed the car off the road, lost control of it and it ran away with him, smashing into a gateway and breaking his leg. He was not a man to do things by halves.

I suspect that Ken Barrington wouldn't have run out of petrol in the first place, for he was a conscientious man, a worrier and an excellent car mechanic. He sacrificed many of his shots for efficiency's sake. As a result he was not the spectator's favourite, with his open stance and bottom-handed cuts and deflections – though he could, if he wanted to, play all the shots – but he was dependable (his Test average of 58.67 surpasses that of all his contemporaries) and totally committed. The Australian wicketkeeper, Wally Grout, once observed, 'Whenever I see Ken coming to the wicket, I imagine the Union Jack fluttering behind him'. A friend of mine christened his Morris 1000 'Ken' out of deference to Barrington; he explained that his car took a while to get going, was slow between the wickets (i.e. overtaking), but it was mighty reliable. After his retirement he became a much-loved assistant manager on England tours, delighting his players with a series of malapropisms ('You're getting caught in two man's land'). He died tragically of a heart attack on the England tour of the West Indies in 1981.

The most graceful was Tom Graveney, easing on to the front foot and despatching the bowlers to the boundary with a casual swing of the bat, perhaps too casual for the England selectors, for he missed the majority of the Test matches in the early sixties, much to the benefit of his adopted county, Worcestershire.

The most difficult man to get out was Geoff Boycott, who was gradually overcoming all obstacles, real and imagined, to find technical perfection, insatiably compiling runs for Yorkshire and England, fretting over the England captaincy and temporarily withdrawing his services for three years.

The most unflappable was John Edrich, playing and missing outside the off-stump, bravely fending off the fast bowlers and carting the New Zealanders for 310 not out at Headingley in 1965.

The most capped and arguably the most complete was Colin Cowdrey, who was always experimenting with some new theory – whilst everyone else urged him just to go out and bat – aching to lead an England side to Australia, but inevitably ending up as vice-captain (four times). At the age of 42 he was so flattered to be chosen by the players as a replacement for the 1974–75 tour of Australia that he couldn't refuse. Just four days and 10,000 miles after his arrival he batted for two hours against Thomson, Lillee and Walker on the fastest pitch in the world at Perth, an innings as praiseworthy as any of his 22 Test hundreds.

With players of this calibre around, even though they are not all exact contemporaries, you would have thought that England's record in the sixties would have been better than it was. Until 1966 the captaincy was shared by three 'amateurs' – even though the distinction no longer existed – the gallant Ted Dexter, M.J.K. Smith of Warwickshire, shy but very popular with his players, and Cowdrey, who was forever on the brink of making the job his own. The Oxbridge chain was broken by Brian Close, who led England to six victories in seven Tests, but his refusal to apologise for blatant time wasting in a Championship match at Edgbaston ended his reign. Cowdrey was reinstated, but when in May 1969 he snapped the Achilles' tendon in his left leg in a Sunday match, the selectors went for a stop-gap, Ray Illingworth, newly appointed as Leicestershire's captain after his dispute with the Yorkshire committee. He lasted five years. In the previous 11 years he had made 30 appearances for England without ever truly establishing himself as a regular. Once he was appointed England captain, his batting was a revelation, often digging the side out of a hole from number six or seven, while his bowling, if sparingly used on occasions, remained utterly reliable, and his captaincy was meticulously shrewd. The responsibility of captaincy can affect a player's performance either way. A decade later Ian Botham's career faltered when he felt a duty to perform 'responsibly'. However, captaincy brought Illingworth security; he was no longer playing for his place, for he was involved in picking the team, and that feeling of security undoubtedly enhanced his play.

His greatest achievement was to retrieve the Ashes in 1970–71, though there were a few hiccups along the way. The captain was none too pleased to see his manager, David Clark, quoted in the paper saying he'd rather see England lose the series three-one, than for all the Tests to be drawn. That's not how Yorkshiremen think, nor Peter May for that matter. Throughout the tour the relationship between the manager, captain and vice-captain (Cowdrey) was at best an uneasy one. In addition

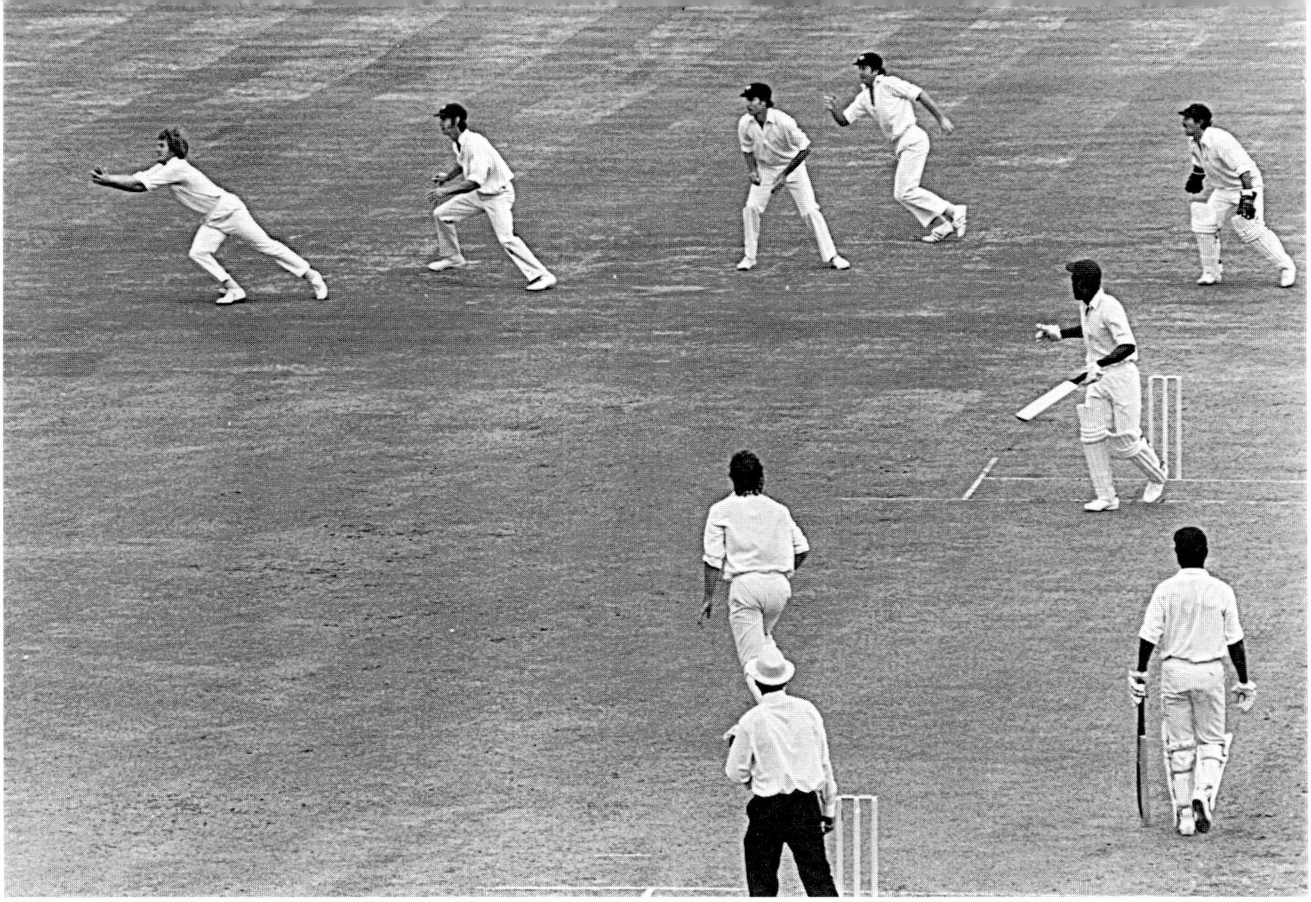

Above *Gary Gilmour catches Viv Richards at Brisbane in 1975. The Australians were a superb fielding side at this time*

Below *Ray Illingworth basks in reflected glory, after leading England to victory against the 1969 West Indians*

Illingworth had one famous argument with an umpire about Snow's short-pitched bowling, and at Sydney in the seventh Test, arranged after a wash-out at Melbourne, Illingworth led his side from the field after a scuffle between Snow and some Sydney Hillites.

Despite, or perhaps because of, all these obstacles there was, according to E.M. Wellings in the 1972 *Wisden*, 'a brand of team spirit, which has been equalled during the post-war years only by sides led by M.J.K. Smith. Illingworth had his players solidly behind him, and Edrich and Boycott in the role of lieutenants were invaluable to him.' That his matchwinners were Boycott and Snow speaks volumes for Illingworth's leadership. Both had repu-

Left *Ted Dexter, a stylish and aggressive batsman and, on his day, a hostile fast-medium bowler*

Below left *Geoffrey Boycott in 1965, by when he had already acquired a reputation as an introverted, unpredictable character*

Below right *Ken Barrington, loyal and reliable*

tations as being independent and potentially difficult, yet both respected Illingworth, although in Boycott's case the odd reservation was to surface a decade or so later. Boycott averaged 93.85 and Snow carried the bowling, taking 31 wickets. His seven for 40, in the first victory at Sydney impressed as stern a critic as E.W. Swanton, who wrote that in the second innings he had, 'not seen any English bowler bowl either faster or better since that tour of Len Hutton's in 1954–55.'

In 1972 England, still under the stewardship of the 'caretaker' Illingworth, retained the Ashes by drawing the series two-all, though there were definite signs of an Australian revival. Ian Chappell impressed as a forthright captain, his younger brother Greg as a stylish batsman, and the Western Australian combination of Dennis Lillee and Bob Massie accounted for 54 of the 83 wickets that fell in the series. At Lord's, on his Test debut, Bob Massie's return was a staggering 16 for 137, figures surpassed only by Jim Laker and S.F. Barnes in Test cricket. In overcast weather he was swinging the ball so much that he opted to bowl around the wicket, like an off-spinner on a turning wicket, to improve his chances of hitting the stumps.

Right and below *John Snow, in action and repose. He was one of the finest post-war English fast bowlers, taking 202 wickets in 49 Tests*

ENGLAND v AUSTRALIA
Played at Lord's, 22, 23, 24, 26 June, 1972.
Result: Australia won by eight wickets.

England: First innings

G. Boycott b Massie	11
J.H. Edrich lbw b Lillee	10
B.W. Luckhurst b Lillee	1
M.J.K. Smith b Massie	34
B.L. D'Oliveira lbw b Massie	32
A.W. Greig c Marsh b Massie	54
A.P.E. Knott† c Colley b Massie	43
R. Illingworth* lbw b Massie	30
J.A. Snow b Massie	37
N. Gifford c Marsh b Massie	3
J.S.E. Price not out	4
Extras (lb 6, w 1, nb 6)	13
Total	272

Fall of Wickets: 1/22, 2/23, 3/28, 4/84, 5/97, 6/193, 7/200, 8/260, 9/265, 10/272.
Bowling: Lillee 28-3-90-2, Massie 32.5-7-84-8, Colley 16-2-42-0, G.S. Chappell 6-1-18-0, Gleeson 9-1-25-0.

Australia: First innings

K.R. Stackpole c Gifford b Price	5
B.C. Francis b Snow	0
I.M. Chappell* c Smith b Snow	56
G.S. Chappell b D'Oliveira	131
K.D. Walters c Illingworth b Snow	1
R. Edwards c Smith b Illingworth	28
J.W. Gleeson c Knott b Greig	1
R.W. Marsh† c Greig b Snow	50
D.J. Colley c Greig b Price	25
R.A.L. Massie c Knott b Snow	0
D.K. Lillee not out	2
Extras (lb 7, nb 2)	9
Total	308

Fall of Wickets: 1/1, 2/7, 3/82, 4/84, 5/190, 6/212, 7/250, 8/290, 9/290, 10/308.
Bowling: Snow 32-13-57-5, Price 26.1-5-87-2, Greig 29-6-74-1, D'Oliveira 17-5-48-1, Gifford 11-4-20-0, Illingworth 7-2-13-1.

England: Second innings

G. Boycott b Lillee	6
J.H. Edrich c Marsh b Massie	6
B.W. Luckhurst c Marsh b Lillee	4
M.J.K. Smith c Edwards b Massie	30
B.L. D'Oliveira c G.S. Chappell b Massie	3
A.W. Greig c I.M. Chappell b Massie	3
A.P.E. Knott† c G.S. Chappell b Massie	12
R. Illingworth* c Stackpole b Massie	12
J.A. Snow c Marsh b Massie	0
N. Gifford not out	16
J.S.E. Price c G.S. Chappell b Massie	19
Extras (w 1, nb 4)	5
Total	116

Fall of Wickets: 1/12, 2/16, 3/18, 4/25, 5/31, 6/52, 7/74, 8/74, 9/81, 10/116.
Bowling: Lillee 21-6-50-2, Massie 27.2-9-53-8, Colley 7-1-8-0.

Australia: Second innings

K.R. Stackpole not out	57
B.C. Francis c Knott b Price	9
I.M. Chappell c Luckhurst b D'Oliveira	6
G.S. Chappell not out	7
K.D. Walters, J.W. Gleeson, R.W. Marsh, D.J. Colley, R.A.L. Massie, D.K. Lillee	did not bat
Extras (lb 2)	2
Total (2 wickets)	81

Fall of Wickets: 1/20, 2/51.
Bowling: Snow 8-2-15-0, Price 7-0-28-1, Greig 3-0-17-0, D'Oliveira 8-3-14-1, Luckhurst 0.5-0-5-0.

However, by 1974 when Mike Denness, a Scot like Jardine, but less controversial and less successful, took the side back to Australia, Massie had faded away. The Australians had found a new partner for Lillee – and much to the Englishmen's consternation, he was even quicker than Lillee himself. The sight of Jeff Thomson's dramatic sling-shot action had me cowering behind the sofa whilst watching the Test match highlights. Before the series began no one had heard of him in England; we vaguely assumed that this Thomson played for Victoria, had appeared without distinction against Illingworth's tourists and answered to the name 'Froggy'. We soon realised our mistake. At Brisbane in the first Test, on an unreliable wicket, Thomson (Jeff) took nine wickets, broke a couple of fingers and established his superiority over the England batsmen, which was maintained until he injured himself playing tennis on the rest day of the Adelaide Test. By then the Australians were assured of the Ashes. Thomson took 33 wickets in the series, Lillee 25.

Lillee's performances were as remarkable as his partner's. Two years earlier it had been discovered that he had four stress fractures at the base of his spine and the specialists doubted whether he could bowl again. He spent six weeks in a plaster cast, played a season of grade cricket purely as a batsman, and trained with complete dedication to strengthen his back. In that first Test at Brisbane he didn't attempt to bowl flat out and he suffered no reaction, so that in the following matches he let himself go and almost matched Thomson for pace.

Lillee and Thomson were fast, they were ruthless and they were good. At the end of the series, the shrewdest of judges, Don Bradman, who had captained Lindwall and Miller, was asked to assess them:

> Lillee and Thomson were probably, as a pair, the fastest and most lethal opening pair in Australia's history. They possessed remarkable physique, strength and stamina and ability and (may I add within the confines of diplomacy) a willingness to exploit the short-pitched delivery to an extent which would have unnerved any side.

They were not shy about bowling bouncers. In the Brisbane Test the English fast bowlers, Bob Willis and Peter Lever, had treated the Australian tail-enders to several bouncers, a decision they may

Opposite above *Bob Massie leaves the field after taking 16 wickets in the 1972 Lord's Test.*

Opposite below *Another wicket for Underwood, as he has Marsh caught behind, at Leeds in 1972*

have regretted, since they were soon to discover that the Australians had rather more ammunition in their arsenal. The Australian public, who enjoy seeing Englishmen humiliated as much as they enjoy drinking their beloved lager (in an ideal world they do both simultaneously), loved them. John Thicknesse, reporting for *Wisden,* wrote: 'When Thomson and Lillee were bowling, the atmosphere was more like that of a soccer ground than of a cricket match, especially at Sydney, where England's batsmen must have experienced the same sort of emotions as they waited for the next ball as early Christians felt as they waited in the Colosseum for the lions.' The Australian press went to town as well. Jeff Thomson was quoted as saying, 'I enjoy hitting a batsman more than getting him out. I like to see blood on the pitch.'

Despite the image created, Thomson conducted himself with dignity on the field and rarely said a word to opposing batsmen. Dennis Lillee was less reticent; he was quite prepared to voice his opinion of his opponent's batting prowess and there's no evidence that he was discouraged from doing so by his captain, Ian Chappell. Chappell cultivated a side that was tough, rugged and uncompromising; he liked that image and was happy to encourage it. 'Sledging', the art of abusing a batsman, became commonplace, and when Australia, after too many years of mediocrity, started winning again there was no one in Australia prepared to stop this trend.

A worried Mike Denness, pictured after dropping himself from the England team for the Sydney Test in 1975

England's tormentors: Dennis Lillee (left) and Jeff Thomson. They destroyed the England batting on the 1974-75 tour

England batsmen suffer at the hands of the Australian quick bowlers on the 1974-75 tour: ***(Above)*** *Cowdrey hit by Walker and* ***(below)*** *Edrich suffers a fractured rib, courtesy of Lillee*

England returned home in the spring, battered and bemused. They were soon joined by all the other Test playing countries, plus Sri Lanka and East Africa, minus South Africa, for the first World Cup. By now limited-overs cricket was well established in England and had helped rescue the counties' finances. In 1972 a series of three one-day internationals had been played against Australia, and a World Cup seemed a logical extension. England provided an ideal venue – not too much travelling, plenty of adequate grounds, long evenings that permitted a 60-overs match, and a multiracial population, ready and eager to support the visiting sides. Only the English weather could mar the event, but in 1975 even that obliged. So the event was a splendid success.

Highlights of 1975: ***Opposite above*** *David Steele, the England batting success of the summer. (****Opposite below****) The Lord's streaker in the firm embrace of the Law. (****Above****) Dennis Lillee hits Underwood for six during his 73 not out in the 1975 Lord's Test*

Below *Police guard the Headingley wicket after it had been vandalised by 'Free George Davis' supporters during the 1975 Test*

Doug Walters, one of Australia's finest batsmen in the 1960s and 1970s, during his marvellous hundred against England at Perth in 1974

The final at Lord's, before another capacity crowd, was contested between the two best sides in the world, Australia and the West Indies. England, with much the most experience in one-day cricket, had dominated their group, but their semi-final against Australia scarcely resembled a one-day game. On one of Headingley's notorious seaming wickets, much criticised by both sides, they were dismissed for 93, with Gary Gilmour taking six for 14. When Australia were 39 for six, the match was in the balance – until Gilmour the batsman took charge, cracking a vital 28. The other semi-finalists, New Zealand, performed tenaciously, but their batting was over-reliant upon their captain, Glenn Turner. Pakistan, with an array of attacking batsmen, led by Majid Khan, almost caused an upset in the preliminary rounds, losing to the West Indies by just one wicket, the last pair (Deryck Murray and Andy Roberts) adding 64 to win the match. India, for the moment, were not suited to one-day cricket. Spinners, in the form of Bedi, Chandra, Prasanna and Venkat, supported by a clutch of close-catchers, had brought them Test success in the early seventies, but they could not be as effective in a short match; their batsmen were renowned more for their patience than their belligerence. Sri Lanka had their moments. They scored 276 for four against Austra-

AUSTRALIA v WEST INDIES
The Prudential World Cup Final

Played at Lord's, 21 June, 1975.
Result: West Indies won by 17 runs.

West Indies

R.C. Fredericks hit wkt b Lillee	7
C.G. Greenidge c Marsh b Thomson	13
A.I. Kallicharran c Marsh b Gilmour	12
R.B. Kanhai b Gilmour	55
C.H. Lloyd* c Marsh b Gilmour	102
I.V.A. Richards b Gilmour	5
K.D. Boyce c G.S Chappell b Thomson	34
B.D. Julien not out	26
D.L. Murray† c and b Gilmour	14
V.A. Holder not out	6
A.M.E. Roberts did not bat	
Extras (lb 5, nb 11)	17
Total (8 wickets, 60 overs)	291

Fall of Wickets: 1/12, 2/27, 3/50, 4/199, 5/206, 6/209, 7/261, 8/285.
Bowling: Lillee 12-1-55-1, Gilmour 12-2-48-5, Thomson 12-1-44-2, Walker 12-1-71-0, G.S. Chappell 7-0-33-0, Walters 5-0-23-0.

Australia

R.B. McCosker c Kallicharran b Boyce	7
A. Turner run out	40
I.M. Chappell* run out	62
G.S. Chappell run out	15
K.D. Walters b Lloyd	35
R.W. Marsh† b Boyce	11
R. Edwards c Fredericks b Boyce	28
G.J. Gilmour c Kanhai b Boyce	14
M.H.N. Walker run out	7
J.R. Thomson run out	21
D.K. Lillee not out	16
Extras (b 2, lb 9, nb 7)	18
Total (58.4 overs)	274

Fall of Wickets: 1/25, 2/81, 3/115, 4/162, 5/170, 6/195, 7/221, 8/231, 9/233.
Bowling: Julien 12-0-58-0, Roberts 11-1-45-0, Boyce 12-0-50-4, Holder 11.4-1-65-0, Lloyd 12-1-38-1.

lia, despite two batsmen retiring hurt having been hit on the head by Thomson, though they still lost the game by 52 runs.

The final took place on 21 June, the longest day, which was just as well for the game didn't finish until a quarter to nine. From the moment Roy Fredericks hooked Lillee for six, only to tread on his stumps, to the run-out of Jeff Thomson as the shadows enveloped Lord's, the match was full of scintillating cricket. Clive Lloyd scored a hundred from 82 balls, rising to the occasion just as he had for Lancashire in one-day finals, thereby steering his side to the formidable total of 291 for eight. However, the Australians were undaunted, and it was only a series of brilliant run-outs by Kallicharran and Viv Richards that undermined them. They finished 17 runs short, and amidst 'hilarious scenes' Prince Philip presented the trophy and the Man of the Match award to Clive Lloyd. This was an experiment that simply had to be repeated.

Clive Lloyd in full flow during his match-winning century in the 1975 World Cup final

One event that can never be repeated was the Centenary Test match at Melbourne in 1977 – 'An occasion', according to Reg Hayter writing in *Wisden,* 'of warmest reunion and nostalgia .... Hans Ebeling, former Australian Test bowler and the inspiration of it all, should have been christened Hans Andersen Ebeling'. It was, if nothing else, a masterpiece of organisation. Invitations were sent to the 244 living cricketers who had played for England or Australia in the series, and a mere 26 failed to make it. Some only just managed it, though; Colin McCool was marooned by floods at his Queensland home and had to be helicoptered to the airport from his lawn, whilst Denis Compton arrived at the pre-flight champagne party only to realise that he had left his passport in a hotel at Cardiff. You would have thought that by then Compton would have realised that you don't really need your passport to get into Wales. A good friend and a fast driver retrieved it just in time. The oldest Australian Test player present was the 87-year-old Jack Ryder, whilst the most senior Englishman was Percy Fender, aged 84. From the moment everyone arrived there were constant parties and celebrations, during which thousands of runs must have been scored and hundreds of wickets taken. Even better, the cricket on the field matched the occasion.

By now England were led by Tony Greig, who had succeeded Mike Denness in 1975. England had just completed a most successful tour of India, defeating the home side three-one, a feat that only Jardine's side had matched. Australia were now captained by Greg Chappell. I suspect that the Melbourne groundsman – or curator – must have had a sleepless night after the first day's play, for it seemed as if the match might be all over within three days. Greig spotted that there was moisture in the pitch, even though he didn't then have recourse to all the modern gadgetry that he now uses as an Australian commentator, and, on winning the toss, put Australia in to bat. John Lever, Willis, Old and Underwood shared the wickets and Australia were dismissed for 138. England, no doubt still attuned to the grassless wickets of India, fared worse, scoring just 95 as Lillee ran riot, taking six for 26. Fortunately for the organisers and the guests, the wicket then dried and the batsmen began to dominate. Rodney Marsh, who had already surpassed Grout's record of 187 victims during the first innings, celebrated with his only century against England, proving what Western Australians already knew – that he was a man for the big occasion. A

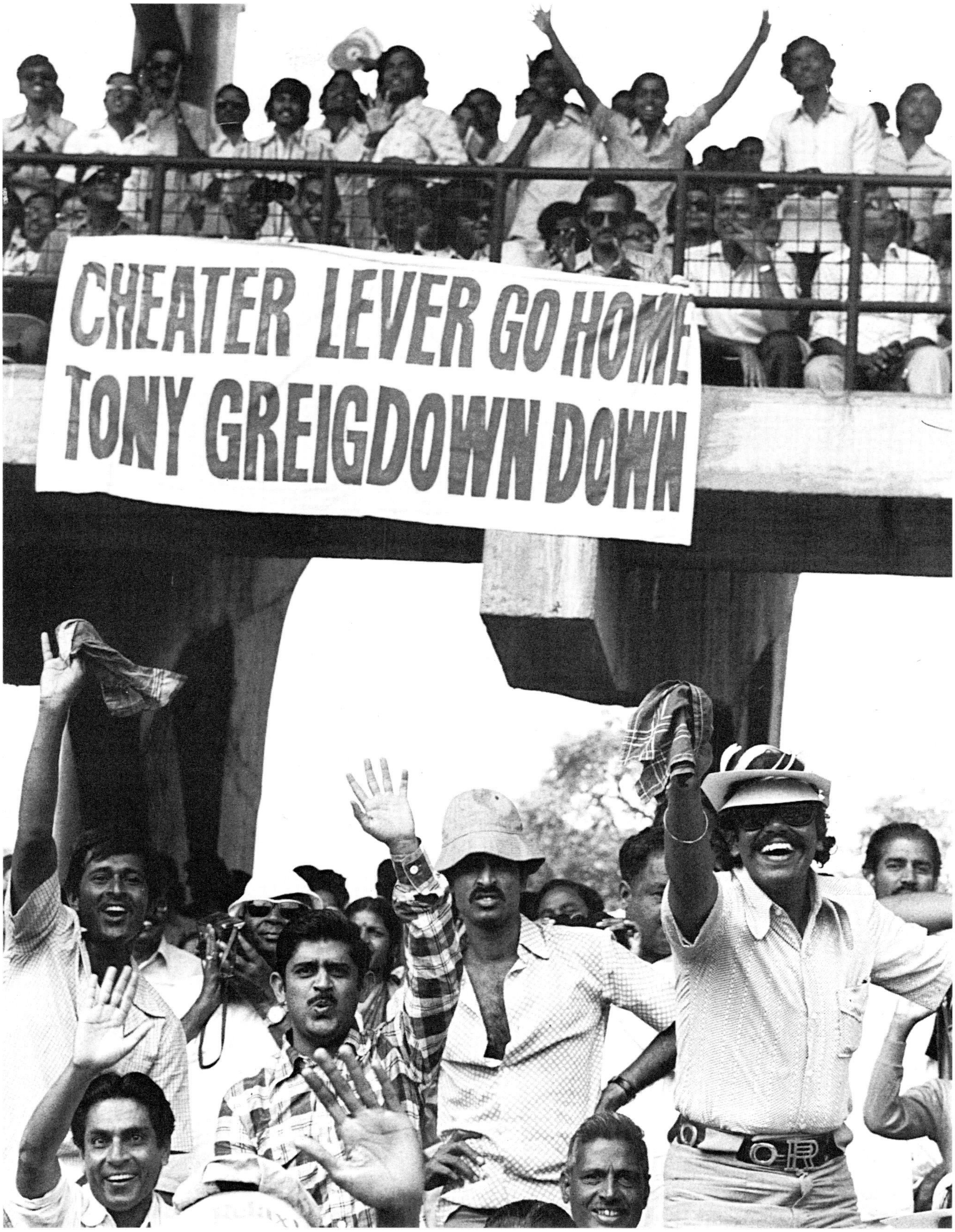

Opposite *Tony Greig illustrates his love-hate relationship with the Indian crowds on England's 1977 tour*

Above *The Indian crowd protest against John Lever, after he had been accused of applying vaseline to the ball during the Madras Test of 1977*

newcomer, David Hookes, from South Australia, added spice to proceedings. Having apparently been subjected to a few harsh words from Greig, no doubt in an attempt to unnerve him, he responded in the best possible manner by hitting the England captain for five consecutive fours. There was a gem from Doug Walters and heroism from Rick McCosker, who batted in the second innings with a broken jaw, a wound inflicted by a Willis bouncer.

Chappell declared, leaving England 463 to win at a rate of 40 per hour. Theoretically there was plenty of time for England to win – but that seemed a most unlikely outcome. However, the innings of a lifetime from Nottinghamshire's Derek Randall kept England's hopes alive. He enchanted those present, and for those of us tucked up in bed in England he was a cause of national insomnia as we tuned in to our radios. His confrontation with Lillee was marvellous entertainment; he refused to be intimidated by him, responding to Lillee's bouncers in a variety of ways. He 'tennis-batted' one to the mid-wicket boundary; to another he ducked, then rose to his full height, doffed his cap and bowed politely; another knocked him down, which prompted him to perform a spontaneous reverse roll. With his score on 161 he was given out by umpire Tom Brooks, but immediately Marsh intimated that the ball had not carried and he was recalled. Finally he was dismissed for 174, reciprocating Marsh's true sportsmanship by walking for a bat-pad catch off O'Keeffe. This innings won Randall the Man of the Match award, but Australia won the game, finally dismissing England for 417, giving them victory by 45 runs, exactly the same margin as the first-ever Test match. Reg Hayter observed that 'Hans "Andersen" Ebeling had even scripted the final curtain'.

Dennis Lillee captures the wicket of Mike Brearley, caught by David Hookes, in the Centenary Test

Such a match lifted the spirits of every enthusiast: marvellous cricket conducted in an atmosphere that was both competitive and chivalrous. All seemed well with the world. The administrators at Lord's might have reflected that cricket was in a far healthier state than at the beginning of this period, with eager sponsors and improved attendances. The future of the game seemed secure. By the end of May they faced pandemonium.

The effervescent Derek Randall, during his 174 in the Centenary Test: ***(above and right)*** *his individual method of bouncer evasion.* ***(Below)*** *A more orthodox moment in his innings*

AUSTRALIA v ENGLAND

Played at Melbourne,
12, 13, 14, 16, 17 March, 1977.
Result: Australia won by 45 runs.

Australia: First innings

I.C. Davis lbw b Lever	5
R.B. McCosker b Willis	4
G.J. Cosier c Fletcher b Lever	10
G.S. Chappell* b Underwood	40
D.W. Hookes c Greig b Old	17
K.D. Walters c Greig b Willis	4
R.W. Marsh† c Knott b Old	28
G.J. Gilmour c Greig b Old	4
K.J. O'Keeffe c Brearley b Underwood	0
D.K. Lillee not out	10
M.H.N. Walker b Underwood	2
Extras (b 4, lb 2, nb 8)	14
Total	138

Fall of Wickets: 1/11, 2/13, 3/23, 4/45, 5/51, 6/102, 7/114, 8/117, 9/136, 10/138.
Bowling: Lever 12-1-36-2, Willis 8-0-33-2, Old 12-4-39-3, Underwood 11.6-2-16-3.

England: First innings

R.A. Woolmer c Chappell b Lillee	9
J.M. Brearley c Hookes b Lillee	12
D.L. Underwood c Chappell b Walker	7
D.W. Randall c Marsh b Lillee	4
D.L. Amiss c O'Keeffe b Walker	4
K.W.R. Fletcher c Marsh b Walker	4
A.W. Greig* b Walker	18
A.P.E. Knott† lbw b Lillee	15
C.M. Old c Marsh b Lillee	3
J.K. Lever c Marsh b Lillee	11
R.G.D. Willis not out	1
Extras (b 2, lb 2, w 1, nb 2)	7
Total	95

Fall of Wickets: 1/19, 2/30, 3/34, 4/40, 5/40, 6/61, 7/65, 8/78, 9/86, 10/95.
Bowling: Lillee 13.3-2-26-6, Walker 15-3-54-4, O'Keeffe 1-0-4-0, Gilmour 5-3-4-0.

Australia: Second innings

I.C. Davis c Knott b Greig	68
R.B. McCosker (10) c Greig b Old	25
G.J. Cosier (4) c Knott b Lever	4
G.S. Chappell* (3) b Old	2
D.W. Hookes (6) c Fletcher b Underwood	56
K.D. Walters (5) c Knott b Greig	66
R.W. Marsh† not out	110
G.J. Gilmour b Lever	16
K.J. O'Keeffe (2) c Willis b Old	14
D.K. Lillee (9) c Amiss b Old	25
M.H.N. Walker not out	8
Extras (lb 10, nb 15)	25
Total (9 wickets declared)	419

Fall of Wickets: 1/33, 2/40, 3/53, 4/132, 5/187, 6/244, 7/277, 8/353, 9/407.
Bowling: Lever 21-1-95-2, Willis 22-0-91-0, Old 27.6-2-104-4, Underwood 12-2-38-1, Greig 14-3-66-2.

England: Second innings

R.A. Woolmer lbw b Walker	12
J.M. Brearley lbw b Lillee	43
D.L. Underwood (10) b Lillee	7
D.W. Randall (3) c Cosier b O'Keeffe	174
D.L. Amiss (4) b Chappell	64
K.W.R. Fletcher (5) c Marsh b Lillee	1
A.W. Greig* (6) c Cosier b O'Keeffe	41
A.P.E. Knott† (7) lbw b Lillee	42
C.M. Old (8) c Chappell b Lillee	2
J.K. Lever (9) lbw b O'Keeffe	4
R.G.D. Willis not out	5
Extras (b 8, lb 4, w 3, nb 7)	22
Total	417

Fall of Wickets: 1/28, 2/113, 3/279, 4/290, 5/346, 6/369, 7/380, 8/385, 9/410, 10/417.
Bowling: Lillee 34.4-7-139-5, Walker 22-4-83-1, O'Keeffe 33-6-108-3, Gilmour 4-0-29-0, Chappell 16-7-29-1, Walters 3-2-7-0.

Above *David Hookes, enjoying himself at Tony Greig's expense in the Centenary Test*

Opposite *1976 was an historic year for cricket, when women played at Lord's for the first time. England beat Australia by eight wickets in a 60-over match*

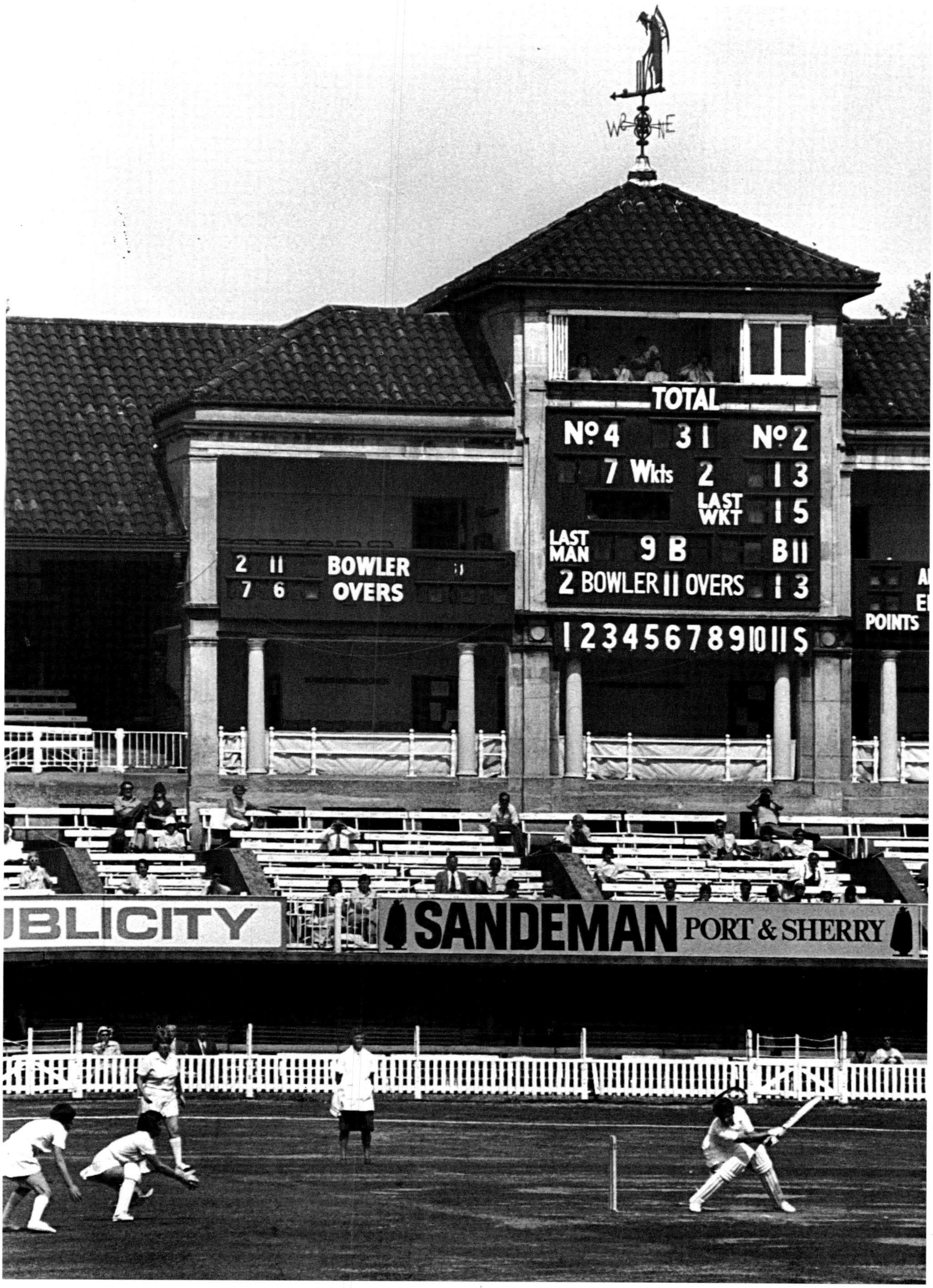
TOTAL
Nº4 31 Nº2
7 Wkts 2 13
LAST WKT 15
LAST MAN 9 B B11
2 BOWLER 11 OVERS 13
1 2 3 4 5 6 7 8 9 10 11 S
2 11 BOWLER
7 6 OVERS
POINTS
UBLICITY
SANDEMAN PORT & SHERRY

6

PACKER AND BEYOND

At the time we all thought the end of the cricketing world was at hand. A wet spring in 1977 had frustrated both the counties and the touring Australians, who were at Hove, desperate for match practice but spending most of their time improving their soccer skills. Warm memories of the Centenary Test still lingered on, and an Australian series in Jubilee year whetted the appetite, if only the rain would stop falling. The Australians were 'inexperienced'; Lillee had stayed at home to rest his back, so there seemed a good chance of recovering the Ashes. Certainly everyone was eagerly awaiting the series.

However, on 9 May the cricket world was thrown into wild confusion when a superbly kept secret finally became public knowledge. Kerry Packer, the chairman of JP Sports and Television Corporation, the proprietors of Channel 9 in Sydney, had signed up 35 of the best players in the world to play in a series of matches in Australia. These included most of the Australian touring party, including their captain, Greg Chappell, who when questioned on 7 May by Australian journalist Peter McFarline, who was hot on the trail, simply smiled and replied, 'It sounds like an interesting proposition – I'd like to know more about it'. In addition to the touring Australians, Ian Chappell, who was to captain Packer's Australians, Ian Redpath and Ross Edwards were coming out of retirement. The Rest of the World squad was drawn from cricketers from South Africa, the West Indies, Pakistan and England. It was to be led by Tony Greig, England's captain, who was joined by fellow countrymen Alan Knott, Derek Underwood and John Snow. It transpired that Greig had acted as a recruiting agent, even whilst the Centenary Test had been absorbing the cricket world. The only player who had declined the offer was Geoff Boycott and opinions varied as to the reason why – was it his devout allegiance to his native Yorkshire, or the possibility that he was reluctant to play under Greig's leadership for England or Packer's Rest of the World team?

Shock soon gave way to universal hostility to the scheme, both in the national press and throughout the cricketing hierarchy. The English players who had signed were christened 'the dogs of cricket' on the front pages, and predictably most of the venom was directed at Tony Greig. After all he was the England captain, one of the selectors of the national team. At the same time he had been gathering a group of cricketers to play in an alternative series of games that would inevitably clash with 'traditional' cricket. To no one's surprise he was sacked as England captain, to be replaced by his vice-captain in India, Mike Brearley. Freddie Brown, the chairman of the Cricket Council, made this explanatory statement:

> The captaincy of the England team involves close liaison with the selectors in the management, selection and development of England players for the future and clearly Greig is unlikely to be able to do this as his stated intention is to be contracted elsewhere during the next three winters.

Throughout the storm Greig remained typically articulate, though a little more tight-lipped than usual, and completely unrepentant. He claimed that Packer would be good for cricket, bringing better pay to both international and county cricketers; he had made personal sacrifices, for he recognised that the England captaincy would be taken away and his imminent benefit at Sussex jeopardised; and he didn't need the money. No one really believed that his motives were quite so altruistic, especially when it dawned that the whole escapade centred around a battle for TV rights in Australia. Kerry Packer wanted exclusive television rights for conventional Test cricket in Australia and had felt rebuffed by the Australian Board of Control's response. Frustrated, he devised this remarkable plan to achieve his ends, and he was absolutely determined that it should work.

For a while there was talk of compromise, but none was forthcoming and the battle-lines were drawn. Sixteen more players, including Englishmen Dennis Amiss and Bob Woolmer, were added to his troupe. No one – apart from Geoff Boycott – was prepared to refuse an offer from Kerry Packer, who observed that cricket was the easiest sport in the world to take over, because 'nobody had bothered to pay the cricketers what they were worth'.

The division amongst cricketers was remarkable to behold. At Warwickshire Dennis Amiss was practically ostracised for a year because of his decision to join. In Kent the members were confused. Knott and Underwood, both gentle souls, had been the most devoted servants of the club for 15 years. Somehow the tag of 'traitor' didn't fit too easily around the necks of such men.

In truth it's hardly surprising that they all signed; all the players were coming towards the end of illustrious England careers. They were being offered lucrative contracts – far more lucrative than playing for England – to ply their trade over a

Above *Two great servants of their countries, both pictured during the Old Trafford Test of 1977: Rodney Marsh (left) and Alan Knott*

guaranteed three-year period. Air tickets and accommodation for their families were all provided – in stark contrast to an England tour. The signatories, when pressed, simply pointed out that it was 'an offer too good to refuse'. How can you blame them? Yet they were subjected to continuous abuse throughout 1977. Indeed, it strikes me as odd that they appeared to receive far more opprobrium for joining Packer than did those who opted to play in South Africa for 'rebel' touring sides a few years later, which reflects a peculiar set of priorities.

In August the TCCB launched their counter-attack. They proposed that Packer players should be banned from playing both international and county cricket; this was all subject to a High Court hearing, which began on 26 September and took 31 days to complete. Justice Slade, in a judgement which ran to 221 pages, ruled that the changes of the rules of the ICC and all their resolutions banning the players from Test cricket were *ultra vires* and void as being in unreasonable restraint of trade. So too were the TCCB's proposed rules governing qualification and registration of cricketers in Test and county cricket. The authorities had lost comprehensively and ended up paying the costs; their only consolation was that Cornhill, recognising a golden opportunity for a high profile and widespread public support, offered to sponsor Test cricket in England, investing a figure of around one million pounds over a period of five years.

The controversy and confusion rumbled on for two years. In Karachi the England team threatened strike action if the Pakistanis opted to play their Packer players. At Edgbaston two apparently contradictory motions were passed by the Cricketers' Association, one urging the TCCB and the ICC to seek a compromise, the other supporting a ban of the Packer players. In Australia some grade clubs refused to let their Packer players use their practice facilities. The pessimists foresaw the end of official Test cricket, which, in turn, was the lifeblood of the county game.

In Australia in the winters of 1977–78 and 1978–79 the two forms of cricket took place side by side amidst the sternest of competition. Which cricket would the Australian public prefer? In fact by the end of 1978 they were none too impressed by either. In the traditional Tests an inexperienced Australian side, somewhat naïvely led by Graham Yallop, were trounced five-one by Brearley's tourists. Perhaps if the Australians had used the experience of John Inverarity, the series might have been closer and the ACB's bargaining position enhanced. Simultaneously Packer's Australians were being outgunned either by the Rest of the World or the West Indies. The Australian public very swiftly tires of losers, and the combined failure of both the Australian teams probably hastened a resolution. Both the Australian Cricket Board and Kerry Packer were losing money fast, the only difference being that Packer had rather more in reserve.

An agreement was reached in April 1979: it could scarcely be called a compromise since Packer gained everything he set out to achieve – exclusive rights for television coverage of the major games in Australia. In addition he managed to annex sole rights for marketing Australian cricket for the next 10 years. He insisted that England and the West Indies should tour in 1979 and that he should launch a tournament of one-day matches between the three most glamorous sides in the world. India, due to tour Australia in 1979, would have to wait their turn. The Australian board saw no alternative but to capitulate, and England reluctantly agreed to tour Australia for the second year in succession.

So normal cricket was resumed, though several of the consequences of the Packer affair still remain with us, not all of them to be decried. On the credit side was the innovation of night cricket in Australia. Added to the Sydney skyline were five massive pylons over the cricket ground, supporting powerful lights; Melbourne and Perth later followed suit. Night cricket is a magnificent spectacle; the white ball flying through the sky is more easily visible to the spectator than a red one in daylight. For the players the ground is reminiscent of an amphitheatre; the crowd become invisible and strangely this seems to magnify the volume of their reaction to the play – or maybe the spectators are just better oiled at that time of day. Whatever the reason, night cricket is an unforgettable experience. The first English tourists were initially sceptical; the lights would dazzle you when attempting a catch and the coloured clothing was jolly undignified. However, once they had played they had to admit that the whole experience aroused their adrenalin and was certainly more exciting than a damp Tuesday at Northampton.

As Greig had claimed, the top cricketers did become better paid after Packer, although the rewards were still far short of those available to tennis, golf and soccer players of equivalent status. Cornhill maintained their sponsorship of Test cricket, and it was now possible for an England regular to become a relatively wealthy man. English professionals could be seen carrying a briefcase and a portable phone to the dressing room; several acquired agents. Lower down the scale the increased awareness of the cricketers' plight saw the Cricketers' Association negotiate a minimum wage for county players. Although the minimum wage did not suddenly transform their income, it was a step in the right direction.

Balanced against this was the legacy of bitterness felt most acutely in Australia between players and administrators and sometimes between the players themselves. Although the innovation of the triangular one-day tournament during the Australian summer has kept JP Sports happy, it has not enhanced the game. A surfeit of one-day games has left the players stale, the discerning public bored and has reduced the status of an 'international' match. All this, as well as adverts at the end of every over, has tested the patience of the traditionalist in Australia. The camerawork of Channel 9 has set new standards, but even that has brought controversy; the action-replay machine has made the umpire's job even harder, and the idea of putting microphones in the pitch has been an unmitigated disaster.

However, perhaps the most important consequence of the whole affair was that it revealed to the top players that they were saleable commodities who had at definite value in the market place. It didn't take long for those in outlawed South Africa, who were desperate for international cricket, to realise this. They now discovered that if there were enough noughts on the cheque, then it was possible to tempt players away from traditional cricket. Within three years, Graham Gooch was leading the English SA Breweries XI on a 'rebel tour' of South Africa, this time including Geoff Boycott. A little later Kim Hughes, who had steadfastly ignored the lure of Packer and had thrown in his lot with the Australian Cricket Board, was to be found captaining a team of Australian 'rebels' in South Africa.

As a result, in Australia the ACB now offers contracts and retainers to its best 35 players to tie them to traditional cricket, whilst in England the threat of a ban from Test cricket remains the only safeguard. Anything more stringent would lead to the law courts, and after Packer the authorities are a little wary of that option. Strangely the English players who signed for both Packer and South Africa are apparently the least likely 'rebels'; Dennis Amiss, Derek Underwood, Alan Knott and Bob Woolmer have been hailed as models of the English professional cricketer, conscientious, honest and self-effacing; they are a most unlikely combination, which suggests that the authorities were slow to recognise the threat from without.

In England any bitterness was soon forgotten. In the eighties it became hard to recall which players were 'Packer' men, which 'rebels' and which both. In May 1977 the Packer affair appeared cataclysmic, but by 1987 it was a dim memory. Soon the professionals were more concerned about where they could acquire a decent helmet.

David Hookes hits Derek Underwood for four during the Grand Final Supertest at Sydney in February 1979

Clive Lloyd, sporting Packer pink – a colour the West Indies were particularly unhappy about wearing, owing to its connotations in the Caribbean

Dennis Amiss, thrust into the world of Packer, where a plethora of short-pitched bowling was reckoned to be part of the attraction of this new 'macho' game, was among the first to wear one, and it undoubtedly helped his confidence against fast bowling. When he first wore it to bat at Edgbaston, looking like an ageing Hell's Angel, many of the pros struggled to stifle a giggle. Yet within three or four years a player batting without a helmet was an oddity. Indeed, of all the modern players only Viv Richards has chosen never to wear one – he feels it might encourage the bowlers – and his rejection of the helmet has become a tacit statement of his inner confidence.

Many of the old-timers and commentators lamented the arrival of the helmet, partly because it made it more difficult for them to tell who was who. One or two suggested that the modern player had 'gone soft' – not a view shared by modern cricketing sages from Brearley downwards. Is there any difference between a box and a helmet, except that one is visible and the other isn't? In addition, the fashion of continuous short-pitched bowling showed no sign of abating, and it no longer mattered if you were a tailender – as Pakistani left-arm spinner Iqbal Qasim would testify.

One other significant change in equipment concerns the bat. The trend has been towards heavier bats, anything up to three pounds (Bradman's bats never weighed more than two pounds four ounces). This has been most discouraging for spin bowlers (I write from bitter personal experience), as it is now possible for mishits to clear the boundary.

The most successful county in English domestic cricket at this time were Middlesex, led by Mike Brearley, who could turn to an international bowling attack of Wayne Daniel, Mike Selvey, Norman Cowans, John Emburey and Phil Edmonds. They were the first side to benefit from a new generation of coloured Englishmen of West Indian origins; in 1980–81 Roland Butcher represented England in the West Indies, and he was soon to be followed, into the side by Norman Cowans and Wilf Slack. Nottinghamshire returned to their former glory under the uncompromising leadership of Clive Rice, who in turn was indebted to the all-round skills of Richard Hadlee. Happily in 1979 Somerset and Essex both won their first-ever trophies, so that every county had something to boast about. At Essex the wily Keith Fletcher moulded his collection of practical jokers into a formidable side, without sacrificing their sense of humour, whilst at Somerset the triumvirate of Richards, Garner and Botham performed wonders in the one-day competitions, under the calm leadership of Brian Rose. Essex have managed to sustain their success rather longer (as I write, Somerset are struggling to avoid the follow-on against Glamorgan).

The West Indies dominated international cricket under the captaincy of Clive Lloyd. He led the team a record 74 times, winning 36 Tests and losing 12, seven of these defeats occurring in his first 13 Tests when he was settling into the job. After humiliation at the hands of Ian Chappell's Australians in 1975–76, he evolved a system of playing Test cricket that could not be countered. Spin bowling, he decided,

Bobby Simpson came down to earth on the 1977-78 Australian tour of the West Indies, when his team lost the series three-two. He had earlier captained the Packerless Australians successfully at home to India

After peace had been made between the ABC and Packer, Greg Chappell returned to captain his country to victory in the 1979-80 Tests against England. Here he scores another boundary during his century at Melbourne

Above *Racial 'integration', South African style. Black groundstaff clear the wicket of water before the Durban 'Test' on the English SA Breweries tour, under the eye of the head (white) groundsman*

Below *Dennis Amiss tries out his new helmet*

was a luxury, especially if four genuinely fast bowlers were available. A West Indies/India series emphasises the point; in April 1976 at Port-of-Spain the Indians succeeded in scoring 406 to win the Test against a side containing just two fast bowlers, Michael Holding and Bernard Julien. A fortnight later these two were augmented by Daniel and Vanburn Holder, and on a lively Sabina Park pitch, the Indians were battered into submission. The Indian second innings ended at 97 for five with five men injured, leaving the West Indians just 13 runs to win the match. Bishen Bedi had actually declared his team's first innings closed at 306 for six because he was so alarmed by the brutality of the bowling.

Once Lloyd had settled on this pattern of play, he was not required to display much subtle tactical expertise; he simply had to act as the foreman of his rota system. Yet it is a mistake to underestimate his qualities as a captain. Under Lloyd the West Indies were a united, purposeful and professional unit; he commanded the respect of all his players and demanded the highest standards of fitness and application. Whilst the rest of the world's cricketers complained (with some justification) about the volume of cricket they were being asked to play, saying that they were stale and jaded, the West Indian juggernaut rolled smoothly on in Test cricket, as well as in the endless triangular one-day tournaments of Australia and in the World Cup of 1979.

Above *Joel Garner's pace unsettles Graeme Fowler at Lord's in 1984*

Top *Paul Terry, having had his arm broken by Winston Davis, loses his off stump to Joel Garner in the Old Trafford Test of 1984*

Right *Allan Lamb's three centuries against West Indies during 1984 were remarkable feats of skill and bravery. Here he reaches his hundred at Old Trafford*

Above *Graham Gooch could never have been said to have been intimidated by quick bowling. Here he hits a boundary during his century at Barbados in 1981*

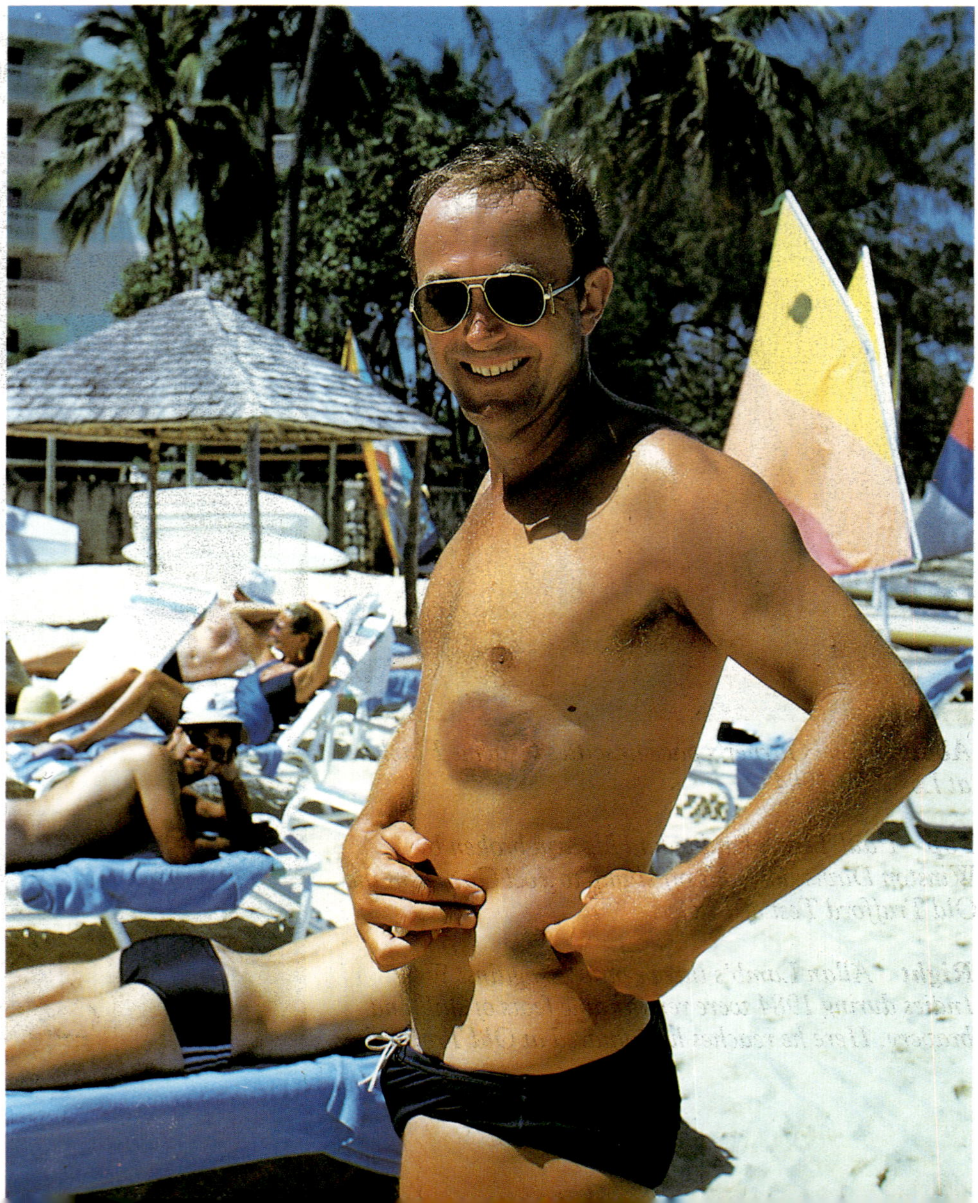

Damage inflicted by the West Indian pacemen on Phil Edmonds at Kingston in 1986. He seems happy enough, though!

The most feared fast bowler of the modern era: Malcolm Marshall

Michael Holding, 'Whispering Death', practises his art

One of the reasons for their continued success was that they were fit. Wherever they went around the world they took with them their own physio/trainer, Denis Waight, who had been allocated to them by Kerry Packer; after the compromise they were so impressed by his work that they decided to keep him. Under his supervision their pre-match limbering up and stretching routines were in themselves an awesome sight for opponents to behold; everyone from the captain to little Gus Logie had to be there to do them. Indeed Clive Lloyd himself is a testament to this regime; in the late 1970s he was alleged to have the knees of an octogenarian, yet he was still playing Test cricket in 1984. Within a year or two, the rest of the world's sides decided to emulate the West Indians, carrying out a whole range of extravagant exercises before the match, which, to begin with, amused the spectators and startled the old-timers. Now at 9.45 each day, the time when I imagine Denis Compton was abusing his alarm clock and contemplating how he should get to the ground (which ground?), most professional cricketers are locked in a hamstring stretch. I presume it's all worthwhile.

Another reason for the success of the West Indies was that they possessed brilliant players, and in particular devastating fast bowlers. During this era Andy Roberts was the first and the most calculating, Michael Holding possibly the fastest and certainly the most graceful, Joel Garner the most awkward (to face) and Colin Croft the most terrifying. When Croft opted to embark on a 'pirate' tour of South Africa, which inevitably resulted in a life-ban in the Caribbean, he was replaced by Malcolm Marshall, who is currently the fastest bowler playing Test cricket. Even worse, he can swing the ball and has an astute cricket brain, as well as remarkable reserves of stamina and determination. At Headingley he bowled England out whilst nursing a broken thumb on his left hand. Any normal professional fast bowler would have retreated to the physio's room for a few days, but not Marshall. Now the names are gradually changing, but the construction of the West Indian attack is not.

As well as keeping the juggernaut securely on the road, Lloyd also scored vital runs at number five or six. If the West Indies batting faltered he invariably came to the rescue, remaining imperturbable in a crisis. Languidly swinging his three-pound bat as if it were a matchstick, he could hit the ball as hard and as far as anyone. However, Gordon Greenidge, who learnt his cricket in Hampshire, and Desmond Haynes from Barbados, a sedate opener by West Indian standards, usually provided a solid platform. Lawrence Rowe and Alvin Kallicharran were prolific in the middle order before defecting to South Africa, but the prized West Indian wicket in this era remained that of Vivian Richards.

When Richards first arrived at Taunton, as a virtually unknown Antiguan in April 1974, everyone from the indestructible Brian Close down to the junior pros soon realised that he was special. His audacious strokeplay, characterised by his ability to crack straight balls through mid-wicket, and his fearless hooking of fellow Antiguan Andy Roberts astounded his new team-mates. Off the field he was shy, polite, shunning the limelight, but when he entered the arena ready to bat he commanded the stage. After a couple of seasons the mere sight of Richards walking out to bat intimidated county bowlers; his entire demeanour was transformed. His entrance, slow and measured, with a hint of a swagger, was in itself a declaration of intent; he was going to dominate the bowlers, and the greater their reputation the more determined he was to assert his mastery. Often his most memorable innings were played against the cream of English bowling, Bob Willis and Derek Underwood. If they were the best around, they must be subjugated.

However, what impressed his colleagues and separated him from many of the contenders for the title of 'best batsman in the world' was his uncanny ability to produce match-winning innings on the big occasion. In eight Lord's finals – five for Somerset and three for the West Indies in the World Cup – he has failed just once – at least by normal standards – and on that occasion, back in 1975, his fielding alone altered the course of the match. He once told me, 'I'll admit that I like showing off and a final at Lord's is the best possible platform. When I was batting I wanted to make sure that no one else was going to come in. It was my stage.'

He has, of course, played many astonishing innings: his double centuries in 1976, which established that he was the best; the fastest Test century (56 balls) against England in Antigua; his 322 in a day for Somerset against Warwickshire. I batted with him at the end on that occasion and remember two things – terror that I might run him out on 299 and his disappointment on being dismissed. Yet the innings which most emphasised his genius to me was his 189 not out against England in a one-day international at Old Trafford in 1984. No other West Indian batsman passed 26 and single-handedly he demoralised an English attack that had the West Indies reeling at 102 for seven. The unbeaten last-wicket partnership with Holding added 106 in 14 overs, Richards' contribution being 93. Without any trace of arrogance he later declared that he would have scored a double century had he not been compelled to take singles to keep the strike.

At the end of 1986 he was controversially sacked by Somerset along with Joel Garner, a decision which sparked a civil war of Yorkshire proportions in sleepy Somerset. However, he remains, at the time of writing, the West Indian captain, more remote than the fatherly Clive Lloyd, and inheriting a team in a state of flux. He has a remarkable record of success to live up to and there are murmurs that the West Indians are not as invincible as they once were. As I write they have just landed in England for a five-Test series. If they were to lose, it would mark the end of an era, for England have not managed a Test victory against the West Indies since the 1973–74 tour. However, Ladbrokes make them the favourites.

So over this period the West Indies were unquestionably the most powerful team in the world, but it's hard to say who were next. There was a levelling-out of standards amongst all the other Test playing countries, excluding Sri Lanka, who were accorded full international status in 1981. Gone were the days when Pakistan, India and New Zealand were guaranteed to be beaten in England. Indeed, in the spring of 1988 Pakistan drew a three-Test series in the Caribbean one-all, so it could be

Above *How are the mighty fallen! The 'King' in an undignified position during his first game for Rishton CC – played in a snowstorm – in 1987*

Below *Sri Lanka's Test baptism: Chris Tavaré is fêted on his return after making a match-winning 85 in the inaugural Test at Colombo in 1982*

argued that they are currently the second-best side. The previous year they won their first Test series in England, having been granted the privilege of a five-match series.

The Pakistan team have been galvanised by their captain, Imran Khan, who has managed to mould the undoubted talents of his players into a match-winning side. Such was his standing in Pakistan that the President, General Zia, himself intervened to persuade him to undertake the Caribbean tour, making Mrs Thatcher appear a remarkably reticent leader by comparison.

Imran began his career at Oxford University and Worcestershire; in the seventies he was a useful inswing bowler of no great pace. But he soon discovered that he could bowl fast, and this combined with greater application with the bat made him one of the great all-rounders in an era that can boast four genuine all-rounders of astonishing ability. Imran has set himself severe standards of physical fitness, which accounts for his longevity; at the age of 35, he was still capable of dominating batsmen by sheer speed, and in addition he could make an old ball swing as much as the new one. His own example, allied to a fierce Pathan determination to win, ensured that he commanded greater respect from his colleagues than any other Pakistan captain in history. Even Javed Miandad, a streetfighter and a rebel by nature, does as he's told when Imran speaks. Javed remains Pakistan's most consistent runscorer; he has also proved to be the most annoying adversary, though that doesn't excuse the behaviour of Dennis Lillee, who aimed a kick in his direction during the Perth Test of 1981. Amazingly Lillee was fined just 200 dollars for this misdemeanour. Nor did Javed win many friends amongst the Englishmen during the wretched tour of Pakistan in 1987–88, when he was captaining Pakistan in Imran's absence.

Above *Gordon Greenidge driving during his match-winning double century at Lord's in 1984. He has been a world-class player for over a decade*

Below *The incomparable Richards – on the way to his 189 not out at Old Trafford in 1984*

Above *Imran's pace takes another wicket. Better relations initiated the first Pakistan versus India series in 1977-78 – won by Pakistan – for 17 years*

Below *The most reliable method of dismissing Javed Miandad on home territory, here demonstrated against Australia in Lahore in 1987*

Duleep Mendis leads Sri Lanka out at Lord's for the first time. Wettimuny scored 190 for the visitors and Mendis narrowly missed a century in each innings

For all that, he is a brilliant player, who riles opponents partly because he is so good. He is the mischievous imp of modern cricket, darting down the wicket to the spinners, stealing singles with quicksilver running, taunting fielders to shy at the stumps, and in the field glaring at the batsmen from silly-point. His opponents would like him much more if he didn't score so many hundreds.

Imran's other match-winner is currently the most enchanting bowler in the world, Abdul Qadir, a wrist-spinner with countless variations and the temperament of a fast bowler. Qadir is not the sort of leg-spinner who surreptitiously lulls you into a false sense of security like Tich Freeman, or more recently Bob Holland of Australia. He attacks the batsman with three close fielders on the prowl, fizzing down leg-spinners, googlies and flippers with very few changes of action (none discernible to this writer). Sometimes his excitable temperament takes over; in 1988 he thumped a spectator who had been abusing him during the closing stages of a Test at Bridgetown, Barbados. But at his best he is a rarity in the modern age, a slow bowler – even better, a leg-spinner – capable of changing the course of a Test match. He has also been remarkably effective in limited-overs cricket for two reasons: he is surprisingly accurate for a wrist-

INDIA v WEST INDIES

The Prudential World Cup Final

Played at Lord's, 25 June, 1983.

Result: India won by 43 runs.

India

S.M. Gavaskar c Dujon b Roberts	2
K. Srikkanth lbw b Marshall	38
M. Amarnath b Holding	26
Yashpal Sharma c sub b Gomes	11
S.M. Patil c Gomes b Garner	27
Kapil Dev* c Holding b Gomes	15
K.B.J. Azad c Garner b Roberts	0
R.M.H. Binny c Garner b Roberts	2
Madan Lal b Marshall	17
S.M.H. Kirmani† b Holding	14
B.S. Sandhu not out	11
Extras (b 5, lb 5, w 9, nb 1)	20
Total (54.4 overs)	183

Fall of Wickets: 1/2, 2/59, 3/90, 4/92, 5/110, 6/111, 7/130, 8/153, 9/161.

Bowling: Roberts 10-3-32-3, Garner 12-4-24-1, Marshall 11-1-24-2, Holding 9.4-2-26-2, Gomes 11-1-49-2, Richards 1-0-8-0.

West Indies

C.G. Greenidge b Sandhu	1
D.L. Haynes c Binny b Madan Lal	13
I.V.A. Richards c Kapil Dev b Madan Lal	33
C.H. Lloyd* c Kapil Dev b Binny	8
H.A. Gomes c Gavaskar b Madan Lal	5
S.F.A. Bacchus c Kirmani b Sandhu	8
P.J. Dujon† b Amarnath	25
M.D. Marshall c Gavaskar b Amarnath	18
A.M.E. Roberts lbw b Kapil Dev	4
J. Garner not out	5
M.A. Holding lbw b Amarnath	6
Extras (lb 4, w 10)	14
Total (52 overs)	140

Fall of Wickets: 1/5, 2/50, 3/57, 4/66, 5/66, 6/76, 7/119, 8/124, 9/126.

Bowling: Kapil Dev 11-4-21-1, Sandhu 9-1-32-2, Madan Lal 12-2-31-3, Binny 10-1-23-1, Amarnath 7-0-12-3, Azad 3-0-7-0.

Pakistani magician, Abdul Qadir

spinner, and it is very hard for modern batsmen to premeditate a shot when they don't know which way the ball is going to move on bouncing. It would be marvellous to chart his progress in an English county season, because a large proportion of players have never encountered a genuine wrist-spinner.

India have also enjoyed more success in England recently; in 1986 they won the series two-nil for the second time in their history. Their most remarkable achievement, though, was to win the World Cup in 1983. Before this they had not been noted for their one-day skills, so it was a surprise to everyone when they reached the final. When they were dismissed for 183, those at Lord's, from Richie Benaud on TV down to the ice-cream vendors, considered it an insufficient total against the West Indies. Greenidge's early dismissal seemed inconsequential as Richards despatched three boundaries from four balls from Madan Lal. Viv was commanding his favourite stage again. However, after scoring 33 from 28 balls and looking his most imperious, Richards was caught near the boundary and the West Indies, who had appeared to be coasting, became jittery. By tea they had slumped to 76 for five from 25 overs. Afterwards India's unlikely crew of medium-pacers maintained the pressure, and despite resistance from Dujon and Marshall, India, 66 to one outsiders before the competition began, won the game by a margin of 43 runs. The Man of the Match was Mohinder Amarnath, whose gentle seamers rarely struck terror into Minor Counties batsmen when he was playing for Wiltshire. Against the West Indies at Lord's he bowled seven overs and took three for twelve.

Back in India the captain, Kapil Dev, was practically deified; he was showered with gifts on his return, one of which was a luxury hotel in his native Chandigarh. He is the second formidable all-rounder of the period, a lively away-swing bowler who can conjure wickets from the dead, grassless pitches of India, and an instinctive, joyful attacking batsman. In that 1983 World Cup he played one innings of Richards proportions; with India on the verge of humiliation at 17 for five against the novices of Zimbabwe, he cracked six sixes and 17 fours to score 175 not out from a total of 266 for eight.

Kapil Dev and Sunil Gavaskar alternated as India's captain throughout the eighties, and this remained a sensitive issue in a country where regional rivalries make the north-south divide in Britain seem a figment of the *Yorkshire Post's* imagination. Kapil is from the north, Gavaskar from Bombay, and their relationship has caused endless comment and speculation on the back pages of the Indian press. On the England tour of 1984–85, when Gavaskar was in charge, Kapil was actually dropped because of his 'undisciplined play'. As a result the walls around Eden Gardens, Calcutta were daubed 'No Kapil; No Test', an indication of how seriously the Indian public view their cricket. But the Test match went ahead peacefully and Kapil was duly recalled for the next Test at Madras. To his first ball he played a scything drive which just cleared mid-off, hardly the act of a contrite man.

Gavaskar's approach to batting was a little more calculating. When he notched his 8,115th Test run, he became the most prolific runscorer in Test cricket, surpassing Geoff Boycott. He has also

Gundappa Viswanath, one of India's post-war batting heroes, driving the Pakistan bowling at Lahore in 1978

exceeded Don Bradman's number of Test centuries (29); having achieved this feat, he immediately observed that any comparisons were futile because he had played far more innings than Bradman. None the less the record is a true reflection of his durability and his skill. He played for Somerset in 1980, whilst the West Indies were touring, and delighted everyone with his superb technique, the surprising power of his strokeplay and his mischievous sense of humour. I think he enjoyed the year, if only because he had the luxury of being able to go shopping with his wife in Taunton without being molested by hordes of well-wishers and autograph hunters; in Bombay such an excursion could never be attempted. He seemed so relaxed and easy-going that it was difficult to detect the hard core of ruthlessness that had enabled him to thwart the best bowlers in the world for more than a decade. We were amazed that this little Indian had been involved in several arguments with the Indian Cricket Board; that in Melbourne he had taken his partner off the field in protest, after being the victim of a dubious lbw decision, and that he once used a World Cup qualifying match, irredeemably lost in his opinion, for batting practice. However, he will be remembered for the quality of his batting. Only five feet five inches (he always claimed to be taller than his talented brother-in-law, Gundappa Viswanath), he combated the West Indians as effectively as anyone. In defence he was technically perfect, in attack capable of all the shots, but his hallmark was an effortless clip through square-leg. Occasionally in 1980 a gentle flick of the wrists would send the ball into Botham country, 10 rows back.

The power of Kapil Dev, here illustrated against England at Delhi in 1984

The advent of one-day cricket, coupled with their World Cup success, has transformed Indian cricket. The Indian crowds, who would once queue for hours to procure a Test match ticket, are now much more interested in the limited-overs game, and this has been reflected in the changed style of Indian batsmanship. Dilip Vengsarkar, the unpredictable Srikkanth, and Ravi Shastri, who has equalled Sobers' six-hitting spree, all go for their shots with an abandon that must astonish the likes of Polly Umrigar and Co.

Of all the 'lesser' countries New Zealand have made the greatest advance in this period. At Wellington in 1977–78 they defeated England for the first time in a Test match; they registered their first victory on English soil in 1983 and then followed this with two series wins in 1983–84 and 1986. Remarkably they have won a series against every Test playing country over the last decade, including the West Indies in all ill-tempered series in 1979–80, when unfortunately the matches were marred by West Indian dissent at local umpiring decisions. On one occasion Holding demolished the stumps with an elegance that only he could muster when performing such a crude act; on another Croft consciously barged into umpire Fred Goodall during his run-up. These incidents highlighted a depressing trend in modern cricket, the questioning of the umpire's authority – though remember W.G. wasn't blameless in this regard. Most recently the Shakoor Rana/Mike Gatting confrontation and Chris Broad's initial refusal to leave the crease during the 1987–88 tour of Pakistan, have provided fresh examples. This has led to a call for a panel of neutral umpires for international cricket. During the 1987 World Cup this system was used successfully, though Javed Miandad was a little nonplussed to be given out lbw in Pakistan. However, in England there are reservations, because we think our umpires are the most experienced and the best.

Sunil Gavaskar, the 'Little Master', on his way to 188 in the 1987 MCC Bicentenary Match

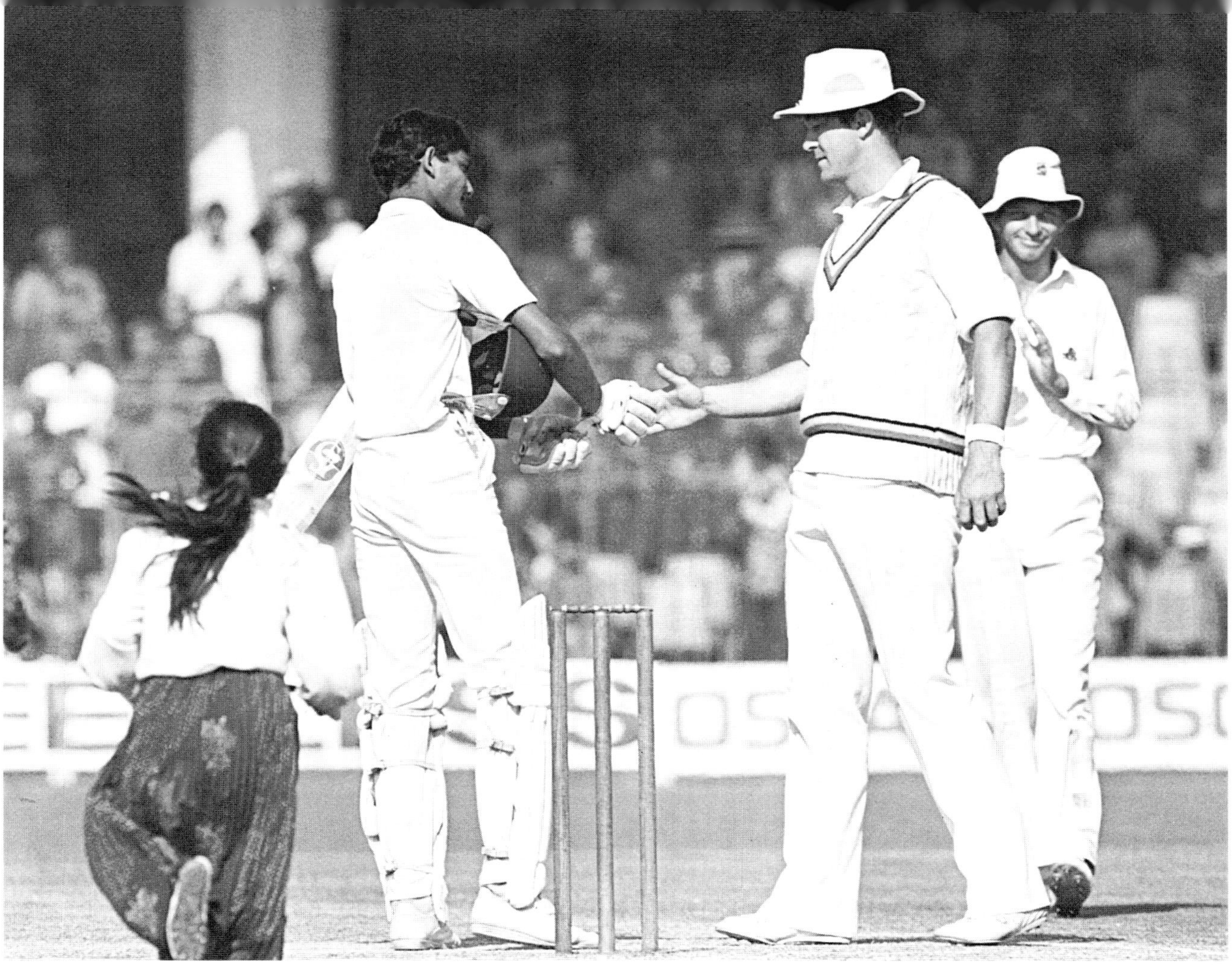

Above *India unearthed another superlative young talent in 1984 – Mohammed Azharuddin, scorer of three centuries in his first three Tests*

Below *Michael Holding's tasteless display of petulance against New Zealand in 1980*

New Zealand's success cannot, of course, be attributed to their umpires. The calm leadership of Geoff Howarth, allied to brilliant catching and accurate seam bowling, were all factors, but the most telling contribution inevitably came from the third great all-rounder, Richard Hadlee. As I write Hadlee needs one more wicket to overhaul Ian Botham's Test record. In contrast to two of his rivals, Botham and Kapil Dev, his bowling has improved with age; he is more effective at the age of 37 than he was at 27 – an unusual phenomenon amongst fast bowlers. Even more laudable is the fact that he has achieved his remarkable Test record without the help of another strike bowler at the other end. Ewen Chatfield and Lance Cairns were both honest and reliable seamers, but invariably it was left to Hadlee to make the breakthrough.

He was also the most efficient all-rounder in county cricket during the eighties, becoming the first man to achieve the double (in 1984) since Fred Titmus in 1967, and the only man to achieve this landmark since the reduction of the County Championship in 1969. Facing Hadlee is a privilege, even though it's likely to lead to dismissal; not a ball is wasted; bouncers are used sparingly just to remind the batsman that he can be quick if necessary, but usually extreme pace is not needed. The ball slides up to the batsman and then darts away, as if attached to a piece of string. His run-up now consists of no more than 12 paces and his action is classically side-on; there is no respite. In contrast his batting depends not on a carefully developed technique, but on a superb eye and natural timing. With a generous swing of the bat, the ball often whistles over extra-cover rather than past him, but such is his power that aerial hits represent a reasonable risk. His innings for Nottinghamshire in the NatWest final of 1987 emphasised this. Notts appeared doomed, but Hadlee, as if capable of tinkering with fate, brought his distinguished county career to a fairy-tale ending by hitting the winning boundary in the final over.

Hadlee, the bowler, is a superb machine, but despite his ice-cool exterior he is as sensitive as the next man. In 1983, jaded by continuous cricket and elevated to superstardom in New Zealand, he suffered a minor breakdown; he consulted a psychologist and was rejuvenated for the 1984 season. Deciding to use statistics in a positive way, as a source of motivation, he set himself a carefully constructed series of targets, which provided a stimulus, and as his actual performances measured up to the standards he had set himself, Nottinghamshire and New Zealand continued to prosper.

At the same time New Zealand's batting became more reliable, thanks to their left-handed openers, John Wright and Bruce Edgar, and players such as Howarth and Jeremy Coney in the middle order.

Richard Hadlee: the ultimate craftsman

However, in the eighties they began to be outshone by Martin Crowe, who now rivals the likes of Martin Donnelly, Bert Sutcliffe and John Reid as New Zealand's most accomplished player.

Crowe is another Somerset player; I hope I'm not accused of bias in pointing out that Taunton has been the temporary home of four remarkable batsmen, Greg Chappell, Richards, Gavaskar and now Crowe.

Crowe is remarkable because he manages to be both a perfectionist and a 'team man', a rare combination. The most obvious batting 'perfectionist', Geoff Boycott, was able to detach himself from his surroundings and steel himself to score runs, whatever the circumstances. Usually this ability was of value to the side; just occasionally it was a hindrance. Crowe, whilst determined to be the best of his era, is affected by externals – the state of the game, the mood and form of his team; he cannot play his cricket in a vacuum like Boycott. At the age of 25 he is unquestionably one of the finest batsmen in the world, and if the teams in which he plays (New Zealand and currently Somerset and Central Districts) become sufficiently strong to give him the freedom to play his shots, rather than constantly burdening him with the responsibility of having to bat for five hours, then we shall see him destroying more attacks, instead of merely subduing them.

Finally, back to the oldest rivals, England and Australia. There were times during this period when they appeared to be battling it out for the 'wooden spoon' of international cricket; yet an Ashes series remains the most reliable crowd-puller in both England and Australia.

In four series from 1977 to 1981 England were led by Mike Brearley, and won three of them. Initially the shadow of Packer affected the Australians; in 1977 the controversy erupted and proved a constant distraction to the tourists, who lost three-nil. At Headingley Geoff Boycott, having terminated his self-imposed exile, enjoyed his happiest moment, scoring his 100th hundred in a Test match against Australia on his own ground. John Woodcock once wrote that 'Boycott's idea of bliss might be to bat all night (so long as it was not for Mr Packer) having batted all day'; he might have added 'against Australia at Headingley'.

1983: New Zealand celebrate their well-deserved first Test win in England

Three faces of Geoffrey Boycott, one of the most remarkable players of recent times: ***(opposite below)*** joy at reaching his 100th hundred in 1977, (***opposite above***) dedication pushed to the limits in another 'net' in the West Indies and (***above***) a moment of despair*

In 1978–79 Australia were without their Packer players and lost five-one, though they gained their revenge three-nil the next year after the truce, and in 1981 England won three-one. Even though Brearley never captained England against the West Indies his record is exceptional; out of 31 Tests he won 18 and lost just four. His only problem as an England player was that he didn't score enough runs, which is odd considering his county record. On one occasion in Australia he considered dropping himself – the precedent had been set by Mike Denness in 1974–75 – but his fellow selectors quickly stifled that idea. His captaincy was too important to the team's success. It's not surprising that he was good at it. At Cambridge he was an excellent academic, and intelligence is undoubtedly a key asset for a captain, though not everything. Rodney Hogg once observed that 'he's got a degree in people', which is possibly even more important. In fact he could relate to the more down-to-earth elements in his side, particularly and crucially to Ian Botham, rather more easily than fellow Cantab Phil Edmonds. Despite obvious differences, he could be 'one of the team' as well as its leader.

Below *Brearley reveals his cutting edge in the row with Greg Chappell and Dennis Lillee over the use of the latter's aluminium bat at Perth in 1979*

Above *A typical mix-up between openers Rick Darling and Graeme Wood, at Melbourne in 1978*

Below *Melbourne, 1982: the end of a classic Test. Miller catches Thomson – after the ball has slipped from Tavaré's grasp – for England to win by 3 runs*

All of which was confirmed by the 1981 series in England. In the first two matches a lacklustre English side, led by Ian Botham, went one down in the series, having been defeated at Trent Bridge and comfortably held to a draw at Lord's. In this match Botham collected a pair, and afterwards he resigned the captaincy just before being sacked, a circumstance that was repeated at Somerset in 1985. Brearley, to the delight of Botham and presumably all the other players except perhaps Geoff Boycott, was recalled. In the next three matches Brearley's reputation was sealed – either he was a genius or incredibly lucky – and Botham's standing as a legendary all-rounder (by the way he's the fourth) was established beyond any doubt.

In the third Test at Headingley England appeared doomed. Australia scored 401 and England's reply was a paltry 174, of which an unshackled Botham scored 50. On the Monday, England slumped to 135 for seven, still 92 runs away from avoiding an innings defeat; the bookmakers quoted them at 500 to one to win the match, odds which attracted very few takers, though remarkably Lillee and Marsh were amongst them. With nothing to lose, Botham blazed away and Graham Dilley joined in willingly. Defiant last gestures, we all assumed; even Botham had booked out of the hotel in the morning. Together they added 117 in 18 overs. On Dilley's dismissal Botham kept blasting away, supported first by Chris Old and then more passively by last

Rodney Hogg, who for a time was one of the most devastating fast bowlers in international cricket, bowls John Emburey at Melbourne in 1978

Above *Botham drives Alderman into the stands during his 149 not out at Headingley in 1981*

Bob Willis gives Trevor Chappell a steely glare during his inspired spell on the last day of the 1981 Headingley Test

man Bob Willis, the final session of the day producing 175 runs. On the Tuesday morning five more precious runs were added, with Botham finishing on 149 not out from just 148 balls, a momentous combination of fierce hitting, outside edges and hearty guffaws.

Australia needed 130 to win and at 56 for one appeared safe. Now Bob Willis enjoyed his finest hour. Literally like a man possessed, with glazed eyes and an expressionless face, he pounded down the hill from the Kirkstall Lane end. Throughout this series he had been no-balling frequently, a problem that he never overcame throughout his career. Brearley told him to forget about them; this was not the time to sacrifice speed and hostility for the sake of a few extras. Thus 56 for one became 58 for four at lunch. Now it was obvious that the possibility of defeat had entered the minds of the Australians for the first time in the match. Willis maintained his onslaught, finally finishing the innings by yorking Ray Bright and leaving the field, still glazed, with career-best figures of eight for 43. England had won the most remarkable Test of the modern era by 18 runs.

Two weeks later Edgbaston saw another astonishing English victory. The Headingley wicket had offered assistance to the seam bowlers throughout the match, and Brearley has observed that a collapse was always possible on such a surface. Edgbaston was different; the bounce was lower and more predictable, easier for batting. Australia this time required 151 to win, and after experiencing problems against Emburey had reached 105 for five. Now Brearley turned to Botham, who, uncharacteristically, was reluctant to bowl; he hadn't been happy with his rhythm in this match and didn't feel he was the best option. Brearley, it transpired, knew best. Botham charged in with the hostility of a wounded bear and destroyed the Australian batting, removing the last five wickets for seven runs. After this it was no surprise to hear Brearley describe Botham as 'the greatest matchwinner of all time'. In turn a correspondent to the *Guardian* made this observation of the England captain:

> On Friday I watched J.M. Brearley directing his fieldsmen very carefully. He then looked up at the sun and made a gesture which seemed to indicate that it should move a little squarer. Who is this man?

Botham hadn't finished yet. At Old Trafford, with England's batsmen dawdling and uncertain, he again transformed the game, scoring 118 in two hours. If at Headingley he had ridden his luck and 'had a bit of a slog', this was classical hitting. *Wisden* commented that this innings 'for its ferocious yet

ENGLAND v AUSTRALIA
Played at Leeds, 16, 17, 18, 20, 21 July, 1981.
Result: England won by 18 runs.

Australia: First innings

J. Dyson b Dilley	102
G.M. Wood lbw b Botham	34
T.M. Chappell c Taylor b Willey	27
K.J. Hughes* c and b Botham	89
R.J. Bright b Dilley	7
G.N. Yallop c Taylor b Botham	58
A.R. Border lbw b Botham	8
R.W. Marsh† b Botham	28
G.F. Lawson c Taylor b Botham	13
D.K. Lillee not out	3
T.M. Alderman not out	0
Extras (b 4, lb 13, w 2, nb 12)	32
Total (9 wickets declared)	401

Fall of Wickets: 1/55, 2/149, 3/196, 4/220, 5/332, 6/354, 7/357, 8/396, 9/401.
Bowling: Willis 30-8-72-0, Old 43-14-91-0, Dilley 27-4-78-2, Botham 39.2-11-95-6, Willey 13-2-31-1, Boycott 3-2-2-0.

England: First innings

G.A. Gooch lbw b Alderman	2
G. Boycott b Lawson	12
J.M. Brearley* c Marsh b Alderman	10
D.I. Gower c Marsh b Lawson	24
M.W. Gatting lbw b Lillee	15
P. Willey b Lawson	8
I.T. Botham c Marsh b Lillee	50
R.W. Taylor† c Marsh b Lillee	5
G.R. Dilley c and b Lillee	13
C.M. Old c Border b Alderman	0
R.G.D. Willis not out	1
Extras (b 6, lb 11, w 6, nb 11)	34
Total	174

Fall of Wickets: 1/12, 2/40, 3/42, 4/84, 5/87, 6/112, 7/148, 8/166, 9/167, 10/174.
Bowling: Lillee 18.5-7-49-4, Alderman 19-4-59-3, Lawson 13-3-32-3.

England: Second innings

G.A. Gooch c Alderman b Lillee	0
G. Boycott lbw b Alderman	46
J.M. Brearley* c Alderman b Lillee	14
D.I. Gower c Border b Alderman	9
M.W. Gatting lbw b Alderman	1
P. Willey c Dyson b Lilley	33
I.T. Botham not out	149
R.W. Taylor† c Bright b Alderman	1
G.R. Dilley b Alderman	56
C.M. Old b Lawson	29
R.G.D. Willis c Border b Alderman	2
Extras (b 5, lb 3, w 3, nb 5)	16
Total	356

Fall of Wickets: 1/0, 2/18, 3/37, 4/41, 5/105, 6/133, 7/135, 8/252, 9/319, 10/356.
Bowling: Lillee 25-6-94-3, Alderman 35.3-6-135-6, Lawson 23-4-96-1, Bright 4-0-15-0.

Australia: Second innings

J. Dyson c Taylor b Willis	34
G.M. Wood c Taylor b Botham	10
T.M. Chappell c Taylor b Willis	8
K.J. Hughes* c Botham b Willis	0
R.J. Bright (8) b Willis	19
G.N. Yallop (5) c Gatting b Willis	0
A.R. Border (6) b Old	0
R.W. Marsh† (7) c Dilley b Willis	4
G.F. Lawson c Taylor b Willis	1
D.K. Lillee c Gatting b Willis	17
T.M. Alderman not out	0
Extras (lb 3, w 1, nb 14)	18
Total	111

Fall of Wickets: 1/13, 2/56, 3/58, 4/58, 5/65, 6/68, 7/74, 8/75, 9/110, 10/111.
Bowling: Willis 15.1-3-43-8, Old 9-1-21-1, Dilley 2-0-11-0, Botham 7-3-14-1, Willey 3-1-4-0.

Above *The young Botham could be delicate! Here he is batting on the England tour to Pakistan in 1977–78*

Below *Botham has Sunil Gavaskar caught behind by Bob Taylor in the Jubilee Test at Bombay in 1980*

effortless power and dazzling cleanness of stroke, can surely never have been bettered in a Test match'. By contrast Chris Tavaré's admirable 78 had taken 423 minutes. Despite centuries by Yallop and Border, England won by 103 runs and secured the Ashes. The BBC wisely issued a video of the series with the unsurprising title *Botham's Ashes*. How could he ever repeat such feats?

What else can one say about Ian Botham? To describe him as a forceful right-hand batsman and a fast-medium away-swing bowler is not quite sufficient. Take into account a catalogue of remarkable achievements on the field, beginning with a Benson and Hedges match against Hampshire at Taunton in 1974, following with five wickets on his Test debut at Trent Bridge in 1977, 100 and 10 wickets in the Jubilee Test in Bombay in 1979–80, and the unparalleled performances of 1981. Off the field there have been various controversies, involving drug-taking, assault charges, marathon walks in aid of leukaemia. His name over the last decade has seldom been out of the newspapers. Wherever he plays, people come to watch; this was nicely illustrated in Australia in 1987–88 when Botham was with Queensland, as a result of which the attendances at their Sheffield Shield matches trebled. His decision to play for Queensland seemed a master-

'Guy the Gorilla' meets an old friend of the family, at Old Trafford in 1981

stroke, but again that ability to self-destruct surfaced. As ever Ian was unrepentant.

He is the hardest man to write about because his life moves so swiftly that within six months everything is out of date. However, whatever happens in the next few years, cricket historians will speak of him in the same breath as Grace, Bradman and Sobers. Those off-field escapades will fade from the memory and people will recall only the power and audacity of his hitting and his indomitable will to win. Botham's greatest asset as a cricketer has been that he has never feared failure, something which regularly haunts the average professional sportsman. He sets no limits on what he can achieve, which means that he allows himself to succeed – or fail – spectacularly; most of us settle for safe mediocrity. For this reason he attracts spectators in Grace-like proportions. Indeed, I suspect that W.G. would have loved him, welcoming him as a rival and a drinking partner. We know that Mike Brearley was a devotee; wearing his psychoanalytical helmet, he observed that 'he needs a father figure and I need a younger brother'. In a sense Botham's career has been shackled by his deeds in 1981; every time he enters a cricket field he's expected to produce the extraordinary – and it's remarkable how often he still manages it. Perhaps his back operation will finally reduce him to mortal realms.

Botham's tenure of the England captaincy was brief; typically he refused to believe that captaincy was the reason for his loss of form. Indeed, it is true that his performances against the West Indies are the only flaw in his record, and he captained nine of his 19 Tests against them. In addition the 1980–81 tour of the Caribbean was fraught with problems that would probably have affected any captain – the tragic death of Ken Barrington and Guyana's refusal to admit Robin Jackman because of his South African connections. However, the captaincy did not rest happily on his shoulders; the last thing that Botham needs to do is to try to play 'responsibly' all the time.

After Brearley the selectors turned to Keith Fletcher, acknowledged as the doyen of English county captains; he hadn't played Test cricket for a while, and a desultory series in India, marred by

Ian Botham has never been exactly the soul of discretion – here illustrated on his John O'Groats to Lands End walk in 1986

Keith Fletcher, involved in heated discussion with umpires Krishan and Ramaswami at Bombay in 1981

slow batting and even slower over-rates, persuaded them to change. Left with no obvious candidate, the selectors turned to the senior pro, Bob Willis.

Willis had made himself into England's leading wicket-taker, despite an unorthodox gangling action and wonky knees; he set an excellent personal example on the field, but it was a problem leading the side from the end of a 40-yard run-up. Willis, the life and soul of many England tours, at the back of the bus or in the team room, became a more introspective, withdrawn character when appointed captain. His relationship with the media was always uneasy, and it came as something of a surprise that he should join their ranks after his retirement. However, that someone of such limited technique should survive as long as he did, taking 325 Test wickets, is a tribute to his determination.

Next came Gower. His record would have been excellent, if we hadn't colonised the West Indies. The Indians were defeated two-one, which meant that he joined the rather more controversial figures of Jardine and Greig as the only England captains to win a series in India. He recovered the Ashes in 1985, scoring 732 runs in the series, though it has to be admitted that the 1985 Australians were not a formidable side. During the 1984–85 season Allan Border had taken over the captaincy after the tearful resignation of Kim Hughes, who complained of the 'political factions' in Australian cricket; somehow the aftermath of Packer still lingered on. Border, a

The victorious David Gower in India in 1985

The elegance of David Gower, illustrated during his 215 against Australia at Edgbaston in 1985

Above *Allan Border sweeps another boundary on the way to his 196 at Lord's in 1985*

Kim Hughes: elegant batsman, but uncharismatic leader. Here he drives Chris Old into the pavilion during his magnificent hundred at Lord's in the ill-fated Centenary Test of 1980

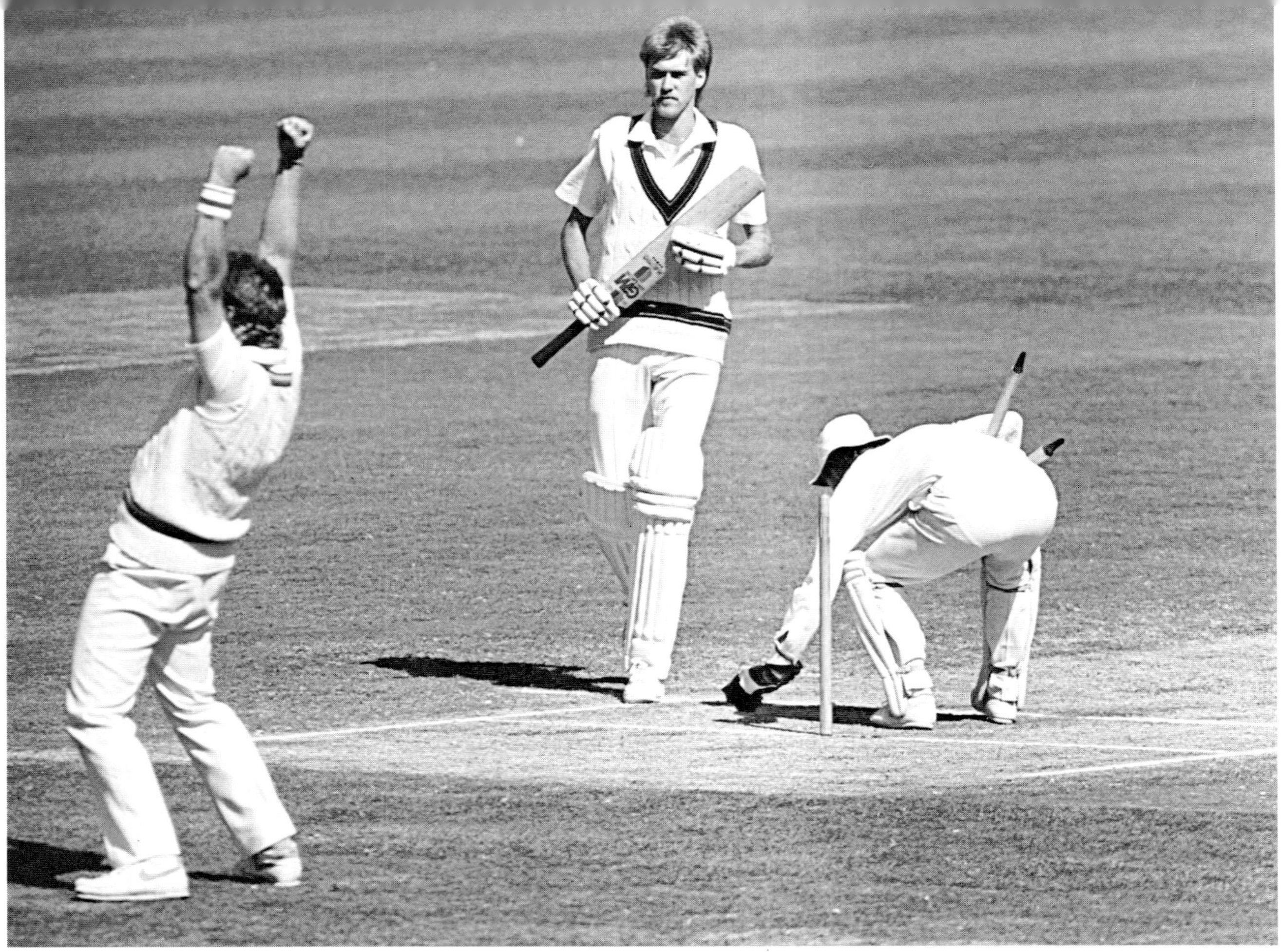

Melbourne, 1986: Merv Hughes has fallen to Phil Edmonds and England have retained the Ashes. **(Right)** *Elton John celebrating with Mike Gatting*

pugnacious, pragmatic left-hander, admirable in a crisis, continued to be Australia's outstanding player, but Test successes remained elusive.

Ten consecutive defeats at the hands of the West Indies led to the end of Gower's tenure. The critics said he was too mild, too laid-back for the England captaincy – 'it's difficult for someone to be more laid-back without being actually comatose', wrote the most unlikely cricket observer, Frances Edmonds, wife of left-arm spinner, Phil. Gower'sproblem, if indeed it is a problem, is that he has a wonderful sense of perspective about the game; it is important to him, but not all-important. The casual shrug of the shoulders was not a sufficiently dramatic reaction after another defeat at the hands of the West Indians. The critics would have been happier if the captain was ranting and raving, which is not Gower's style.

I wonder whether we fully appreciate Gower's worth as a batsman and an entertainer; contemporary players can easily be underestimated. Back in 1963 a headline blazoned from the *Cricketer*, 'Where are the batsmen?' Well, there were Cowdrey, Dexter, Graveney, Barrington for a start. In the year 2000 we shall no doubt be pining for the likes of Gooch, Gatting, Lamb and Gower. Of them all, the slight figure of Gower has been the most durable. When he has failed the doubters have complained that he's too casual, too lazy, forgetting that when he cover-drives to the boundary he also looks casual and lazy. One of Brearley's and Boycott's attributes was that they always looked as if they had been dismissed by an exceptionally good ball; Gower's dismissals appear to be the consequence of a momentary loss of concentration.

The aesthete would always pick Gower – that has never been questioned; but there's a good case for the statistician to pick him as well. So far he's scored over 6,500 Test runs at an average of almost 45, which puts him on a par with the greats of any era. Of all the modern players, I would choose to watch Gower score a century.

Gower was replaced by Mike Gatting, who survived for two years; the greatest threat to his tenure appeared to be the visit of the 1988 West Indians, a frequent stumbling block for recent English Test captains. However, a more devious source ended his reign. Allegations of 'sexual misconduct' during the rest day of the first Test match at Trent Bridge in 1988 were printed in a national newspaper and, after a brief enquiry, Gatting was replaced as England captain by his Middlesex colleague John Emburey. Remarkably the selectors and the TCCB accepted Gatting's version of the incident – and indeed his innocence – but sacked him anyway, presumably adopting the 'Caesar's Wife' approach. I suppose a few newspaper editors enjoyed the whole affair, revelling in increased sales for a day or two, but they were certainly the only benefactors. The England captaincy, once the most sought-after job in cricket, was now an unenviable task. Even without the threat of 'trial by the tabloids' it has become such an arduous job that anyone who survives more than two years must be applauded for his resilience, if nothing else. A bewildering number of Test matches are played each year and the strain on our top cricketers is beginning to tell; in recent years Botham, Gooch and Gower have all chosen to be unavailable for winter tours; financially they had acquired the freedom to take a winter off and they needed to recharge. Gatting's main achievement was the retention of the Ashes in 1985-86 though Test victories against anyone else proved elusive.

Yet it's fatal to draw too many conclusions about the relative merits of the Test playing countries. Who were the finalists in the 1987 World Cup? Australia and England. Australia won, which was a tribute to the doggedness of Allan Border, who had stuck with a job that he didn't particularly want in the first place. The tournament was a great success, superbly organised in an amazing display of cooperation between India and Pakistan – perhaps there is a place for cricket in the modern world, after all.

Who knows what John Wisden would have made of it all in 1988? Certainly he would have been delighted to see the almanack appearing each year bearing his name. The Packer affair would not have stunned him as much as it did the Lord's heirarchy in 1977, though he might have been a little surprised that it hadn't happened before; after all, the escapades of the itinerant All England XI were not that dissimilar. However, he might have been confused by the advent of helmets, night cricket, coloured clothing and white balls. He would be

RELIANCE WORLD CUP FINAL

AUSTRALIA v ENGLAND

Played at Calcutta, 8 November, 1988
Result: Australia won by 7 runs

Australia

D.C. Boon c Downton b Hemmings	75
G.R. Marsh b Foster	24
D.M. Jones c Athey b Hemmings	33
C.J. McDermott b Gooch	14
A.R. Border* run out (Robinson/Downton)	31
M.R. J. Veletta not out	45
S.R. Waugh not out	5
S.P. O'Donnell, G.C. Dyer†, T.B. May, B.A. Reid did not bat	
Extras (b 1, lb 13, w 5, nb 7)	26
Total (50 overs; 5 wickets)	253

Fall of Wickets: 1/75, 2/151, 3/166, 4/168, 5/241.
Bowling: DeFreitas 6-1-34-0, Small 6-0-33-0, Foster 10-0-38-1, Hemmings 10-1-48-2, Emburey 10-0-44-0, Gooch 8-1-42-1.

England

G.A. Gooch lbw b O'Donnell	35
R.T. Robinson lbw b McDermott	0
C.W.J. Athey run out (Waugh/Reid)	58
M.W. Gatting* c Dyer b Border	41
A.J. Lamb b Waugh	45
P.R. Downton† c O'Donnell b Border	9
J.E. Emburey run out (Boon/McDermott)	10
P.A.J. DeFreitas c Reid b Waugh	17
N.A. Foster not out	7
G.C. Small not out	3
E.E. Hemmings did not bat	
Extras (b 1, lb 14, w 2, nb 4)	21
Total (50 overs; 8 wickets)	246

Fall of Wickets: 1/1, 2/66, 3/135, 4/170, 5/188, 6/218, 7/220, 8/235.
Bowling: McDermott 10-1-51-1, Reid 10-0-43-0, Waugh 9-0-37-2, O'Donnell 10-1-35-1, May 4-0-27-0, Border 7-0-38-2.

Above *Jaipur, the sumptuous setting for an England v West Indies match in the 1987 World Cup*

Below *Mike Gatting's fatal reverse sweep – it may well have cost England the 1987 World Cup final*

Above *The Faisalabad row in December 1987: Mike Gatting squares up to Shakoor Rana*

Below *Graeme Hick lofts Somerset's perspiring off-spinner for another six during his 405 not out*

bemused to learn that England had no more than an even chance of defeating Pakistan – if he'd been able to fathom where it was in the first place.

However, the stumps are still 22 yards apart and batsmen still complain about the fickleness of fate and the umpires' decisions. Remarkable deeds on a cricket field still attract widespread public attention despite the proliferation of new 'TV' sports like snooker, darts and bowls; cricket is sufficiently complex and unpredictable to outlast them. New heroes continue to spring up to rival Grace, Bradman and Sobers. I write still smarting from bowling 50 fruitless overs at Graeme Hick, a batsman of Zimbabwe and Worcestershire, who scored 405 not out against Somerset in May 1988 – the highest county score since A.C. MacLaren's 424 at Taunton in 1895. How do we find out such crucial snippets of information? A quick flick through the pages of *Wisden*.

6
THE RECORDS

FIRST-CLASS MATCHES

These records are updated to 6 May 1988, with the exception of career aggregates which are complete to the start of the 1988 season.

TEAM RECORDS

Highest Innings Totals

1107	Victoria v New South Wales	Melbourne	1926-27
1059	Victoria v Tasmania	Melbourne	1922-23
951-7d	Sind v Baluchistan	Karachi	1973-74
918	New South Wales v South Australia	Sydney	1900-01
912-8d	Holkar v Mysore	Indore	1945-46
910-6d	Railways v Dera Ismail Khan	Lahore	1964-65
903-7d	England v Australia	The Oval	1938
887	Yorkshire v Warwickshire	Birmingham	1896
849	England v West Indies	Kingston	1929-30

There have been 23 instances of a team scoring 800 runs or more in an innings, the most recent being by North Zone (800 + 68 penalty runs) v West Zone at Bhilai in the final of the 1987-88 Duleep trophy.

Highest Second Innings Total

770	New South Wales v South Australia	Adelaide	1920-21

Highest Fourth Innings Total

654-5	England v South Africa	Durban	1938-39

Highest Match Aggregate

2376	Maharashtra v Bombay	Poona	1948-49

Record Margin of Victory

Innings and 851 runs	Railways v Dera Ismail Khan	Lahore	1964-65

Most Runs in a Day

721	Australians v Essex	Southend	1948

Most Hundreds in an Innings

6	Holkar v Mysore	Indore	1945-46
5	New South Wales v South Australia	Sydney	1900-01
5	Australia v West Indies	Kingston	1954-55

Lowest Innings Totals

12	+	Oxford University v MCC and Ground	Oxford	1877
12		Northamptonshire v Gloucestershire	Gloucester	1907
13		Auckland v Canterbury	Auckland	1877-78
13		Nottinghamshire v Yorkshire	Nottingham	1901
14		Surrey v Essex	Chelmsford	1983
15	+	MCC v Surrey	Lord's	1839
15		Victoria v MCC	Melbourne	1903-04
15	+	Northamptonshire v Yorkshire	Northampton	1908
15		Hampshire v Warwickshire	Birmingham	1922

+Batted one man short

There have been 26 instances of a team being dismissed for under 20, the most recent being by Surrey in 1983 (above).

Lowest Match Aggregate by One Team

34	(16 and 18) Border v Natal	East London	1959-60

Lowest Completed Match Aggregate by Both Teams

105	MCC v Australians	Lord's	1878

Fewest Runs in an Uninterrupted Day's Play

95	Australia (80) v Pakistan (15-2)	Karachi	1956-57

Tied Matches

Before 1948 a match was considered to be tied if the scores were level after the fourth innings, even if the side batting last had wickets in hand when play ended. Law 22 was amended in 1948 and since then a match has been tied only when the scores are level after the fourth innings has been completed. There have been 46 tied first-class matches, five of which would not have qualified under the current law. The most recent are:

Australia	(574-7d/170-5d) v India (397/347)	Madras	1986-87
Derbyshire	(340/226-5d) v Gloucestershire (288/278)	Bristol	1987

BATTING RECORDS

Highest Individual Innings

499	Hanif Mohammad	Karachi v Bahawalpur	Karachi	1958-59
452*	D.G. Bradman	New South Wales v Queensland	Sydney	1929-30
443*	B.B.Nimbalkar	Maharashtra v Kathiawar	Poona	1948-49
437	W.H. Ponsford	Victoria v Queensland	Melbourne	1927-28
429	W.H.Ponsford	Victoria v Tasmania	Melbourne	1922-23
428	Aftab Baloch	Sind v Baluchistan	Karachi	1973-74
424	A.C. MacLaren	Lancashire v Somerset	Taunton	1895
405*	G.A.Hick	Worcestershire v Somerset	Taunton	1988
385	B.Sutcliffe	Otago v Canterbury	Christchurch	1952-53
383	C.W.Gregory	New South Wales v Queensland	Brisbane	1906-07
369	D.G.Bradman	South Australia v Tasmania	Adelaide	1935-36
365*	C.Hill	South Australia v NSW	Adelaide	1900-01
365*	G.St A.Sobers	West Indies v Pakistan	Kingston	1957-58
364	L.Hutton	England v Australia	The Oval	1938
359*	V.M.Merchant	Bombay v Maharashtra	Bombay	1943-44
359	R.B.Simpson	New South Wales v Queensland	Brisbane	1963-64
357*	R.Abel	Surrey v Somerset	The Oval	1899

357	D.G.Bradman	South Australia v Victoria	Melbourne	1935-36
356	B.A.Richards	S Australia v W Australia	Perth	1970-71
355	B.Sutcliffe	Otago v Auckland	Dunedin	1949-50
352	W.H.Ponsford	Victoria v New South Wales	Melbourne	1926-27
350	Rashid Israr	Habib Bank v National Bank	Lahore	1976-77

There have been 99 triple hundreds in first-class cricket, the most recent being 405* by G.A.Hick on 5/6 May 1988 as above. The most recent overseas is 320 by R.Lamba for North Zone v West Zone at Bhilai in 1987-88.

Most Hundreds in Successive Innings

6	C.B.Fry	Sussex and Rest of England	1901
6	D.G.Bradman	South Australia and D.G.Bradman's XI	1938-39
6	M.J.Procter	Rhodesia	1970-71
5	E.de C.Weekes	West Indians (in New Zealand)	1955-56

Two Double Hundreds in a Match

244,202*	A.E.Fagg	Kent v Essex	Colchester	1938

Double Hundred and Hundred in a Match Most Times

4	Zaheer Abbas	Gloucestershire	1976-81

Two Hundreds in a Match Most Times

8	Zaheer Abbas	Gloucestershire and PIA	1976-82
7	W.R.Hammond	Gloucestershire, England and MCC	1927-45

Most Hundreds in a Season

18	D.C.S.Compton	1947
16	J.B.Hobbs	1925
15	W.R.Hammond	1938

Most Hundreds in a Career

(The season in which the player's 100th hundred was scored is given in brackets)

197	J.B. Hobbs (1923)
170	E.H. Hendren (1928-29)
167	W.R.Hammond (1935)
153	C.P.Mead (1927)
151	G.Boycott (1977)
149	H.Sutcliffe (1932)
145	F.E.Woolley (1929)
129	L.Hutton (1951)
126	W.G.Grace (1895)
123	D.C.S.Compton (1952)
122	T.W.Graveney (1964)
117	D.G. Bradman (1947-48)
108	Zaheer Abbas (1982-83)
107	A.Sandham (1935)
107	M.C.Cowdrey (1973)
104	T.W.Hayward (1913)
103	J.H.Edrich (1977)
103	G.M.Turner (1982)
102	E.Tyldesley (1934)
102	L.E.G.Ames (1950)
102	D.L.Amiss (1986)

Most Runs in a Month

1294	(avge 92.42)	L.Hutton	Yorkshire	June 1949

Most Runs in a Season

Runs			*I*	*NO*	*HS*	*Avge*	*100*	*Season*
3816	D.C.S.Compton	Middlesex	50	8	246	90.85	18	1947
3539	W.J.Edrich	Middlesex	52	8	267*	80.43	12	1947
3518	T.W.Hayward	Surrey	61	8	219	66.37	13	1906

The feat of scoring 3000 runs in a season has been achieved on 28 occasions, the most recent instance being by W.E.Alley (3019) in 1961. The highest aggregate in a season since 1969, when the number of County Championship matches was substantially reduced, is 2559 by G.A.Gooch in 1984.

1000 Runs in a Season Most Times

28 W.G.Grace (Gloucestershire), F.E.Woolley (Kent)

Highest Batting Average in a Season

(Qualification: 12 innings)

Avge			*I*	*NO*	*HS*	*Runs*	*100*	*Season*
115.66	D.G.Bradman	Australians	26	5	278	2429	13	1938
102.53	G.Boycott	Yorkshire	20	5	175*	1538	6	1979
102.00	W.A.Johnston	Australians	17	16	28*	102	-	1953
100.12	G.Boycott	Yorkshire	30	5	233	2503	13	1971

Fastest Hundred

35 min	P.G.H.Fender	Surrey v Northamptonshire	Northampton	1920
35 min	S.J. O'Shaughnessy	Lancashire v Leicestershire	Manchester	1983

Fastest Double Hundred

113 min	R.J.Shastri	Bombay v Baroda	Bombay	1984-85

Fastest Triple Hundred

181 min	D.C.S.Compton	MCC v NE Transvaal	Benoni	1948-49

Most Sixes in an Innings

15	J.R.Reid	Wellington v N Districts	Wellington	1962-63
13	Majid Khan	Pakistanis v Glamorgan	Swansea	1967
13	C.G. Greenidge	D.H. Robins' XI v Pakistanis	Eastbourne	1974
13	C.G.Greenidge	Hampshire v Sussex	Southampton	1975
13	G.W.Humpage	Warwickshire v Lancashire	Southport	1982
13	R.J.Shastri	Bombay v Baroda	Bombay	1984-85

Most Sixes in a Match

17	W.J.Stewart	Warwickshire v Lancashire	Blackpool	1959

Most Sixes in a Season

80	I.T.Botham	Somerset and England	1985

Most Boundaries in an Innings

68	P.A.Perrin	Essex v Derbyshire	Chesterfield	1904

Most Runs off One Over

36	G.St A.Sobers	Nottinghamshire v Glamorgan	Swansea	1968
36	R.J.Shastri	Bombay v Baroda	Bombay	1984-85

Both batsmen hit all six balls of an over (bowled by M.A.Nash and Tilak Raj respectively) for six.

Most Runs in a Day

345	C.G.Macartney	Australians v Nottinghamshire	Nottingham	1921

There have been 17 instances of a batsman scoring 300 or more runs in a day, the most recent being by K.R.Rutherford (317) for the New Zealanders v D.B.Close's XI at Scarborough in 1986.

Highest Partnerships

First Wicket				
561	Waheed Mirza/Mansoor Akhtar	Karachi W v Quetta	Karachi	1976-77
555	P.Holmes/H.Sutcliffe	Yorkshire v Essex	Leyton	1932
554	J.T.Brown/J.Tunnicliffe	Yorkshire v Derbys	Chesterfield	1898
Second Wicket				
465*	J.A.Jameson/R.B.Kanhai	Warwickshire v Glos	Birmingham	1974
455	K.V.Bhandarkar/B.B.Nimbalkar	Maha'tra v Kathiawar	Poona	1948-49
451	D.G. Bradman/W.H .Ponsford	Australia v England	The Oval	1934
Third Wicket				
456	Khalid Irtiza/Aslam Ali	United Bank v Multan	Karachi	1975-76
451	Mudassar Nazar/Javed Miandad	Pakistan v India	Hyderabad	1982-83
445	P.E.Whitelaw/W.N.Carson	Auckland v Otago	Dunedin	1936-37
434	J.B.Stollmeyer/G.E.Gomez	Trinidad v Br Guiana	Port-of-Spain	1946-47
424*	W.J.Edrich/D.C.S.Compton	Middlesex v Somerset	Lord's	1948
Fourth Wicket				
577	V.S.Hazare/Gul Mahomed	Baroda v Holkar	Baroda	1946-47
574*	C.L.Walcott/F.M.M.Worrell	Barbados v Trinidad	Port-of-Spain	1945-46
502*	F.M.M.Worrell/J.D.C.Goddard	Barbados v Trinidad	Bridgetown	1943-44
470	A.I.Kallicharran/G.W.Humpage	Warwickshire v Lancs	Southport	1982
Fifth Wicket				
405	S.G.Barnes/D.G.Bradman	Australia v England	Sydney	1946-47
397	W.Bardsley/C.Kelleway	NSW v S Australia	Sydney	1920-21
393	E.G.Arnold/W.B.Burns	Worcs v Warwickshire	Birmingham	1909
Sixth Wicket				
487*	G.A.Headley/C.C.Passailaigue	Jamaica v Tennyson's	Kingston	1931-32
428	W.W.Armstrong/M.A.Noble	Australians v Sussex	Hove	1902
411	R.M.Poore/E.G.Wynyard	Hampshire v Somerset	Taunton	1899
Seventh Wicket				
347	D.St E.Atkinson/C.C.Depeiza	W Indies v Australia	Bridgetown	1954-55
344	K.S.Ranjitsinhji/W.Newham	Sussex v Essex	Leyton	1902
340	K.J.Key/H.Philipson	Oxford U v Middlesex	Chiswick Park	1887
Eighth Wicket				
433	A.Sims/V.T.Trumper	Australians v C'bury	Christchurch	1913-14
292	R.Peel/Lord Hawke	Yorkshire v Warwicks	Birmingham	1896
270	V.T.Trumper/E.P.Barbour	NSW v Victoria	Sydney	1912-13

Ninth Wicket

283	J.Chapman/A.Warren	Derbys v Warwicks	Blackwell	1910
251	J.W.H.T.Douglas/S.N.Hare	Essex v Derbyshire	Leyton	1921
245	V.S.Hazare/N.D.Nagarwalla	Maharashtra v Baroda	Poona	1939-40

Tenth Wicket

307	A.F.Kippax/J.E.H.Hooker	NSW v Victoria	Melbourne	1928-29
249	C.T.Sarwate/S.N.Bannerjee	Indians v Surrey	The Oval	1946
235	F.E.Woolley/A.Fielder	Kent v Worcs	Stourbridge	1909

Most Runs in a Career

	Career	*I*	*NO*	*HS*	*Runs*	*Avge*	*100*
J.B.Hobbs	1905-34	1315	106	316*	61237	50.65	197
F.E.Woolley	1906-38	1532	85	305*	58969	40.75	145
E.H.Hendren	1907-38	1300	166	301*	57611	50.80	170
C.P.Mead	1905-36	1340	185	280*	55061	47.67	153
W.G.Grace	1865-1908	1493	105	344	54896	39.55	126
W.R.Hammond	1920-51	1005	104	336*	50551	56.10	167
H.Sutcliffe	1919-45	1088	123	313	50138	51.95	149
G.Boycott	1962-86	1014	162	261*	48426	56.83	151
T.W.Graveney	1948-71/72	1223	159	258	47793	44.91	122
T.W.Hayward	1893-1914	1138	96	315*	43551	41.79	104
D.L.Amiss	1960-87	1139	126	262*	43423	42.86	102
M.C.Cowdrey	1950-76	1130	134	307	42719	42.89	107
A.Sandham	1911-1937/38	1000	79	325	41284	44.82	107
L.Hutton	1934-60	814	91	364	40140	55.51	129
M.J.K.Smith	1951-75	1091	139	204	39832	41.84	69
W.Rhodes	1898-1930	1528	237	267*	39802	30.83	58
J.H.Edrich	1956-78	979	104	310*	39790	45.47	103
R.E.S.Wyatt	1923-57	1141	157	232	39405	40.04	85
D.C.S.Compton	1936-64	839	88	300	38942	51.85	123
E.Tyldesley	1909-36	961	106	256*	38874	45.46	102
J.T.Tyldesley	1895-1923	994	62	295*	37897	40.60	86
K.W.R.Fletcher	1962-87	1153	167	228*	37362	37.89	63
J.W.Hearne	1909-36	1025	116	285*	37252	40.98	96
L.E.G.Ames	1926-51	951	95	295	37248	43.51	102
D.Kenyon	1946-67	1159	59	259	37002	33.63	74
W.J.Edrich	1934-58	964	92	267*	36965	42.39	86
J.M.Parks	1949-76	1227	172	205*	36673	34.76	51
D.Denton	1894-1920	1163	70	221	36479	33.37	69
G.H.Hirst	1891-1929	1215	151	341	36323	34.13	60
A.Jones	1957-83	1168	72	204*	36049	32.89	56
W.G.Quaife	1894-1928	1203	185	255*	36012	35.37	72
R.E.Marshall	1945/46-72	1053	59	228*	35725	35.94	68
G.Gunn	1902-32	1061	82	220	35208	35.96	62

BOWLING RECORDS

All Ten Wickets in an Innings

This feat has been achieved on 71 occasions at first-class level.
Three Times: A.P.Freeman (1929, 1930, 1931)
Twice: V.E.Walker (1859, 1865); H.Verity (1931, 1932); J.C.Laker (1956)

Instances since 1945:

W.E.Hollies	Warwickshire v Notts	Birmingham	1946
J.M.Sims	East v West	Kingston on Thames	1948

J.K.R.Graveney	Gloucestershire v Derbyshire	Chesterfield	1949
T.E.Bailey	Essex v Lancashire	Clacton	1949
R.Berry	Lancashire v Worcestershire	Blackpool	1953
S.P.Gupte	President's XI v Combined XI	Bombay	1954-55
J.C.Laker	Surrey v Australians	Oval	1956
K.Smales	Nottinghamshire v Glos	Stroud	1956
G.A.R.Lock	Surrey v Kent	Blackheath	1956
J.C.Laker	England v Australia	Manchester	1956
P.M.Chatterjee	Bengal v Assam	Jorhat	1956-57
J.D.Bannister	Warwicks v Combined Services	Birmingham	1959
A.J.G.Pearson	Cambridge U v Leicestershire	Loughborough	1961
N.I.Thomson	Sussex v Warwickshire	Worthing	1964
P.J.Allan	Queensland v Victoria	Melbourne	1965-66
I.J.Brayshaw	Western Australia v Victoria	Perth	1967-68
Shahid Mahmood	Karachi Whites v Khairpur	Karachi	1969-70
E.E.Hemmings	International XI v W Indians	Kingston	1982-83
P.Sunderam	Rajasthan v Vidarbha	Jodhpur	1985-86
S.T.Jefferies	Western Province v OFS	Cape Town	1987-88

Most Wickets in a Match

19	J.C.Laker	England v Australia	Manchester	1956

Most Wickets in a Season

Wkts		*Season*	*Matches*	*Overs*	*Mdns*	*Runs*	*Avge*
304	A.P.Freeman	1928	37	1976.1	423	5489	18.05
298	A.P.Freeman	1933	33	2039	651	4549	15.26

The feat of taking 250 wickets in a season has being achieved on 12 occasions, the last instance being by A.P.Freeman in 1933. 200 or more wickets in a season have been taken on 59 occasions, the last being by G.A.R.Lock (212 wickets, average 12.02) in 1957.

The highest aggregates of wickets taken in a season since the reduction of the County Championship matches in 1969 are as follows:

Wkts		*Season*	*Matches*	*Overs*	*Mdns*	*Runs*	*Avge*
134	M.D.Marshall	1982	22	822	225	2108	15.73
131	L.R.Gibbs	1971	23	1024.1	295	2475	18.89
121	R.D.Jackman	1980	23	746.2	220	1864	15.40

Since 1969 there have been 42 instances of bowlers taking 100 wickets in a season.

Most Hat-Tricks in a Career

7 D.V.P.Wright
6 T.W.J.Goddard, C.W.L.Parker
5 S.Haigh, V.W.C.Jupp, A.E.G.Rhodes, F.A.Tarrant

Most Wickets in a Career

	Career	*Runs*	*Wkts*	*Avge*	*100w*
W.Rhodes	1898-1930	69993	4187	16.71	23
A.P.Freeman	1914-36	69577	3776	18.42	17
C.W.L.Parker	1903-35	63817	3278	19.46	16
J.T.Hearne	1888-1923	54352	3061	17.75	15
T.W.J.Goddard	1922-52	59116	2979	19.84	16
W.G.Grace	1865-1908	51545	2876	17.92	10
A.S.Kennedy	1907-36	61034	2874	21.23	15
D.Shackleton	1948-69	53303	2857	18.65	20
G.A.R.Lock	1946-70/71	54709	2844	19.23	14

F.J.Titmus	1949-82	63313	2830	22.37	16
M.W.Tate	1912-37	50571	2784	18.16	13*
G.H.Hirst	1891-1929	51282	2739	18.72	15
C.Blythe	1899-1914	42136	2506	16.81	14
D.L.Underwood	1963-87	49993	2465	20.28	10
W.E.Astill	1906-39	57783	2431	23.76	9
J.C.White	1909-37	43759	2356	18.57	14
W.E.Hollies	1932-57	48656	2323	20.94	14
F.S.Trueman	1949-69	42154	2304	18.29	12
J.B.Statham	1950-68	36995	2260	16.36	13
R.T.D.Perks	1930-55	53770	2233	24.07	16
J.Briggs	1879-1900	35430	2221	15.95	12
D.J.Shepherd	1950-72	47302	2218	21.32	12
E.G.Dennett	1903-26	42571	2147	19.82	12
T.Richardson	1892-1905	38794	2104	18.43	10
T.E.Bailey	1945-67	48170	2082	23.13	9
R.Illingworth	1951-83	42023	2072	20.28	10
F.E.Woolley	1906-38	41066	2068	19.85	8
G.Geary	1912-38	41339	2063	20.03	11
D.V.P.Wright	1932-57	49307	2056	23.98	10
N.Gifford	1960-87	47755	2037	23.44	4
J.A.Newman	1906-30	51111	2032	25.15	9
A.Shaw	1864-97	24579	2027*	12.12	9
S.Haigh	1895-1913	32091	2012	15.94	11

* Excluding one wicket for which no analysis is available

ALL-ROUND RECORDS

The 'Double'

3000 runs and 100 wickets: J.H.Parks (1937)
2000 runs and 200 wickets: G.H.Hirst (1906)
2000 runs and 100 wickets: F.E.Woolley (4), J.W.Hearne (3), W.G.Grace (2), G.H.Hirst (2), W.Rhodes (2), T.E.Bailey, D.E.Davies, G.L.Jessop, V.W.C.Jupp, James Langridge, F.A.Tarrant, C.L.Townsend, L.F.Townsend
1000 runs and 200 wickets: M.W.Tate (3), A.E.Trott (2), A.S.Kennedy
Most Doubles: W.Rhodes (16), G.H.Hirst (14), V.W.C.Jupp (10)
Double in debut season: D.B.Close (1949) – aged 18, he is the youngest to achieve this feat

The feat of scoring 1000 runs and taking 100 wickets in a season has been achieved on 304 occasions, the last instance being by R.J.Hadlee in 1984.

WICKET-KEEPING RECORDS

Most Dismissals in an Innings

8	(8ct)	A.T.W.Grout	Queensland v W Australia	Brisbane	1959-60
8	(8ct)	D.E.East	Essex v Somerset	Taunton	1985

Most Dismissals in a Match

12	(8ct, 4st)	E.Pooley	Surrey v Sussex	The Oval	1868
12	(9ct, 3st)	D.Tallon	Queensland v NSW	Sydney	1938-39
12	(9ct, 3st)	H.B.Taber	NSW v South Australia	Adelaide	1968-69

Most Catches in a Match

11	A.Long	Surrey v Sussex	Hove	1964
11	R.W.Marsh	W Australia v Victoria	Perth	1975-76
11	D.L.Bairstow	Yorkshire v Derbyshire	Scarborough	1982

Most Dismissals in a Season

128 (79ct, 49st) L.E.G. Ames 1929

Most Dismissals in a Career

	Career	*Dismissals*	*Ct*	*St*
R.W.Taylor	1960-86	1648	1473	175
J.T.Murray	1952-75	1527	1270	257
H.Strudwick	1902-27	1497	1242	255
A.P.E.Knott	1964-85	1344	1211	133
F.H.Huish	1895-1914	1310	933	377
B.Taylor	1949-73	1294	1083	211
D.Hunter	1889-1909	1253	906	347
H.R.Butt	1890-1912	1228	953	275
J.H.Board	1891-1914/15	1207	852	355
H.Elliott	1920-47	1206	904	302
J.M.Parks	1949-76	1181	1088	93
R.Booth	1951-70	1126	948	178
L.E.G.Ames	1926-51	1121	703	418
G.Duckworth	1923-47	1095	753	342
H.W.Stephenson	1948-64	1082	748	334
J.G.Binks	1955-75	1071	895	176
T.G.Evans	1939-69	1066	816	250
A.Long	1960-80	1046	922	124
G.O.Dawkes	1937-61	1043	895	148
R.W.Tolchard	1965-83	1037	912	125
D.L.Bairstow	1970-87	1024	888	136
W.L.Cornford	1921-47	1017	675	342

FIELDING RECORDS

Most Catches

Innings: 7 M.J.Stewart Surrey v Northants Northampton 1957
7 A.S.Brown Glos v Notts Nottingham 1966
Match: 10 W.R.Hammond Glos v Surrey Cheltenham 1928
Season: 78 W.R.Hammond (1928); 77 M.J.Stewart (1957)
Career: 1018 F.E.Woolley; 887 W.G.Grace; 831 G.A.R.Lock; 819 W.R.Hammond; 813 D.B.Close; 784 J.G.Langridge; 764 W.Rhodes; 758 C.A.Milton; 754 E.H.Hendren.

TEST CRICKET RECORDS

updated to 1 June 1988

TEAM RECORDS

Highest Innings Totals

903-7d	England v Australia	The Oval	1938
849	England v West Indies	Kingston	1929-30
790-3d	West Indies v Pakistan	Kingston	1957-58
758-8d	Australia v West Indies	Kingston	1954-55
729-6d	Australia v England	Lord's	1930
708	Pakistan v England	The Oval	1987
701	Australia v England	The Oval	1934
695	Australia v England	The Oval	1930
687-8d	West Indies v England	The Oval	1976
681-8d	West Indies v England	Port-of-Spain	1953-54

676-7	India v Sri Lanka	Kanpur	1986-87
674-6	Pakistan v India	Faisalabad	1984-85
674	Australia v India	Adelaide	1947-48
668	Australia v West Indies	Bridgetown	1954-55
659-8d	Australia v England	Sydney	1946-47
658-8d	England v Australia	Nottingham	1938
657-8d	Pakistan v West Indies	Bridgetown	1957-58
656-8d	Australia v England	Manchester	1964
654-5	England v South Africa	Durban	1938-39
652-7d	England v India	Madras	1984-85
652-8d	West Indies v England	Lord's	1973
652	Pakistan v India	Faisalabad	1982-83
650-6d	Australia v West Indies	Bridgetown	1964-65

The highest innings for other countries are:

622-9d	South Africa v Australia	Durban	1969-70
553-7d	New Zealand v Australia	Brisbane	1985-86
491-7d	Sri Lanka v England	Lord's	1984

Lowest Innings Totals

26	New Zealand v England	Auckland	1954-55
30	South Africa v England	Port Elizabeth	1895-96
30	South Africa v England	Birmingham	1924
35	South Africa v England	Cape Town	1898-99
36	Australia v England	Birmingham	1902
36	South Africa v Australia	Melbourne	1931-32
42	Australia v England	Sydney	1887-88
42	New Zealand v Australia	Wellington	1945-46
42	India v England	Lord's	1974
43	South Africa v England	Cape Town	1888-89
44	Australia v England	The Oval	1896
45	England v Australia	Sydney	1886-87
45	South Africa v Australia	Melbourne	1931-32
47	South Africa v England	Cape Town	1888-89
47	New Zealand v England	Lord's	1958

The lowest innings for other countries are:

53	West Indies v Pakistan	Faisalabad	1986-87
62	Pakistan v Australia	Perth	1981-82
93	Sri Lanka v New Zealand	Wellington	1982-83

BATTING RECORDS

Highest Individual Innings

365*	G.St A.Sobers	WI v P	Kingston	1957-58
364	L.Hutton	E v A	The Oval	1938
337	Hanif Mohammad	P v WI	Bridgetown	1957-58
336*	W.R.Hammond	E v NZ	Auckland	1932-33
334	D.G.Bradman	A v E	Leeds	1930
325	A.Sandham	E v WI	Kingston	1929-30
311	R.B.Simpson	A v E	Manchester	1964
310*	J.H.Edrich	E v NZ	Leeds	1965
307	R.M.Cowper	A v E	Melbourne	1965-66
304	D.G.Bradman	A v E	Leeds	1934
302	L.G.Rowe	WI v E	Bridgetown	1973-74

299*	D.G.Bradman	A v SA	Adelaide	1931-32
291	I.V.A.Richards	WI v E	The Oval	1976
287	R.E.Foster	E v A	Sydney	1903-04
285*	P.B.H.May	E v WI	Birmingham	1957
280*	Javed Miandad	P v I	Hyderabad	1982-83
278	D.C.S.Compton	E v P	Nottingham	1954
274	R.G.Pollock	SA v A	Durban	1969-70
274	Zaheer Abbas	P v E	Birmingham	1971
270*	G.A.Headley	WI v E	Kingston	1934-35
270	D.G.Bradman	A v E	Melbourne	1936-37
268	G.N.Yallop	A v P	Melbourne	1983-84
266	W.H.Ponsford	A v E	The Oval	1934
262*	D.L.Amiss	E v WI	Kingston	1973-74
261	F.M.M.Worrell	WI v E	Nottingham	1950
260	C.C.Hunte	WI v P	Kingston	1957-58
260	Javed Miandad	P v E	The Oval	1987
259	G.M.Turner	NZ v WI	Georgetown	1971-72
258	T.W.Graveney	E v WI	Nottingham	1957
258	S.M.Nurse	WI v NZ	Christchurch	1968-69
256	R.B.Kanhai	WI v I	Calcutta	1958-59
256	K.F.Barrington	E v A	Manchester	1964
255*	D.J.McGlew	SA v NZ	Wellington	1952-53
254	D.G.Bradman	A v E	Lord's	1930
251	W.R.Hammond	E v A	Sydney	1928-29
250	K.D.Walters	A v NZ	Christchurch	1976-77
250	S.F.A.F.Bacchus	WI v I	Kanpur	1978-79

The highest individual innings for other countries are:

236*	S.M.Gavaskar	I v WI	Madras	1983-84
201*	D.S.B.P.Kuruppu	SL v NZ	Colombo (CCC)	1986-87

Most Runs in a Series

Runs			*Series*	*M*	*I*	*NO*	*HS*	*Avge*	*100*	*50*
974	D.G.Bradman	A v E	1930	5	7	0	334	139.14	4	-
905	W.R.Hammond	E v A	1928-29	5	9	1	251	113.12	4	-
834	R.N.Harvey	A v SA	1952-53	5	9	0	205	92.66	4	3
829	I.V.A.Richards	WI v E	1976	4	7	0	291	118.42	3	2
827	C.L.Walcott	WI v A	1954-55	5	10	0	155	82.70	5	2
824	G.St A.Sobers	WI v P	1957-58	5	8	2	365*	137.33	3	3
810	D.G.Bradman	A v E	1936-37	5	9	0	270	90.00	3	1
806	D.G.Bradman	A v SA	1931-32	5	5	1	299*	201.50	4	-
779	E.de C.Weekes	WI v I	1948-49	5	7	0	194	111.28	4	2
774	S.M.Gavaskar	I v WI	1970-71	4	8	3	220	154.80	4	3
761	Mudassar Nazar	P v I	1982-83	6	8	2	231	126.83	4	1
758	D.G.Bradman	A v E	1934	5	8	0	304	94.75	2	1
753	D.C.S.Compton	E v SA	1947	5	8	0	208	94.12	4	2

Record Wicket Partnerships

1st	413	V.Mankad/Pankaj Roy	I v NZ	Madras	1955-56
2nd	451	W.H.Ponsford/D.G.Bradman	A v E	The Oval	1934
3rd	451	Mudassar Nazar/Javed Miandad	P v I	Hyderabad	1982-83

4th	411	P.B.H.May/M.C.Cowdrey	E v WI	Birmingham	1957
5th	405	S.G.Barnes/D.G.Bradman	A v E	Sydney	1946-47
6th	346	J.H.W.Fingleton/D.G.Bradman	A v E	Melbourne	1936-37
7th	347	D.St E.Atkinson/C.C.Depeiza	WI v A	Bridgetown	1954-55
8th	246	L.E.G.Ames/G.O.B.Allen	E v NZ	Lord's	1931
9th	190	Asif Iqbal/Intikhab Alam	P v E	The Oval	1967
10th	151	B.F.Hastings/R.O.Collinge	NZ v P	Auckland	1972-73

Wicket Partnerships of Over 300

451	2nd	W.H.Ponsford/D.G.Bradman	A v E	The Oval	1934
451	3rd	Mudassar Nazar/Javed Miandad	P v I	Hyderabad	1982-83
446	2nd	C.C.Hunte/G.St A.Sobers	WI v P	Kingston	1957-58
413	1st	V.Mankad/Pankaj Roy	I v NZ	Madras	1955-56
411	4th	P.B.H.May/M.C.Cowdrey	E v WI	Birmingham	1957
405	5th	S.G.Barnes/D.G.Bradman	A v E	Sydney	1946-47
399	4th	G.St A.Sobers/F.M.M.Worrell	WI v E	Bridgetown	1959-60
397	3rd	Qasim Omar/Javed Miandad	P v SL	Faisalabad	1985-86
388	4th	W.H.Ponsford/D.G.Bradman	A v E	Leeds	1934
387	1st	G.M.Turner/T.W.Jarvis	NZ v WI	Georgetown	1971-72
382	2nd	L.Hutton/M.Leyland	E v A	The Oval	1938
382	1st	W.M.Lawry/R.B.Simpson	A v WI	Bridgetown	1964-65
370	3rd	W.J.Edrich/D.C.S.Compton	E v SA	Lord's	1947
369	2nd	J.H.Edrich/K.F.Barrington	E v NZ	Leeds	1965
359	1st	L.Hutton/C.Washbrook	E v SA	Jo'burg	1948-49
351	2nd	G.A.Gooch/D.I.Gower	E v A	The Oval	1985
350	4th	Mushtaq Mohammad/Asif Iqbal	P v NZ	Dunedin	1972-73
347	7th	D.St E.Atkinson/C.C.Depeiza	WI v A	Bridgetown	1954-55
346	6th	J.H.W.Fingleton/D.G.Bradman	A v E	Melbourne	1936-37
344*	2nd	S.M.Gavaskar/D.B.Vengsarkar	I v WI	Calcutta	1978-79
341	3rd	E.J.Barlow/R.G.Pollock	SA v A	Adelaide	1963-64
338	3rd	E.de C.Weekes/F.M.M.Worrell	WI v E	Pt-of-Spain	1953-54
336	4th	W.M.Lawry/K.D.Walters	A v WI	Sydney	1968-69
331	2nd	R.T.Robinson/D.I.Gower	E v A	Birmingham	1985
323	1st	J.B.Hobbs/W.Rhodes	E v A	Melbourne	1911-12
319	3rd	A.Melville/A.D.Nourse	SA v E	Nottingham	1947
316+	3rd	G.R.Viswanath/Yashpal Sharma	I v E	Madras	1981-82
308	7th	Waqar Hassan/Imtiaz Ahmed	P v NZ	Lahore	1955-56
308	3rd	R.B.Richardson/I.V.A.Richards	WI v A	St John's	1983-84
303	3rd	I.V.A.Richards/A.I.Kallicharran	WI v E	Nottingham	1976
301	2nd	A.R.Morris/D.G.Bradman	A v E	Leeds	1948

+ 415 runs were added for this wicket in two separate partnerships. D.B.Vengsarkar retired hurt and was replaced by Yashpal Sharma after 99 runs had been added.

4000 Runs in Tests

Runs			*M*	*I*	*NO*	*HS*	*Avge*	*100*	*50*
10122	S.M.Gavaskar	I	125	214	16	236*	51.12	34	45
8114	G.Boycott	E	108	193	23	246*	47.72	22	42
8032	G.St A.Sobers	WI	93	160	21	365*	57.78	26	30
7624	M.C.Cowdrey	E	114	188	15	182	44.06	22	38
7515	C.H.Lloyd	WI	110	175	14	242*	46.67	19	39
7343	A.R.Border	A	94	164	27	205	53.59	22	34

Runs			*M*	*I*	*NO*	*HS*	*Avge*	*100*	*50*
7249	W.R.Hammond	E	85	140	16	336*	58.45	22	24
7110	G.S.Chappell	A	87	151	19	247*	53.86	24	31
7045	I.V.A.Richards	WI	94	141	9	291	53.37	22	31
6996	D.G.Bradman	A	52	80	10	334	99.94	29	13
6971	L.Hutton	E	79	138	15	364	56.67	19	33
6806	K.F.Barrington	E	82	131	15	256	58.67	20	35
6789	D.I.Gower	E	96	164	12	215	44.66	14	34
6621	Javed Miandad	P	92	141	18	280*	53.82	17	35
6256	D.B.Vengsarkar	I	98	158	22	166	46.00	17	30
6227	R.B.Kanhai	WI	79	137	6	256	47.53	15	28
6149	R.N.Harvey	A	79	137	10	205	48.41	21	24
6080	G.R.Viswanath	I	91	155	10	222	41.93	14	35
5904	C.G.Greenidge	WI	83	140	14	223	46.85	14	30
5807	D.C.S.Compton	E	78	131	15	278	50.06	17	28
5410	J.B.Hobbs	E	61	102	7	211	56.94	15	28
5357	K.D.Walters	A	74	125	14	250	48.26	15	33
5345	I.M.Chappell	A	75	136	10	196	42.42	14	26
5234	W.M.Lawry	A	67	123	12	210	47.15	13	27
5138	J.H.Edrich	E	77	127	9	310*	43.54	12	24
5062	Zaheer Abbas	P	78	124	11	274	44.79	12	20
5057	I.T.Botham	E	94	150	5	208	34.87	14	22
4882	T.W.Graveney	E	79	123	13	258	44.38	11	20
4869	R.B.Simpson	A	62	111	7	311	46.81	10	27
4737	I.R.Redpath	A	66	120	11	171	43.45	8	31
4555	H.Sutcliffe	E	54	84	9	194	60.73	16	23
4537	P.B.H.May	E	66	106	9	285*	46.77	13	22
4502	E.R.Dexter	E	62	102	8	205	47.89	9	27
4455	E.de C.Weekes	WI	48	81	5	207	58.61	15	19
4415	K.J.Hughes	A	70	124	6	213	37.41	9	22
4399	A.I.Kallicharran	WI	66	109	10	187	44.43	12	21
4389	A.P.E.Knott	E	95	149	15	135	32.75	5	30
4378	M.Amarnath	I	69	113	10	138	42.50	11	24
4334	R.C.Fredericks	WI	59	109	7	169	42.49	8	26
4288	D.L.Haynes	WI	72	122	13	184	39.33	9	25

Most Hundreds

34	S.M.Gavaskar	I	22	M.C.Cowdrey	E
29	D.G.Bradman	A	22	W.R.Hammond	E
26	G.St A.Sobers	WI	22	I.V.A.Richards	WI
24	G.S.Chappell	A	21	R.N.Harvey	A
22	A.R.Border	A	20	K.F.Barrington	E
22	G.Boycott	E			

BOWLING RECORDS

Most Wickets in an Innings

10-53	J.C.Laker	E v A	Manchester	1956
9-28	G.A.Lohmann	E v SA	Johannesburg	1895-96
9-37	J.C.Laker	E v A	Manchester	1956
9-52	R.J.Hadlee	NZ v A	Brisbane	1985-86
9-56	Abdul Qadir	P v E	Lahore	1987-88
9-69	J.M.Patel	I v A	Kanpur	1959-60
9-83	Kapil Dev	I v WI	Ahmedabad	1983-84
9-86	Sarfraz Nawaz	P v A	Melbourne	1978-79
9-95	J.M.Noreiga	WI v I	Port-of-Spain	1970-71

9-102	S.P.Gupte	I v WI	Kanpur	1958-59
9-103	S.F.Barnes	E v SA	Johannesburg	1913-14
9-113	H.J.Tayfield	SA v E	Johannesburg	1956-57
9-121	A.A.Mailey	A v E	Melbourne	1920-21

Most Wickets in a Test

19-90	J.C.Laker	E v A	Manchester	1956
17-159	S.F.Barnes	E v SA	Johannesburg	1913-14
16-136	N.Hirwani	I v WI	Madras	1987-88
16-137	R.A.L.Massie	A v E	Lord's	1972
15-28	J.Briggs	E v SA	Cape Town	1888-89
15-45	G.A.Lohmann	E v SA	Port Elizabeth	1895-96
15-99	C.Blythe	E v SA	Leeds	1907
15-104	H.Verity	E v A	Lord's	1934
15-123	R.J.Hadlee	NZ v A	Brisbane	1985-86
15-124	W.Rhodes	E v A	Melbourne	1903-04

Most Wickets in a Series

Wkts			*Series*	*M*	*Balls*	*Runs*	*Avge*	*5 wI*	*10 wM*
49	S.F.Barnes	E v SA	1913-14	4	1356	536	10.93	7	3
46	J.C.Laker	E v A	1956	5	1703	442	9.60	4	2
44	C.V.Grimmett	A v SA	1935-36	5	2077	642	14.59	5	3
42	T.M.Alderman	A v E	1981	6	1950	893	21.26	4	-
41	R.M.Hogg	A v E	1978-79	6	1740	527	12.85	5	2
40	Imran Khan	P v I	1982-83	6	1339	558	13.95	4	2
39	A.V.Bedser	E v A	1953	5	1591	682	17.48	5	1
39	D.K.Lillee	A v E	1981	6	1870	870	22.30	2	1
38	M.W.Tate	E v A	1924-25	5	2528	881	23.18	5	1
37	W.J.Whitty	A v SA	1910-11	5	1395	632	17.08	2	-
37	H.J.Tayfield	SA v E	1956-57	5	2280	636	17.18	4	1
36	A.E.E.Vogler	SA v E	1909-10	5	1349	783	21.75	4	1
36	A.A.Mailey	A v E	1920-21	5	1465	946	26.27	4	2
35	G.A.Lohmann	E v SA	1895-96	3	520	203	5.80	4	2
35	B.S.Chandrasekhar	I v E	1972-73	5	1747	662	18.91	4	-

200 Wickets in Tests

Wkts			*M*	*Balls*	*Runs*	*Avge*	*5wI*	*10wM*
373	I.T.Botham	E	94	20801	10392	27.86	27	4
373	R.J.Hadlee	NZ	74	19135	8379	22.46	32	8
355	D.K.Lillee	A	70	18467	8493	23.92	23	7
334	Imran Khan	P	73	17137	7319	21.91	23	6
325	R.G.D.Willis	E	90	17357	8190	25.20	16	-
319	Kapil Dev	I	92	19225	9454	29.63	19	2
309	L.R.Gibbs	WI	79	27115	8989	29.09	18	2
307	F.S.Trueman	E	67	15178	6625	21.57	17	3
297	D.L.Underwood	E	86	21862	7674	25.83	17	6
266	B.S.Bedi	I	67	21364	7637	28.71	14	1
259	J.Garner	WI	58	13169	5433	20.97	7	-
255	M.D.Marshall	WI	53	11828	5478	21.48	15	2
252	J.B.Statham	E	70	16056	6261	24.84	9	1
249	M.A.Holding	WI	60	12680	5898	23.68	13	2
248	R.Benaud	A	63	19108	6704	27.03	16	1
246	G.D.McKenzie	A	60	17681	7328	29.78	16	3
242	B.S.Chandrasekhar	I	58	15963	7199	29.74	16	2

Wkts			*M*	*Balls*	*Runs*	*Avge*	*5wI*	*10wM*
236	A.V.Bedser	E	51	15918	5876	24.89	15	5
235	G.St A.Sobers	WI	93	21599	7999	34.03	6	-
228	R.R.Lindwall	A	61	13650	5251	23.03	12	-
216	C.V.Grimmett	A	37	14513	5231	24.21	21	7
205	Abdul Qadir	P	54	14425	6483	31.62	14	5
202	A.M.E.Roberts	WI	47	11136	5174	25.61	11	2
202	J.A.Snow	E	49	12021	5387	26.66	8	1
200	J.R.Thomson	A	51	10535	5601	28.00	8	-

Hat-Tricks

F.R.Spofforth	Australia v England	Melbourne	1878-79
W.Bates	England v Australia	Melbourne	1882-83
J.Briggs	England v Australia	Sydney	1891-92
G.A.Lohmann	England v South Africa	Port Elizabeth	1895-96
J.T.Hearne	England v Australia	Leeds	1899
H.Trumble	Australia v England	Melbourne	1901-02
H.Trumble	Australia v England	Melbourne	1903-04
T.J.Matthews (2)*	Australia v South Africa	Manchester	1912
M.J.C.Allom+	England v New Zealand	Christchurch	1929-30
T.W.J.Goddard	England v South Africa	Johannesburg	1938-39
P.J.Loader	England v West Indies	Leeds	1957
L.F.Kline	Australia v South Africa	Cape Town	1957-58
W.W.Hall	West Indies v Pakistan	Lahore	1958-59
G.M.Griffin	South Africa v England	Lord's	1960
L.R.Gibbs	West Indies v Australia	Adelaide	1960-61
P.J.Petherick	New Zealand v Pakistan	Lahore	1976-77

*In each innings + Four wickets in five balls

WICKET-KEEPING RECORDS

Most Dismissals in an Innings

7	Wasim Bari	Pakistan v New Zealand	Auckland	1978-79
7	R.W.Taylor	England v India	Bombay	1979-80
6	A.T.W.Grout	Australia v South Africa	Johannesburg	1957-58
6	D.T.Lindsay	South Africa v Australia	Johannesburg	1966-67
6	J.T.Murray	England v India	Lord's	1967
6+	S.M.H.Kirmani	India v New Zealand	Christchurch	1975-76
6	R.W.Marsh	Australia v England	Brisbane	1982-83
6	S.A.R.Silva	Sri Lanka v India	Colombo (SSC)	1985-86

+ Including one stumping

Most Stumpings in an Innings

5	K.S.More	India v West Indies	Madras	1987-88

Most Dismissals in a Test

10	R.W.Taylor	England v India	Bombay	1979-80
9+	G.R.A.Langley	Australia v England	Lord's	1956
9	D.A.Murray	West Indies v Australia	Melbourne	1981-82
9	R.W.Marsh	Australia v England	Brisbane	1982-83
9	S.A.R.Silva	Sri Lanka v India	Colombo (SSC)	1985-86
9+	S.A.R.Silva	Sri Lanka v India	Colombo (SO)	1985-86

+ Including one stumping

Most Dismissals in a Series

28	R.W.Marsh	Australia v England	1982-83
26 inc 3st	J.H.B.Waite	South Africa v New Zealand	1961-62
26	R.W.Marsh	Australia v West Indies (6 Tests)	1975-76
24 inc 2st	D.L.Murray	West Indies v England	1963
24	D.T.Lindsay	South Africa v Australia	1966-67
24 inc 3st	A.P.E.Knott	England v Australia (6 Tests)	1970-71

100 Dismissals in Tests

Total			Tests	Ct	St
355	R.W.Marsh	Australia	96	343	12
269	A.P.E.Knott	England	95	250	19
228	Wasim Bari	Pakistan	81	201	27
219	T.G.Evans	England	91	173	46
198	S.M.H.Kirmani	India	88	160	38
189	D.L.Murray	West Indies	62	181	8
187	A.T.W.Grout	Australia	51	163	24
174	R.W.Taylor	England	57	167	7
159+	P.J.L.Dujon	West Indies	50	154	5
141	J.H.B.Waite	South Africa	50	124	17
130	W.A.S.Oldfield	Australia	54	78	52
127	I.D.S.Smith	New Zealand	43	120	7
114+	J.M.Parks	England	46	103	11

+ Including two catches taken in the field

FIELDING RECORDS
(Excluding Wicket-Keepers)

Most Catches in an Innings

5	V.Y.Richardson	Australia v South Africa	Durban	1935-36
5	Yajurvindra Singh	India v England	Bangalore	1976-77

Most Catches in a Test

7	G.S.Chappell	Australia v England	Perth	1974-75
7	Yajurvindra Singh	India v England	Bangalore	1976-77

Most Catches in a Series

15	J.M.Gregory	Australia v England	1920-21

100 Catches in Tests

Total			Tests
122	G.S.Chappell	Australia	87
120	M.C.Cowdrey	England	114
110	R.B.Simpson	Australia	62
110	W.R.Hammond	England	85
109	G.St A.Sobers	West Indies	93
109	I.T.Botham	England	94
108	S.M.Gavaskar	India	125
105	I.M.Chappell	Australia	75
102	A.R.Border	Australia	94

Most Test Appearances

India	S.M.Gavaskar	125	England	M.C.Cowdrey	114
Pakistan	Javed Miandad	92	Australia	R.W.Marsh	96
Sri Lanka	L.R.D.Mendis	23	South Africa	J.H.B.Waite	50
	A.Ranatunga	23	West Indies	C.H.Lloyd	110
	S.Wettimuny	23	New Zealand	R.J.Hadlee	74

SUMMARY OF ALL TEST MATCHES

To 1 June 1988

		Tests				*Won*	*by*				*Tied*	*Drawn*
			E	*A*	*SA*	*WI*	*NZ*	*I*	*P*	*SL*		
England	v Australia	263	88	97	-	-	-	-	-	-	-	78
	v South Africa	102	46	-	18	-	-	-	-	-	-	38
	v West Indies	90	21	-	-	35	-	-	-	-	-	34
	v New Zealand	66	30	-	-	-	4	-	-	-	-	32
	v India	75	30	-	-	-	-	11	-	-	-	34
	v Pakistan	47	13	-	-	-	-	-	5	-	-	29
	v Sri Lanka	2	1	-	-	-	-	-	-	0	-	1
Australia	v South Africa	53	-	29	11	-	-	-	-	-	-	13
	v West Indies	62	-	27	-	19	-	-	-	-	1	15
	v New Zealand	24	-	10	-	-	5	-	-	-	-	9
	v India	45	-	20	-	-	-	8	-	-	1	16
	v Pakistan	28	-	11	-	-	-	-	8	-	-	9
	v Sri Lanka	2	-	2	-	-	-	-	-	0	-	0
South Africa	v New Zealand	17	-	-	9	-	2	-	-	-	-	6
West Indies	v New Zealand	24	-	-	-	8	4	-	-	-	-	12
	v India	58	-	-	-	23	-	6	-	-	-	29
	v Pakistan	25	-	-	-	9	-	-	6	-	-	10
New Zealand	v India	25	-	-	-	-	4	10	-	-	-	11
	v Pakistan	27	-	-	-	-	3	-	10	-	-	14
	v Sri Lanka	6	-	-	-	-	4	-	-	0	-	2
India	v Pakistan	40	-	-	-	-	-	4	7	-	-	29
	v Sri Lanka	7	-	-	-	-	-	2	-	1	-	4
Pakistan	v Sri Lanka	9	-	-	-	-	-	-	5	1	-	3
		1097	229	196	38	94	26	41	41	2	2	428

	Tests	*Won*	*Lost*	*Drawn*	*Tied*	*Toss Won*
England	645	229	170	246	-	319
Australia	477	196	139	140	2	240
South Africa	172	38	77	57	-	80
West Indies	259	94	64	100	1	139
New Zealand	189	26	77	86	-	93
India	250	41	85	123	1	123
Pakistan	176	41	41	94	-	90
Sri Lanka	26	2	14	10	-	13

LIMITED-OVERS INTERNATIONALS

updated to 1 June 1988

TEAM RECORDS

Highest Total	360-4	West Indies v Sri Lanka	Karachi	1987-88
Lowest Total	45	Canada v England	Manchester	1979
Lowest Total Batting Second	297-6	New Zealand v England	Adelaide	1982-83

Highest Aggregate	626	Pakistan v Sri Lanka	Swansea	1983
Lowest Aggregate	91	England v Canada	Manchester	1979
Tied Match		Australia (229-9) v West Indies (222-5)	Melbourne	1983-84

BATTING RECORDS

Highest Individual Score for each Country

189*	I.V.A.Richards	West Indies v England	Manchester	1984
175*	Kapil Dev	India v Zimbabwe	Tunbridge Wells	1983
171*	G.M.Turner	New Zealand v East Africa	Birmingham	1975
158	D.I.Gower	England v New Zealand	Brisbane	1982-83
138*	G.S.Chappell	Australia v New Zealand	Sydney	1980-81
123	Zaheer Abbas	Pakistan v Sri Lanka	Lahore	1981-82
121	R.L.Dias	Sri Lanka v India	Bangalore	1982-83

Highest Partnership For Each Wicket

1st	212	G.R.Marsh/D.C.Boon	A v I	Jaipur	1986-87
2nd	221	C.G.Greenidge/I.V.A.Richards	WI v I	Jamshedpur	1983-84
3rd	224*	D.M.Jones/A.R.Border	A v SL	Adelaide	1984-85
4th	173	D.M.Jones/S.R.Waugh	A v P	Perth	1986-87
5th	152	I.V.A.Richards/C.H.Lloyd	WI v SL	Brisbane	1984-85
6th	144	Imran Khan/Shahid Mahboob	P v SL	Leeds	1983
7th	115	P.J.L.Dujon/M.D.Marshall	WI v P	Gujranwala	1986-87
8th	117	D.L.Houghton/I.P.Butchart	Z v NZ	Hyderabad	1987-88
9th	126*	Kapil Dev/S.M.H.Kirmani	I v Z	Tunbridge Wells	1983
10th	106*	I.V.A.Richards/M.A.Holding	WI v E	Manchester	1984

BOWLING RECORDS

Best Bowling Analyses for each Country

7-15	W.W.Davis	West Indies v Australia	Leeds	1983
6-14	G.J.Gilmour	Australia v England	Leeds	1975
6-14	Imran Khan	Pakistan v India	Sharjah	1984-85
5-20	V.J.Marks	England v New Zealand	Wellington	1983-84
5-23	R.O.Collinge	New Zealand v India	Christchurch	1975-76
5-26	U.S.H.Karnain	Sri Lanka v New Zealand	Moratuwa	1983-84
5-43	Kapil Dev	India v Australia	Nottingham	1983

Hat-Tricks

Jalaluddin	Pakistan v Australia	Hyderabad	1982-83
B.A.Reid	Australia v New Zealand	Sydney	1985-86
C.Sharma	India v New Zealand	Nagpur	1987-88

WICKET-KEEPING RECORDS

Most Dismissals

5(5ct)	R.W.Marsh	Australia v England	Leeds	1981
5(5ct)	R.G.de Alwis	Sri Lanka v Australia	Colombo (SO)	1982-83
5(5ct)	S.M.H.Kirmani	India v Zimbabwe	Leicester	1983
5(3ct,2st)	S.Viswanath	India v England	Sydney	1984-85

FIELDING RECORDS

Most Catches

4	Salim Malik	Pakistan v New Zealand	Sialkot	1984-85
4	S.M.Gavaskar	India v Pakistan	Sharjah	1984-85

INDEX